MY
UTMOST
FOR HIS
HIGHEST®

MY
UTMOST
FOR HIS
HIGHEST®

An Updated Edition
In Today's Language

The Golden Book of
Oswald
CHAMBERS

Discovery House.
from Our Daily Bread Ministries

Edited by James Reimann
Authorized by the Oswald Chambers Publications Association, Ltd.

United States publication rights are held by Discovery House,
which is affiliated with Our Daily Bread Ministries,
Grand Rapids, Michigan.

Unless otherwise indicated, Scripture quotations are from
The New King James Version. © 1979, 1980, 1982, Thomas
Nelson, Inc., Publishers.

Request for permission to quote from this book should be
directed to: Permissions Department, P.O. Box 3566, Grand
Rapids, Michigan, MI 49501, or contact us by e-mail at
permissionsdept@dhp.org

Library of Congress Cataloging-in-Publication Data

Chambers, Oswald, 1874-1917.
    My utmost for his highest : an updated edition in today's
language : the golden book of Oswald Chambers / edited by
James G. Reimann.
        p. cm.
    "Authorized by the Oswald Chambers Publications
Association, Ltd."
    Includes index.
    1. Devotional calendars. I. Reimann, James G. II. Title
BV4811.455 1992
242'.2—dc20   92-15394
                                                            CIP

ISBN: 978-1-57293-771-0

Printed in the United States of America

Sixth printing in 2015

This book is dedicated to the reader, especially
my parents, Gil and Violet,
my wife, Pam,
my children, Jeremy, Aaron, and Bethany,
and each generation of readers they represent.

May you know God better and draw closer to
Him as a result of applying the truths of
God's Word expressed in this book.

ACKNOWLEDGMENTS

A SPECIAL THANK YOU TO those who have daily lifted this project to God in prayer and have continually given me words of encouragement. Your prayers and support were essential in taking this project from vision to reality. I am especially appreciative of:

Maurice Garton, Chairman, Oswald Chambers Publications Association, London, England, for your openness to this project.

Bob DeVries, Publisher, Discovery House Publishers, for your unwavering faith in, and support of, this project.

Carol Holquist, Associate Publisher, Discovery House Publishers, for your friendship and guidance.

Tim Beals, Editor, Discovery House Publishers, and Arthur Neil, Editor, Oswald Chambers Publications Association, for your careful and diligent work.

Bill Anderson, President, Christian Booksellers Association, and each member of the CBA Board.

Charles F. Stanley, Pastor, First Baptist Church, Atlanta, Georgia, for many years of sound teaching.

Ben and Donna Reed, Cheryl Gainey, Robert Brenner, Winston and Delores Maddox, Bob and C. Kay Streight, Bob Allums, Chuck Graham, Tim Skinner, Jane Bateman, Carol Williams, Bobby and Kathy Respess, and Bill Price. Thank you for your prayers, your counsel, and your love.

The staff of the Christian Armory, Inc., Tucker, Georgia, particularly Greg Holland, General Manager. Thanks for continuing to grow our ministry while I was writing this book.

Teresa Holland, the world's sweetest "word-processor."

My parents, Gil and Violet Reimann, for raising me in a Christian home. My wife Pam and my children, Jeremy, Aaron, and Bethany. Thanks for allowing this author two-and-a-half years of "relative" peace and quiet while I worked at home. I love you dearly.

Jesus Christ, who is my life.

James Reimann
Colossians 3:4

FOREWORD

With the exception of the Bible, no book has had as profound an effect on my life as *My Utmost for His Highest*. My wife introduced it to me before we were married, and it has been a part of my daily diet from the first reading.

It was here that God impressed on my heart that precious truth essential to the life of every believer who truly desires to follow Christ: the most important aspect of the Christian life is our personal relationship with Christ.

Few individuals have had the insight into the Person of Christ as Oswald Chambers, and fewer still have been able to make its application so inescapable. This volume is not a treasure to be admired but a message to be lived.

I am greatly encouraged to see these powerful daily devotions updated with more contemporary expressions. The purpose of this edition is to make it more readable and easily understood. Not a single truth has been altered even to the slightest degree. It has been done with the hope that it will receive even wider distribution to this and future generations.

James Reimann has approached this task with the greatest of care to protect the message of Oswald Chambers. He is to be commended. As a part of our ministry for over twenty years, I have known him as a friend, a diligent student of the Word, and a faithful follower of Christ in his walk and his work. It is my earnest prayer that this volume will be received with delight and shared freely.

Charles F. Stanley
February 1, 1992

INTRODUCTION

MY UTMOST FOR HIS HIGHEST has been a close companion to me through most of my Christian life. It was first recommended to me by my pastor, Charles Stanley, who has often expressed his love for its powerful content. It is a work that has endured far beyond the author's death in 1917. Oswald Chambers, who died at the age of 43, originally shared these thoughts as lectures at the Bible Training College in Clapham, England, from 1911 to 1915, and as devotional talks while serving with the Young Men's Christian Association from 1915 to 1917. The YMCA had appointed him to serve in Egypt with the Australian and New Zealand troops who were guarding the Suez Canal during World War I. These lectures and talks were later compiled by Chambers' wife and published in book form in 1927 in England, and in 1935 in the United States. It has since become the best-selling devotional book of all time.

The idea of a new edition was prompted by the changes in the English language over the last century. As a Christian bookstore owner, I have sold thousands of copies of My Utmost for His Highest through the years. However, because of these language changes, I have had an ever-increasing concern that readers were not gleaning all they could from the book. One morning, after reading the devotional selection for that day, I asked the Lord to impress on someone a burden to write a new edition. Much to my surprise, I immediately sensed God's directive to write it myself. I began that same day.

What you hold in your hand is the culmination of approximately 1800 hours of research and editing. It is not a paraphrase of the original work, but could be considered a translation of it. Thousands of word studies have been done to render an accurate yet readable edition. This edition also includes the reference for every Scripture quotation to allow the reader to further his study of the biblical passage. (Note: Scripture quotations without references are passages that have been referred to earlier in the selection.) I encourage you to read with this book in one hand and your Bible in the other.

INTRODUCTION

This book is not the Bible—it is intended to point you to the Bible. The desire of my heart is that this work will unlock for you the treasure of the truth of God's Word and the insights into that truth that Oswald Chambers explored. May you use this book as a help in meditating on God's Word, and as a help in applying it to your life.

James Reimann
Joshua 1:8

A Word About Oswald and Biddy Chambers

OSWALD CHAMBERS WAS NOT FAMOUS during his lifetime. At the time of his death in 1917, at the age of forty-three, only three books bearing his name had been published. Among a relatively small circle of Christians in Britain and the U.S., Chambers was much appreciated as a teacher of rare insight and expression, but he was not widely known.

His wide-ranging influence came during the decades following his death as his widow compiled Oswald's spoken words into thirty published books, many of which have become Christian classics: *Baffled to Fight Better, If Ye Shall Ask, Studies in the Sermon on the Mount,* and of course, *My Utmost for His Highest.*

Oswald Chambers was born in Aberdeen, Scotland, on July 24, 1874, the eighth of nine children of Rev. Clarence Chambers, a rather stern Baptist minister, and his gracious wife, Hannah. During Oswald's boyhood years in Perth, he first exhibited his keen talent in art. When he was fifteen, the family moved to London where Oswald made his public profession of faith in Christ and became a member of Rye Lane Baptist Church. This marked a period of rapid spiritual growth, along with an intense struggle to find God's will and way for his life.

As a gifted artist and musician, Chambers trained at London's National Art Training School, later named the Royal Academy of Art. He sensed God's call to be an ambassador for Christ in the world of art, music, and aesthetics. But while studying at the University of Edinburgh (1895–96), he experienced a major redirection in life. Following an agonizing internal battle, he decided to train for the Christian ministry, a profession he said he would never enter "unless God takes me by the scruff of the neck and throws me in." He left the university and entered Dunoon College, near Glasgow, where he spent nine years, first as a theological student, then as a tutor of philosophy. Under the wise guidance of Rev. Duncan MacGregor, his mentor and friend, Oswald matured greatly and came through a long "dark night of the soul" into a deeper and more joyful knowledge of Christ.

A WORD ABOUT OSWALD
AND BIDDY CHAMBERS

In 1906 and 1907 Oswald spent six months teaching at God's Bible School in Cincinnati, Ohio. From there he went to Japan, visiting the Tokyo Bible School, founded by Charles and Lettie Cowman. This journey around the world marked his transition from Dunoon College to full-time work with the London-based Pentecostal League of Prayer.

While serving as a travelling speaker and representative of the League of Prayer in Britain, Oswald met Gertrude Hobbs. Their friendship blossomed during a voyage to the United States in the summer of 1908, and two years later they were married. Oswald called her "Beloved Disciple," shortened to the initials B.D., and spoken as "Biddy." For the rest of her life, she was known by this affectionate nickname.

A long-time dream of Oswald's became reality in January 1911 with the opening of the Bible Training College (BTC) near Clapham Common in London. Sponsored by the League of Prayer, it housed twenty-five residential students and reached hundreds more through evening classes and Bible correspondence courses. Oswald served as Principal and main teacher while Biddy filled the role of Lady Superintendent, overseeing a myriad of logistical details, from the preparation of meals to temporary housing for missionary families in transit through London.

During Oswald's lectures Biddy sat in the back of the room recording his words verbatim in her precise Pittman's shorthand. Trained as a court stenographer, she could take dictation rapidly while remaining engaged with her husband's purpose as he taught. Biddy's storehouse of notes grew as Oswald taught Biblical Psychology, Studies in Genesis, Biblical Ethics, and a host of other classes. Of special significance were her records of the sermon class and the weekly devotional hour when Oswald spoke to the residential students from his heart.

Their only child, Kathleen, was born in May 1913, and promptly began her reign as queen of the BTC. Oswald found himself completely charmed by this new arrival. He had always loved children, but the feelings

A WORD ABOUT OSWALD AND BIDDY CHAMBERS

produced by his own daughter were something entirely new. When she cried at the top of her lungs during a meal at the college, Oswald would say, "And now my daughter will sing." But the happy days of a settled life in London were soon to end.

The outbreak of World War I in August 1914 changed Britain dramatically and led to the closing of the BTC within a year. Oswald volunteered as a YMCA secretary in Egypt, where Biddy, Kathleen, and several former students from the BTC joined him to assist in the work. At Zeitoun Camp, near Cairo, Oswald quickly established himself as a friend of the troops and a man of uncommon spiritual insight. One soldier described him as "the personification of the Sherlock Holmes of fiction—tall, erect, virile, with clean-cut face, framing a pair of piercing bright eyes . . . a detective of the soul."

Biddy continued to fill shorthand notebooks with Oswald's talks to the troops, including "The Shadow of an Agony," "Shade of His Hand" (Studies in Ecclesiastes), and "Baffled to Fight Better" (Studies in Job). Against the formidable foes of heat, insects, and blowing sand, she continued a ministry of hospitality that produced the special touches of home for the troops so far from their families.

In a letter to Biddy's mother, Oswald freely praised his wife: "As for Biddy I love her and I am her husband but I do not believe it is possible to exaggerate what she has been in the way of a Sacrament out here—God conveying His presence through the common elements of an ordinary life. The letters she has received from mothers and wives and sisters and fathers and brothers are in themselves a deep testimony to a most unconscious ministry of wife and mother and woman."

In the desert camp Oswald supervised the construction of rock-lined walkways and a myriad of flower beds. Some critics said it was a waste of time, but Chambers believed that if physical improvements were not made and new touches occasionally given to the huts, they would reflect slovenly care, unpleasing to God. "A grave defect

A WORD ABOUT OSWALD AND BIDDY CHAMBERS

in much work of today," he said, "is that men do not follow Solomon's admonition, 'Whatsoever thy hand findeth to do, do it with thy might.' The tendency is to argue, 'It's only for so short a time, why trouble?' If it is only for five minutes, let it be well done."

In late October 1917 Oswald underwent an emergency appendectomy and appeared to be recovering. But two weeks later, while still in Gizeh Red Cross Hospital, he suffered a relapse and died early in the morning on November 15. All those who knew and loved him were stunned.

Dazed with disbelief and sorrow, Biddy began dealing with the numbing tasks facing a young widow with a four-year-old daughter. Her telegram to family and friends in Britain said simply, "Oswald in His Presence." The next afternoon, Chambers was buried with full military honors in the British Military Cemetery in Old Cairo.

For the next two years, Biddy and Kathleen continued to work among the troops at Zeitoun. In the ways of God's providence, which Oswald frequently referred to as "the haphazard," Biddy's personal sending of one of his sermons as a Christmas gift to the troops in Egypt mushroomed into a monthly printing and mailing of 10,000 copies by the YMCA. Gradually it became clear to Biddy that her calling in life was to give her husband's words to the world. In so doing, she continued the dream she and Oswald had shared of working together to help others.

Upon her return to England in 1919, Biddy continued transcribing her shorthand notes and preparing them for publication. She worked to support herself and Kathleen, using any money from sales to help finance the next book.

While maintaining a boarding house for students in Oxford, Biddy compiled a book of daily readings which she titled *My Utmost for His Highest*. Since it was first published in 1927, *My Utmost* has been continuously in print and has sold millions of copies. It exists today in more than forty different languages, and every day, mul-

A Word About Oswald and Biddy Chambers

tiplied thousands of people around the world open its pages seeking a word from the Lord through His servant Oswald Chambers.

From the earliest days of publication after World War I, Mrs. Chambers was advised and assisted by a small group of personal friends. In later years, this group became known as the Oswald Chambers Publications Association. It was incorporated in 1942, and exists today as a Registered British Charity overseeing the publication and distribution of Oswald Chambers's material around the world. Royalties are used to help fund new translations of Chambers's books in developing nations and to provide gift copies of the OC books to students and pastors.

My Utmost for His Highest, along with all the other OC books, sprang from the shared life and vision of two remarkable people—Oswald and Biddy Chambers. The books are the result of their love for God, for each other, and for people everywhere. Together Oswald and Biddy touched individuals from varied backgrounds and many nations through hospitality, biblical teaching, encouragement, and joyful good humor. The pages of *My Utmost* are infused with their belief that taking the gospel to the whole earth involves following God's example of "keeping open house for the universe."

Kathleen described her mother as always having time for people. A knock at the door would take her from the typewriter to the teakettle. She considered it just as important to chat with a child from the neighborhood as it was to prepare the next book for publication. Biddy personally answered the hundreds of letters that came to her, and often included a complimentary copy of one of Oswald's books with her reply.

By the time Biddy Chambers died in 1966, she had compiled and published some fifty books that bore the name of Oswald Chambers but never mentioned her own. Occasional words of greeting at the beginning of a volume, followed by her initials "B.C.," were the only evidence of her role.

A Word About Oswald and Biddy Chambers

In the weeks just after Oswald's death in Egypt, Biddy wrote to her mother of a friend whose life had been radically changed by reading some of Oswald's sermons. "It confirms me so much in the assurance I have that I am to go on getting everything I can printed," Biddy said. "It will be like casting bread upon the waters and we'll know someday all it has meant in people's lives."

To her sister, she wrote: "Living with Oswald and seeing his faith in God and knowing that 'by his faithfulness he is speaking to us still' is the secret of life these days, and I feel as if it will be overwhelming to one day see what God has wrought, and one will only be sorry not to have trusted more utterly. So just go on praying and believing and we will surely find that God is doing His wondrous things all the time."

By their faithfulness in the ordinary circumstances of each unfolding day, Oswald and Biddy Chambers have demonstrated the significance and power of giving our utmost for God's highest.

David McCasland

LET US KEEP TO THE POINT

"... my earnest expectation and hope that in nothing I shall be ashamed, but with all boldness, as always, so now also Christ will be magnified in my body, whether by life or by death" (Philippians 1:20).

My Utmost for His Highest. "... my earnest expectation and hope that in nothing I shall be ashamed ...." We will all feel very much ashamed if we do not yield to Jesus the areas of our lives He has asked us to yield to Him. It's as if Paul were saying, "My determined purpose is to be my utmost for His highest—my best for His glory." To reach that level of determination is a matter of the will, not of debate or of reasoning. It is absolute and irrevocable surrender of the will at that point. An undue amount of thought and consideration for ourselves is what keeps us from making that decision, although we cover it up with the pretense that it is others we are considering. When we think seriously about what it will cost others if we obey the call of Jesus, we tell God He doesn't know what our obedience will mean. Keep to the point—He does know. Shut out every other thought and keep yourself before God in this one thing only—my utmost for His highest. I am determined to be absolutely and entirely for Him and Him alone.

My Unstoppable Determination for His Holiness. "Whether it means life or death—it makes no difference!" (see 1:21). Paul was determined that nothing would stop him from doing exactly what God wanted. But before we choose to follow God's will, a crisis must develop in our lives. This happens because we tend to be unresponsive to God's gentler nudges. He brings us to the place where He asks us to be our utmost for Him and we begin to debate. He then providentially produces a crisis where we have to decide—for or against. That moment becomes a great crossroads in our lives. If a crisis has come to you on any front, surrender your will to Jesus absolutely and irrevocably.

WILL YOU GO OUT
WITHOUT KNOWING?

"He went out, not knowing where he was going" (Hebrews 11:8).

Have you ever "gone out" in this way? If so, there is no logical answer possible when anyone asks you what you are doing. One of the most difficult questions to answer in Christian work is, "What do you expect to do?" You don't know what you are going to do. The only thing you know is that God knows what He is doing. Continually examine your attitude toward God to see if you are willing to "go out" in every area of your life, trusting in God entirely. It is this attitude that keeps you in constant wonder, because you don't know what God is going to do next. Each morning as you wake, there is a new opportunity to "go out," building your confidence in God. ". . . do not worry about your life . . . nor about the body . . ." (Luke 12:22). In other words, don't worry about the things that concerned you before you did "go out."

Have you been asking God what He is going to do? He will never tell you. God does not tell you what He is going to do—He reveals to you who He is. Do you believe in a miracle-working God, and will you "go out" in complete surrender to Him until you are not surprised one iota by anything He does?

Believe God is always the God you know Him to be when you are nearest to Him. Then think how unnecessary and disrespectful worry is! Let the attitude of your life be a continual willingness to "go out" in dependence upon God, and your life will have a sacred and inexpressible charm about it that is very satisfying to Jesus. You must learn to "go out" through your convictions, creeds, or experiences until you come to the point in your faith where there is nothing between yourself and God.

"CLOUDS AND DARKNESS"

**"Clouds and darkness surround Him . . ."
(Psalm 97:2).**

A person who has not been born again by the Spirit of God will tell you that the teachings of Jesus are simple. But when he is baptized by the Holy Spirit, he finds that "clouds and darkness surround Him . . . ." When we come into close contact with the teachings of Jesus Christ we have our first realization of this. The only possible way to have full understanding of the teachings of Jesus is through the light of the Spirit of God shining inside us. If we have never had the experience of taking our casual, religious shoes off our casual, religious feet—getting rid of all the excessive informality with which we approach God—it is questionable whether we have ever stood in His presence. The people who are flippant and disrespectful in their approach to God are those who have never been introduced to Jesus Christ. Only after the amazing delight and liberty of realizing what Jesus Christ *does*, comes the impenetrable "darkness" of realizing who He *is*.

Jesus said, "The words that I speak to you are spirit, and they are life" (John 6:63). Once, the Bible was just so many words to us—"clouds and darkness"—then, suddenly, the words become spirit and life because Jesus re-speaks them to us when our circumstances make the words new. That is the way God speaks to us; not by visions and dreams, but by words. When a man gets to God, it is by the most simple way—words.

"WHY CAN I NOT FOLLOW YOU NOW?"

"Peter said to Him, 'Lord, why can I not follow You now?' " (John 13:37).

There are times when you can't understand why you cannot do what you want to do. When God brings a time of waiting, and appears to be unresponsive, don't fill it with busyness, just wait. The time of waiting may come to teach you the meaning of sanctification—to be set apart from sin and made holy—or it may come after the process of sanctification has begun to teach you what service means. Never run before God gives you His direction. If you have the slightest doubt, then He is not guiding. Whenever there is doubt—wait.

At first you may see clearly what God's will is—the severance of a friendship, the breaking off of a business relationship, or something else you feel is distinctly God's will for you to do. But never act on the impulse of that feeling. If you do, you will cause difficult situations to arise which will take years to untangle. Wait for God's timing and He will do it without any heartache or disappointment. When it is a question of the providential will of God, wait for God to move.

Peter did not wait for God. He predicted in his own mind where the test would come, and it came where he did not expect it. "I will lay down my life for Your sake." Peter's statement was honest but ignorant. "Jesus answered him, ' . . . the rooster shall not crow till you have denied Me three times' " (13:38). This was said with a deeper knowledge of Peter than Peter had of himself. He could not follow Jesus because he did not know himself or his own capabilities well enough. Natural devotion may be enough to attract us to Jesus, to make us feel His irresistible charm, but it will never make us disciples. Natural devotion will deny Jesus, always falling short of what it means to truly follow Him.

THE LIFE OF POWER TO FOLLOW

"Jesus answered him, 'Where I am going you cannot follow Me now, but you shall follow Me afterward' " (John 13:36).

"And when He had spoken this, He said to him, 'Follow Me' " (John 21:19). Three years earlier Jesus had said, "Follow Me" (Matthew 4:19), and Peter followed with no hesitation. The irresistible attraction of Jesus was upon him and he did not need the Holy Spirit to help him do it. Later he came to the place where he denied Jesus, and his heart broke. Then he received the Holy Spirit and Jesus said again, "Follow Me" (John 21:19). Now no one is in front of Peter except the Lord Jesus Christ. The first "Follow Me" was nothing mysterious; it was an external following. Jesus is now asking for an internal sacrifice and yielding (see 21:18).

Between these two times Peter denied Jesus with oaths and curses (see Matthew 26:69–75). But then he came completely to the end of himself and all of his self-sufficiency. There was no part of himself he would ever rely on again. In his state of destitution, he was finally ready to receive all that the risen Lord had for him. ". . . He breathed on them, and said to them, 'Receive the Holy Spirit' " (John 20:22). No matter what changes God has performed in you, never rely on them. Build only on a Person, the Lord Jesus Christ, and on the Spirit He gives.

All our promises and resolutions end in denial because we have no power to accomplish them. When we come to the end of ourselves, not just mentally but completely, we are able to "receive the Holy Spirit." *"Receive the Holy Spirit"*—the idea is that of invasion. There is now only One who directs the course of your life, the Lord Jesus Christ.

WORSHIP

"He moved from there to the mountain east of Bethel, and he pitched his tent with Bethel on the west and Ai on the east; there he built an altar to the LORD and called on the name of the LORD" (Genesis 12:8).

Worship is giving God the best that He has given you. Be careful what you do with the best you have. Whenever you get a blessing from God, give it back to Him as a love-gift. Take time to meditate before God and offer the blessing back to Him in a deliberate act of worship. If you hoard it for yourself, it will turn into spiritual dry rot, as the manna did when it was hoarded (see Exodus 16:20). God will never allow you to keep a spiritual blessing completely for yourself. It must be given back to Him so that He can make it a blessing to others.

Bethel is the symbol of fellowship with God; Ai is the symbol of the world. Abram "pitched his tent" between the two. The lasting value of our public service for God is measured by the depth of the intimacy of our private times of fellowship and oneness with Him. Rushing in and out of worship is wrong every time—there is always plenty of time to worship God. Days set apart for quiet can be a trap, detracting from the need to have daily quiet time with God. That is why we must "pitch our tents" where we will always have quiet times with Him, however noisy our times with the world may be. There are not three levels of spiritual life—worship, waiting, and work. Yet some of us seem to jump like spiritual frogs from worship to waiting, and from waiting to work. God's idea is that the three should go together as one. They were always together in the life of our Lord and in perfect harmony. It is a discipline that must be developed; it will not happen overnight.

INTIMATE WITH JESUS

> "Jesus said to him, 'Have I been with you so long, and yet you have not known Me, Philip?' " (John 14:9).

These words were not spoken as a rebuke, nor even with surprise; Jesus was encouraging Philip to draw closer. Yet the last person we get intimate with is Jesus. Before Pentecost the disciples knew Jesus as the One who gave them power to conquer demons and to bring about a revival (see Luke 10:18-20). It was a wonderful intimacy, but there was a much closer intimacy to come: ". . . I have called you friends . . ." (John 15:15). True friendship is rare on earth. It means identifying with someone in thought, heart, and spirit. The whole experience of life is designed to enable us to enter into this closest relationship with Jesus Christ. We receive His blessings and know His Word, but do we really know Him?

Jesus said, "It is to your advantage that I go away . . ." (John 16:7). He left that relationship to lead them even closer. It is a joy to Jesus when a disciple takes time to walk more intimately with Him. The bearing of fruit is always shown in Scripture to be the visible result of an intimate relationship with Jesus Christ (see John 15:1-4).

Once we get intimate with Jesus we are never lonely and we never lack for understanding or compassion. We can continually pour out our hearts to Him without being perceived as overly emotional or pitiful. The Christian who is truly intimate with Jesus will never draw attention to himself but will only show the evidence of a life where Jesus is completely in control. This is the outcome of allowing Jesus to satisfy every area of life to its depth. The picture resulting from such a life is that of the strong, calm balance that our Lord gives to those who are intimate with Him.

IS MY SACRIFICE LIVING?

"Abraham built an altar . . . ; and he bound Isaac his son and laid him on the altar . . ." (Genesis 22:9).

This event is a picture of the mistake we make in thinking that the ultimate God wants of us is the sacrifice of death. What God wants is the sacrifice *through* death which enables us to do what Jesus did, that is, sacrifice our lives. Not—"Lord, I am ready to go with You . . . to death" (Luke 22:33). But—"I am willing to be identified with Your death so that I may sacrifice my life to God."

We seem to think that God wants us to give up things! God purified Abraham from this error, and the same process is at work in our lives. God never tells us to give up things just for the sake of giving them up, but He tells us to give them up for the sake of the only thing worth having, namely, life with Himself. It is a matter of loosening the bands that hold back our lives. Those bands are loosened immediately by identification with the death of Jesus. Then we enter into a relationship with God whereby we may sacrifice our lives to Him.

It is of no value to God to give Him your life for death. He wants you to be a *"living* sacrifice"—to let Him have all your strengths that have been saved and sanctified through Jesus (Romans 12:1). This is what is acceptable to God.

Prayerful Inner-searching

"May your whole spirit, soul, and body be pre-served blameless . . ." (1 Thessalonians 5:23).

"Your whole spirit . . . ." The great, mysterious work of the Holy Spirit is in the deep recesses of our being which we cannot reach. Read Psalm 139. The psalmist implies—"O Lord, You are the God of the early mornings, the God of the late nights, the God of the mountain peaks, and the God of the sea. But, my God, my soul has horizons further away than those of early mornings, deeper darkness than the nights of earth, higher peaks than any mountain peaks, greater depths than any sea in nature. You who are the God of all these, be my God. I cannot reach to the heights or to the depths; there are motives I cannot discover, dreams I cannot realize. My God, search me."

Do we believe that God can fortify and protect our thought processes far beyond where we can go? *". . . the blood of Jesus Christ His Son cleanses us from all sin"* (1 John 1:7). If this verse means cleansing only on our conscious level, may God have mercy on us. The man who has been dulled by sin will say that he is not even conscious of it. But the cleansing from sin we experience will reach to the heights and depths of our spirit if we will "walk in the light as He is in the light" (1:7). The same Spirit that fed the life of Jesus Christ will feed the life of our spirit. It is only when we are protected by God with the miraculous sacredness of the Holy Spirit that our spirit, soul, and body can be preserved in pure uprightness until the coming of Jesus—no longer condemned in God's sight.

We should more frequently allow our minds to meditate on these great, massive truths of God.

THE OPENED SIGHT

"I now send you, to open their eyes . . . that they may receive forgiveness of sins . . ." (Acts 26:17-18).

This verse is the greatest example of the true essence of the message of a disciple of Jesus Christ in all of the New Testament.

God's first sovereign work of grace is summed up in the words, ". . . that they may receive forgiveness of sins . . . ." When a person fails in his personal Christian life, it is usually because he has never *received* anything. The only sign that a person is saved is that he has received something from Jesus Christ. Our job as workers for God is to open people's eyes so that they may turn themselves from darkness to light. But that is not salvation; it is conversion—only the effort of an awakened human being. I do not think it is too broad a statement to say that the majority of so-called Christians are like this. Their eyes are open, but they have received nothing. Conversion is not regeneration. This is a neglected fact in our preaching today. When a person is born again, he knows that it is because he has received something as a gift from Almighty God and not because of his own decision. People may make vows and promises, and may be determined to follow through, but none of this is salvation. Salvation means that we are brought to the place where we are able to receive something from God on the authority of Jesus Christ, namely, forgiveness of sins.

This is followed by God's second mighty work of grace: ". . . an inheritance among those who are sanctified . . . ." In sanctification, the one who has been born again deliberately gives up his right to himself to Jesus Christ, and identifies himself entirely with God's ministry to others.

What My Obedience to God Costs Other People

"As they led Him away, they laid hold of a certain man, Simon . . . , and on him they laid the cross that he might bear it after Jesus" (Luke 23:26).

I f we obey God, it is going to cost other people more than it costs us, and that is where the pain begins. If we are in love with our Lord, obedience does not cost us anything—it is a delight. But to those who do not love Him, our obedience does cost a great deal. If we obey God, it will mean that other people's plans are upset. They will ridicule us as if to say, "You call this Christianity?" We could prevent the suffering, but not if we are obedient to God. We must let the cost be paid.

When our obedience begins to cost others, our human pride entrenches itself and we say, "I will never accept anything from anyone." But we must, or disobey God. We have no right to think that the type of relationships we have with others should be any different from those the Lord Himself had (see Luke 8:1-3).

A lack of progress in our spiritual life results when we try to bear all the costs ourselves. And actually, we cannot. Because we are so involved in the universal purposes of God, others are immediately affected by our obedience to Him. Will we remain faithful in our obedience to God and be willing to suffer the humiliation of refusing to be independent? Or will we do just the opposite and say, "I will not cause other people to suffer"? We can disobey God if we choose, and it will bring immediate relief to the situation, but it will grieve our Lord. If, however, we obey God, He will care for those who have suffered the consequences of our obedience. We must simply obey and leave all the consequences with Him.

Beware of the inclination to dictate to God what consequences you would allow as a condition of your obedience to Him.

HAVE YOU EVER BEEN ALONE WITH GOD?

"When they were alone, He explained all things to His disciples" (Mark 4:34).

Our Solitude with Him. Jesus doesn't take us aside and explain things to us all the time; He explains things to us as we are able to understand them. The lives of others are examples for us, but God requires us to examine our own souls. It is slow work—so slow that it takes God all of time and eternity to make a man or woman conform to His purpose. We can only be used by God after we allow Him to show us the deep, hidden areas of our own character. It is astounding how ignorant we are about ourselves! We don't even recognize the envy, laziness, or pride within us when we see it. But Jesus will reveal to us everything we have held within ourselves before His grace began to work. How many of us have learned to look inwardly with courage?

We have to get rid of the idea that we understand ourselves. That is always the last bit of pride to go. The only One who understands us is God. The greatest curse in our spiritual life is pride. If we have ever had a glimpse of what we are like in the sight of God, we will never say, "Oh, I'm so unworthy." We will understand that this goes without saying. But as long as there is any doubt that we are unworthy, God will continue to close us in until He gets us alone. Whenever there is any element of pride or conceit remaining, Jesus can't teach us anything. He will allow us to experience heartbreak or the disappointment we feel when our intellectual pride is wounded. He will reveal numerous misplaced affections or desires—things over which we never thought He would have to get us alone. Many things are shown to us, often without effect. But when God gets us alone over them, they will be clear.

HAVE YOU EVER BEEN
ALONE WITH GOD?

"When He was alone . . . the twelve asked Him about the parable" (Mark 4:10).

His Solitude with Us. When God gets us alone through suffering, heartbreak, temptation, disappointment, sickness, or by thwarted desires, a broken friendship, or a new friendship—when He gets us absolutely alone, and we are totally speechless, unable to ask even one question, then He begins to teach us. Notice Jesus Christ's training of the Twelve. It was the disciples, not the crowd outside, who were confused. His disciples constantly asked Him questions, and He constantly explained things to them, but they didn't understand until after they received the Holy Spirit (see John 14:26).

As you journey with God, the only thing He intends to be clear is the way He deals with your soul. The sorrows and difficulties in the lives of others will be absolutely confusing to you. We think we understand another person's struggle until God reveals the same shortcomings in our lives. There are vast areas of stubbornness and ignorance the Holy Spirit has to reveal in each of us, but it can only be done when Jesus gets us alone. Are we alone with Him now? Or are we more concerned with our own ideas, friendships, and cares for our bodies? Jesus cannot teach us anything until we quiet all our intellectual questions and get alone with Him.

CALLED BY GOD

> "I heard the voice of the Lord, saying: 'Whom shall I send, and who will go for Us?' Then I said, 'Here am I! Send me' " (Isaiah 6:8).

God did not direct His call to Isaiah—Isaiah overheard God saying, ". . . who will go for Us?" The call of God is not just for a select few but for everyone. Whether I hear God's call or not depends on the condition of my ears, and exactly what I hear depends upon my spiritual attitude. "Many are called, but few are chosen" (Matthew 22:14). That is, few prove that they are the chosen ones. The chosen ones are those who have come into a relationship with God through Jesus Christ and have had their spiritual condition changed and their ears opened. Then they hear "the voice of the Lord" continually asking, ". . . who will go for Us?" However, God doesn't single out someone and say, "Now, *you* go." He did not force His will on Isaiah. Isaiah was in the presence of God, and he overheard the call. His response, performed in complete freedom, could only be to say, "Here am I! Send me."

Remove the thought from your mind of expecting God to come to force you or to plead with you. When our Lord called His disciples, He did it without irresistible pressure from the outside. The quiet, yet passionate, insistence of His "Follow Me" was spoken to men whose every sense was receptive (Matthew 4:19). If we will allow the Holy Spirit to bring us face to face with God, we too will hear what Isaiah heard—"the voice of the Lord." In perfect freedom we too will say, "Here am I! Send me."

DO YOU WALK IN WHITE?

"We were buried with Him . . . that just as Christ was raised from the dead . . . even so we also should walk in newness of life" (Romans 6:4).

No one experiences complete sanctification without going through a "white funeral"—the burial of the old life. If there has never been this crucial moment of change through death, sanctification will never be more than an elusive dream. There must be a "white funeral," a death with only one resurrection—a resurrection into the life of Jesus Christ. Nothing can defeat a life like this. It has oneness with God for only one purpose—to be a witness for Him.

Have you really come to your last days? You have often come to them in your mind, but have you *really* experienced them? You cannot die or go to your funeral in a mood of excitement. Death means you stop being. You must agree with God and stop being the intensely striving kind of Christian you have been. We avoid the cemetery and continually refuse our own death. It will not happen by striving, but by yielding to death. It is dying—being "baptized into His death" (Romans 6:3).

Have you had your "white funeral," or are you piously deceiving your own soul? Has there been a point in your life which you now mark as your last day? Is there a place in your life to which you go back in memory with humility and overwhelming gratitude, so that you can honestly proclaim, "Yes, it was then, at my 'white funeral,' that I made an agreement with God."

"This is the will of God, your sanctification . . ." (1 Thessalonians 4:3). Once you truly realize this is God's will, you will enter into the process of sanctification as a natural response. Are you willing to experience that "white funeral" now? Will you agree with Him that this is your last day on earth? The moment of agreement depends on you.

THE VOICE OF THE NATURE OF GOD

"I heard the voice of the Lord, saying: 'Whom shall I send, and who will go for Us?'" (Isaiah 6:8).

When we talk about the call of God, we often forget the most important thing, namely, the nature of Him who calls. There are many things calling each of us today. Some of these calls will be answered, and others will not even be heard. The call is the expression of the nature of the One who calls, and we can only recognize the call if that same nature is in us. The call of God is the expression of God's nature, not ours. God providentially weaves the threads of His call through our lives, and only we can distinguish them. It is the threading of God's voice directly to us over a certain concern, and it is useless to seek another person's opinion of it. Our dealings over the call of God should be kept exclusively between ourselves and Him.

The call of God is not a reflection of my nature; my personal desires and temperament are of no consideration. As long as I dwell on my own qualities and traits and think about what I am suited for, I will never hear the call of God. But when God brings me into the right relationship with Himself, I will be in the same condition Isaiah was. Isaiah was so attuned to God, because of the great crisis he had just endured, that the call of God penetrated his soul. The majority of us cannot hear anything but ourselves. And we cannot hear anything God says. But to be brought to the place where we can hear the call of God is to be profoundly changed.

THE CALL OF THE NATURAL LIFE

"When it pleased God . . . to reveal His Son in me . . ." (Galatians 1:15–16).

The call of God is not a call to serve Him in any particular way. My contact with the nature of God will shape my understanding of His call and will help me realize what I truly desire to do for Him. The call of God is an expression of His nature; the service which results in my life is suited to me and is an expression of my nature. The call of the natural life was stated by the apostle Paul—"When it pleased God . . . to reveal His Son in me, that I might *preach* Him [that is, *purely and solemnly express* Him] among the Gentiles . . . ."

Service is the overflow which pours from a life filled with love and devotion. But strictly speaking, there is no *call* to that. Service is what I bring to the relationship and is the reflection of my identification with the nature of God. Service becomes a natural part of my life. God brings me into the proper relationship with Himself so that I can understand His call, and then I serve Him on my own out of a motivation of absolute love. Service to God is the deliberate love-gift of a nature that has heard the call of God. Service is an expression of my nature, and God's call is an expression of His nature. Therefore, when I receive His nature and hear His call, His divine voice resounds throughout His nature and mine and the two become one in service. The Son of God reveals Himself in me, and out of devotion to Him service becomes my everyday way of life.

"It Is the Lord!"

"Thomas answered and said to Him, 'My Lord and my God!' " (John 20:28).

J esus said to her, 'Give Me a drink' " (John 4:7). How many of us are expecting Jesus Christ to quench our thirst when we should be satisfying Him! We should be pouring out our lives, investing our total beings, not drawing on Him to satisfy us. "You shall be witnesses to Me . . ." (Acts 1:8). That means lives of pure, uncompromising, and unrestrained devotion to the Lord Jesus, which will be satisfying to Him wherever He may send us.

Beware of anything that competes with your loyalty to Jesus Christ. The greatest competitor of true devotion to Jesus is the service we do for Him. It is easier to serve than to pour out our lives completely for Him. The goal of the call of God is His satisfaction, not simply that we should do something *for* Him. We are not sent to do battle for God, but to be used by God in His battles. Are we more devoted to service than we are to Jesus Christ Himself?

VISION AND DARKNESS

**"When the sun was going down, a deep sleep
fell upon Abram; and behold, horror and
great darkness fell upon him" (Genesis 15:12).**

Whenever God gives a vision to a Christian, it is
as if He puts him in "the shadow of His hand"
(Isaiah 49:2). The saint's duty is to be still and
listen. There is a "darkness" that comes from too much
light—that is the time to listen. The story of Abram and
Hagar in Genesis 16 is an excellent example of listening
to so-called good advice during a time of darkness, rather
than waiting for God to send the light. When God gives
you a vision and darkness follows, wait. God will bring
the vision He has given you to reality in your life if you
will wait on His timing. Never try to help God fulfill His
word. Abram went through thirteen years of silence, but
in those years all of his self-sufficiency was destroyed. He
grew past the point of relying on his own common sense.
Those years of silence were a time of discipline, not a
period of God's displeasure. There is never any need to
pretend that your life is filled with joy and confidence;
just wait upon God and be grounded in Him (see Isaiah
50:10–11).

Do I trust at all in the flesh? Or have I learned to
go beyond all confidence in myself and other people of
God? Do I trust in books and prayers or other joys in my
life? Or have I placed my confidence in God *Himself*, not
in His blessings? "I am Almighty God . . ." —El-Shaddai,
the All-Powerful God (Genesis 17:1). The reason we are
all being disciplined is that we will know God is real. As
soon as God becomes real to us, people pale by comparison, becoming shadows of reality. Nothing that other
saints do or say can ever upset the one who is built on
God.

ARE YOU FRESH FOR EVERYTHING?

"Jesus answered and said to him, 'Most assuredly, I say to you, unless one is born again, he cannot see the kingdom of God' " (John 3:3).

S ometimes we are fresh and eager to attend a prayer meeting, but do we feel that same freshness for such mundane tasks as polishing shoes?

Being born again by the Spirit is an unmistakable work of God, as mysterious as the wind, and as surprising as God Himself. We don't know where it begins—it is hidden away in the depths of our soul. Being born again from above is an enduring, perpetual, and eternal beginning. It provides a freshness all the time in thinking, talking, and living—a continual surprise of the life of God. Staleness is an indication that something in our lives is out of step with God. We say to ourselves, "I have to do this thing or it will never get done." That is the first sign of staleness. Do we feel fresh this very moment or are we stale, frantically searching our minds for something to do? Freshness is not the result of obedience; it comes from the Holy Spirit. Obedience keeps us "in the light as He is in the light . . ." (1 John 1:7).

Jealously guard your relationship with God. Jesus prayed "that they may be one just as We are one"—with nothing in between (John 17:22). Keep your whole life continually open to Jesus Christ. Don't pretend to be open with Him. Are you drawing your life from any source other than God Himself? If you are depending on something else as your source of freshness and strength, you will not realize when His power is gone.

Being born of the Spirit means much more than we usually think. It gives us new vision and keeps us absolutely fresh for everything through the never-ending supply of the life of God.

RECALL WHAT GOD REMEMBERS

"Thus says the LORD: 'I remember . . . the kindness of your youth . . .' " (Jeremiah 2:2).

Am I as spontaneously kind to God as I used to be, or am I only expecting God to be kind to me? Does everything in my life fill His heart with gladness, or do I constantly complain because things don't seem to be going my way? A person who has forgotten what God treasures will not be filled with joy. It is wonderful to remember that Jesus Christ has needs which we can meet—"Give Me a drink" (John 4:7). How much kindness have I shown Him in the past week? Has my life been a good reflection on His reputation?

God is saying to His people, "You are not in love with Me now, but I remember a time when you were." He says, "I remember . . . the love of your betrothal . . ." (Jeremiah 2:2). Am I as filled to overflowing with love for Jesus Christ as I was in the beginning, when I went out of my way to prove my devotion to Him? Does He ever find me pondering the time when I cared only for Him? Is that where I am now, or have I chosen man's wisdom over true love for Him? Am I so in love with Him that I take no thought for where He might lead me? Or am I watching to see how much respect I get as I measure how much service I should give Him?

As I recall what God remembers about me, I may also begin to realize that He is not what He used to be to me. When this happens, I should allow the shame and humiliation it creates in my life, because it will bring godly sorrow, and "godly sorrow produces repentance . . ." (2 Corinthians 7:10).

AM I LOOKING TO GOD?

"Look to Me, and be saved . . ." (Isaiah 45:22).

Do we expect God to come to us with His blessings and save us? He says, "*Look to Me*, and *be* saved . . . ." The greatest difficulty spiritually is to concentrate on God, and His blessings are what make it so difficult. Troubles almost always make us look to God, but His blessings tend to divert our attention elsewhere. The basic lesson of the Sermon on the Mount is to narrow all your interests until your mind, heart, and body are focused on Jesus Christ. "Look to Me . . . ."

Many of us have a mental picture of what a Christian should be, and looking at this image in other Christians' lives becomes a hindrance to our focusing on God. This is not salvation—it is not simple enough. He says, in effect, "Look to Me and you are saved," not "You will be saved someday." We will find what we are looking for if we will concentrate on Him. We get distracted from God and irritable with Him while He continues to say to us, "Look to Me, and be saved . . . ." Our difficulties, our trials, and our worries about tomorrow all vanish when we look to God.

Wake yourself up and look to God. Build your hope on Him. No matter how many things seem to be pressing in on you, be determined to push them aside and look to Him. "Look to Me . . . ." Salvation is yours the moment you look.

TRANSFORMED BY BEHOLDING

"We all, with unveiled face, beholding as in a mirror the glory of the Lord, are being transformed into the same image . . ." (2 Corinthians 3:18).

The greatest characteristic a Christian can exhibit is this completely unveiled openness before God, which allows that person's life to become a mirror for others. When the Spirit fills us, we are transformed, and by beholding God we become mirrors. You can always tell when someone has been beholding the glory of the Lord, because your inner spirit senses that he mirrors the Lord's own character. Beware of anything that would spot or tarnish that mirror in you. It is almost always something good that will stain it—something good, but not what is best.

The most important rule for us is to concentrate on keeping our lives open to God. Let everything else including work, clothes, and food be set aside. The busyness of things obscures our concentration on God. We must maintain a position of beholding Him, keeping our lives completely spiritual through and through. Let other things come and go as they will; let other people criticize us as they will; but never allow anything to obscure the life that "is hidden with Christ in God" (Colossians 3:3). Never let a hurried lifestyle disturb the relationship of abiding in Him. This is an easy thing to allow, but we must guard against it. The most difficult lesson of the Christian life is learning how to continue "beholding as in a mirror the glory of the Lord . . . ."

GOD'S OVERPOWERING PURPOSE

**"I have appeared to you for this purpose . . ."
(Acts 26:16).**

The vision Paul had on the road to Damascus was not a passing emotional experience, but a vision that had very clear and emphatic directions for him. And Paul stated, "I was not disobedient to the heavenly vision" (Acts 26:19). Our Lord said to Paul, in effect, "Your whole life is to be overpowered or subdued by Me; you are to have no end, no aim, and no purpose but Mine." And the Lord also says to us, "You did not choose Me, but *I chose you* and appointed you that you should go . . ." (John 15:16).

When we are born again, if we are spiritual at all, we have visions of what Jesus wants us to be. It is important that I learn not to be "disobedient to the heavenly vision"—not to doubt that it can be attained. It is not enough to give mental assent to the fact that God has redeemed the world, nor even to know that the Holy Spirit can make all that Jesus did a reality in my life. I must have the foundation of a personal relationship with Him. Paul was not given a message or a doctrine to proclaim. He was brought into a vivid, personal, overpowering relationship with Jesus Christ. Acts 26:16 is tremendously compelling ". . . to make you a minister and a witness . . . ." There would be nothing there without a personal relationship. Paul was devoted to a Person, not to a cause. He was absolutely Jesus Christ's. He saw nothing else and he lived for nothing else. "For I determined not to know anything among you except Jesus Christ and Him crucified" (1 Corinthians 2:2).

LEAVE ROOM FOR GOD

"When it pleased God . . ." (Galatians 1:15).

As servants of God, we must learn to make room for Him—to give God "elbow room." We plan and figure and predict that this or that will happen, but we forget to make room for God to come in as He chooses. Would we be surprised if God came into our meeting or into our preaching in a way we had never expected Him to come? Do not look for God to come in a particular way, but *do look for Him*. The way to make room for Him is to expect Him to come, but not in a certain way. No matter how well we may know God, the great lesson to learn is that He may break in at any minute. We tend to overlook this element of surprise, yet God never works in any other way. Suddenly—God meets our life—". . . when it pleased God . . . ."

Keep your life so constantly in touch with God that His surprising power can break through at any point. Live in a constant state of expectancy, and leave room for God to come in as He decides.

LOOK AGAIN AND CONSECRATE

"If God so clothes the grass of the field . . . , will He not much more clothe you . . . ?" (Matthew 6:30).

A simple statement of Jesus is always a puzzle to us because we will not be simple. How can we maintain the simplicity of Jesus so that we may understand Him? By receiving His Spirit, recognizing and relying on Him, and obeying Him as He brings us the truth of His Word, life will become amazingly simple. Jesus asks us to consider that "if God so clothes the grass of the field . . ." how "much more" will He clothe you, if you keep your relationship right with Him? Every time we lose ground in our fellowship with God, it is because we have disrespectfully thought that we knew better than Jesus Christ. We have allowed "the cares of this world" to enter in (Matthew 13:22), while forgetting the "much more" of our heavenly Father.

"Look at the birds of the air . . ." (6:26). Their function is to obey the instincts God placed within them, and God watches over them. Jesus said that if you have the right relationship with Him and will obey His Spirit within you, then God will care for your "feathers" too.

"Consider the lilies of the field . . ." (6:28). They grow where they are planted. Many of us refuse to grow where God plants us. Therefore, we don't take root anywhere. Jesus said if we would obey the life of God within us, He would look after all other things. Did Jesus Christ lie to us? Are we experiencing the "much more" He promised? If we are not, it is because we are not obeying the life God has given us and have cluttered our minds with confusing thoughts and worries. How much time have we wasted asking God senseless questions while we should be absolutely free to concentrate on our service to Him? Consecration is the act of continually separating myself from everything except that which God has appointed me to do. It is not a one-time experience but an ongoing process. Am I continually separating myself and looking to God every day of my life?

LOOK AGAIN AND THINK

"Do not worry about your life . . ." (Matthew 6:25).

A warning which needs to be repeated is that "the cares of this world and the deceitfulness of riches," and the lust for other things, will choke out the life of God in us (Matthew 13:22). We are never free from the recurring waves of this invasion. If the frontline of attack is not about clothes and food, it may be about money or the lack of money; or friends or lack of friends; or the line may be drawn over difficult circumstances. It is one steady invasion, and these things will come in like a flood, unless we allow the Spirit of God to raise up the banner against it.

"I say to you, do not worry about your life . . . ." Our Lord says to be careful only about one thing—our relationship to Him. But our common sense shouts loudly and says, "That is absurd, I *must* consider how I am going to live, and I *must* consider what I am going to eat and drink." Jesus says you must not. Beware of allowing yourself to think that He says this while not understanding your circumstances. Jesus Christ knows our circumstances better than we do, and He says we must not think about these things to the point where they become the primary concern of our life. Whenever there are competing concerns in your life, be sure you always put your relationship to God first.

"Sufficient for the day is its own trouble" (6:34). How much trouble has begun to threaten you today? What kind of mean little demons have been looking into your life and saying, "What are your plans for next month—or next summer?" Jesus tells us not to worry about any of these things. Look again and think. Keep your mind on the "much more" of your heavenly Father (6:30).

How Could Someone So Persecute Jesus!

> "Saul, Saul, why are you persecuting me?"
> (Acts 26:14).

Are you determined to have your own way in living for God? We will never be free from this trap until we are brought into the experience of the baptism of "the Holy Spirit and fire" (Matthew 3:11). Stubbornness and self-will will always stab Jesus Christ. It may hurt no one else, but it wounds His Spirit. Whenever we are obstinate and self-willed and set on our own ambitions, we are hurting Jesus. Every time we stand on our own rights and insist that this is what we intend to do, we are persecuting Him. Whenever we rely on self-respect, we systematically disturb and grieve His Spirit. And when we finally understand that it is Jesus we have been persecuting all this time, it is the most crushing revelation ever.

Is the Word of God tremendously penetrating and sharp in me as I hand it on to you, or does my life betray the things I profess to teach? I may teach sanctification and yet exhibit the spirit of Satan, the very spirit that persecutes Jesus Christ. The Spirit of Jesus is conscious of only one thing—a perfect oneness with the Father. And He tells us, "Take My yoke upon you and learn from Me, for I am gentle and lowly in heart, and you will find rest for your souls" (Matthew 11:29). All I do should be based on a perfect oneness with Him, not on a self-willed determination to be godly. This will mean that others may use me, go around me, or completely ignore me, but if I will submit to it for His sake, I will prevent Jesus Christ from being persecuted.

HOW COULD SOMEONE BE SO IGNORANT!

"Who are You, Lord?" (Acts 26:15).

"T he LORD spoke thus to me with a strong hand . . ." (Isaiah 8:11). There is no escape when our Lord speaks. He always comes using His authority and taking hold of our understanding. Has the voice of God come to you directly? If it has, you cannot mistake the intimate insistence with which it has spoken to you. God speaks in the language you know best—not through your ears, but through your circumstances.

God has to destroy our determined confidence in our own convictions. We say, "I know that this is what I should do"—and suddenly the voice of God speaks in a way that overwhelms us by revealing the depths of our ignorance. We show our ignorance of Him in the very way we decide to serve Him. We serve Jesus in a spirit that is not His, and hurt Him by our defense of Him. We push His claims in the spirit of the devil; our words sound all right, but the spirit is that of an enemy. "He . . . rebuked them, and said, 'You do not know what manner of spirit you are of' " (Luke 9:55). The spirit of our Lord in His followers is described in 1 Corinthians 13.

Have I been persecuting Jesus by an eager determination to serve Him in my own way? If I feel I have done my duty, yet have hurt Him in the process, I can be sure that this was not my duty. My way will not be to foster a meek and quiet spirit, only the spirit of self-satisfaction. We presume that whatever is unpleasant is our duty! Is that anything like the spirit of our Lord—"I *delight* to do Your will, O my God . . ." (Psalm 40:8).

THE DILEMMA OF OBEDIENCE

**"Samuel was afraid to tell Eli the vision"
(1 Samuel 3:15).**

God never speaks to us in dramatic ways, but in ways that are easy to misunderstand. Then we say, "I wonder if that is God's voice?" Isaiah said that the Lord spoke to him "with a strong hand," that is, by the pressure of his circumstances (Isaiah 8:11). Without the sovereign hand of God Himself, nothing touches our lives. Do we discern His hand at work, or do we see things as mere occurrences?

Get into the habit of saying, "Speak, LORD," and life will become a romance (1 Samuel 3:9). Every time circumstances press in on you, say, "Speak, LORD," and make time to listen. Chastening is more than a means of discipline—it is meant to bring me to the point of saying, "Speak, LORD." Think back to a time when God spoke to you. Do you remember what He said? Was it Luke 11:13, or was it 1 Thessalonians 5:23? As we listen, our ears become more sensitive, and like Jesus, we will hear God all the time.

Should I tell my "Eli" what God has shown to me? This is where the dilemma of obedience hits us. We disobey God by becoming amateur providences and thinking, "I must shield 'Eli,' " who represents the best people we know. God did not tell Samuel to tell Eli—he had to decide that for himself. God's message to you may hurt your "Eli," but trying to prevent suffering in another's life will prove to be an obstruction between your soul and God. It is at your own risk that you prevent someone's right hand being cut off or right eye being plucked out (see Matthew 5:29-30).

Never ask another person's advice about anything God makes you decide before Him. If you ask advice, you will almost always side with Satan. ". . . I did not immediately confer with flesh and blood . . ." (Galatians 1:16).

DO YOU SEE YOUR CALLING?

". . . separated to the gospel of God . . ."
(Romans 1:1).

Our calling is not primarily to be holy men and women, but to be proclaimers of the gospel of God. The one all-important thing is that the gospel of God should be recognized as *the* abiding reality. Reality is not human goodness, or holiness, or heaven, or hell—it is redemption. The need to perceive this is the most vital need of the Christian worker today. As workers, we have to get used to the revelation that redemption is the only reality. Personal holiness is an effect of redemption, not the cause of it. If we place our faith in human goodness we will go under when testing comes.

Paul did not say that he separated himself, but "when it pleased God, who separated me . . ." (Galatians 1:15). Paul was not overly interested in his own character. And as long as our eyes are focused on our own personal holiness, we will never even get close to the full reality of redemption. Christian workers fail because they place their desire for their own holiness above their desire to know God. "Don't ask me to be confronted with the strong reality of redemption on behalf of the filth of human life surrounding me today; what I want is anything God can do for me to make me more desirable in my own eyes." To talk that way is a sign that the reality of the gospel of God has not begun to touch me. There is no reckless abandon to God in that. God cannot deliver me while my interest is merely in my own character. Paul was not conscious of himself. He was recklessly abandoned, totally surrendered, and separated by God for one purpose—to proclaim the gospel of God (see Romans 9:3).

THE CALL OF GOD

"Christ did not send me to baptize, but to preach the gospel . . ." (1 Corinthians 1:17).

Paul states here that the call of God is to preach the gospel. But remember what Paul means by "the gospel," namely, the reality of redemption in our Lord Jesus Christ. We are inclined to make sanctification the goal of our preaching. Paul refers to personal experiences only by way of illustration, never as the end of the matter. We are not commissioned to preach salvation or sanctification—we are commissioned to lift up Jesus Christ (see John 12:32). It is an injustice to say that Jesus Christ labored in redemption to make *me* a saint. Jesus Christ labored in redemption to redeem the whole world and to place it perfectly whole and restored before the throne of God. The fact that we can experience redemption illustrates the power of its reality, but that experience is a byproduct and not the goal of redemption. If God were human, how sick and tired He would be of the constant requests we make for our salvation and for our sanctification. We burden His energies from morning till night asking for things for ourselves or for something from which *we* want to be delivered! When we finally touch the underlying foundation of the reality of the gospel of God, we will never bother Him anymore with little personal complaints.

The one passion of Paul's life was to proclaim the gospel of God. He welcomed heartbreak, disillusionment, and tribulation for only one reason—these things kept him unmovable in his devotion to the gospel of God.

THE COMPELLING
FORCE OF THE CALL

"Woe is me if I do not preach the gospel!"
(1 Corinthians 9:16).

Beware of refusing to hear the call of God. Everyone who is saved is called to testify to the fact of his salvation. That, however, is not the same as the call to preach, but is merely an illustration which can be used in preaching. In this verse, Paul was referring to the stinging pains produced in him by the compelling force of the call to preach the gospel. Never try to apply what Paul said regarding the call to preach to those souls who are being called to God for salvation. There is nothing easier than getting saved, because it is solely God's sovereign work—"Look to Me, and be saved . . ." (Isaiah 45:22). Our Lord never requires the same conditions for discipleship that he requires for salvation. We are condemned to salvation through the Cross of Christ. But discipleship has an option with it—"*If* anyone . . ." (Luke 14:26).

Paul's words have to do with our being made servants of Jesus Christ, and our permission is never asked as to what we will do or where we will go. God makes us as broken bread and poured-out wine to please Himself. To be "separated to the gospel" means being able to hear the call of God (Romans 1:1). Once someone begins to hear that call, a suffering worthy of the name of Christ is produced. Suddenly, every ambition, every desire of life, and every outlook is completely blotted out and extinguished. Only one thing remains—". . . *separated to the gospel* . . . ." Woe be to the soul who tries to head in any other direction once that call has come to him. The Bible Training College exists so that each of you may know whether or not God has a man or woman here who truly cares about proclaiming His gospel and to see if God grips you for this purpose. Beware of competing calls once the call of God grips you.

BECOMING THE "FILTH OF THE WORLD"

"We have been made as the filth of the world . . ." (1 Corinthians 4:13).

These words are not an exaggeration. The only reason they may not be true of us who call ourselves ministers of the gospel is not that Paul forgot or misunderstood the exact truth of them, but that we are too cautious and concerned about our own desires to allow ourselves to become the refuse or "filth of the world." "Fill up in my flesh what is lacking in the afflictions of Christ . . ." (Colossians 1:24) is not the result of the holiness of sanctification, but the evidence of consecration—being "separated *to* the gospel of God . . ." (Romans 1:1).

"Beloved, do not think it strange concerning the fiery trial which is to try you . . ." (1 Peter 4:12). If we do think the things we encounter are strange, it is because we are fearful and cowardly. We pay such close attention to our own interests and desires that we stay out of the mire and say, "I won't submit; I won't bow or bend." And you don't have to—you can be saved by the "skin of your teeth" if you like. You can refuse to let God count you as one who is "separated to the gospel . . . ." Or you can say, "I don't care if I am treated like 'the filth of the world' as long as the gospel is proclaimed." A true servant of Jesus Christ is one who is willing to experience martyrdom for the reality of the gospel of God. When a moral person is confronted with contempt, immorality, disloyalty, or dishonesty, he is so repulsed by the offense that he turns away and in despair closes his heart to the offender. But the miracle of the redemptive reality of God is that the worst and the vilest offender can never exhaust the depths of His love. Paul did not say that God separated him to show what a wonderful man He could make of him, but "*to reveal His Son in me* . . ." (Galatians 1:16).

THE COMPELLING MAJESTY
OF HIS POWER

"The love of Christ compels us . . ."
(2 Corinthians 5:14).

Paul said that he was overpowered, subdued, and held as in a vise by "the love of Christ." Very few of us really know what it means to be held in the grip of the love of God. We tend so often to be controlled simply by our own experience. The one thing that gripped and held Paul, to the exclusion of everything else, was the love of God. "The love of Christ compels us. . . ." When you hear that coming from the life of a man or woman it is unmistakable. You will know that the Spirit of God is completely unhindered in that person's life.

When we are born again by the Spirit of God, our testimony is based solely on what God has done for us, and rightly so. But that will change and be removed forever once you "receive power when the Holy Spirit has come upon you . . ." (Acts 1:8). Only then will you begin to realize what Jesus meant when He went on to say, ". . . you shall be *witnesses to Me* . . . ." Not witnesses to what Jesus can do—that is basic and understood—but "witnesses to Me . . . ." We will accept everything that happens as if it were happening to Him, whether we receive praise or blame, persecution or reward. No one is able to take this stand for Jesus Christ who is not totally compelled by the majesty of His power. It is the only thing that matters, and yet it is strange that it's the last thing we as Christian workers realize. Paul said that he was gripped by the love of God and that is why he acted as he did. People could perceive him as mad or sane—he did not care. There was only one thing he lived for—to persuade people of the coming judgment of God and to tell them of "the love of Christ." This total surrender to "the love of Christ" is the only thing that will bear fruit in your life. And it will always leave the mark of God's holiness and His power, never drawing attention to your personal holiness.

ARE YOU READY TO BE POURED OUT AS AN OFFERING?

"If I am being poured out as a drink offering on the sacrifice and service of your faith, I am glad and rejoice with you all" (Philippians 2:17).

Are you willing to sacrifice yourself for the work of another believer—to pour out your life sacrificially for the ministry and faith of others? Or do you say, "I am not willing to be poured out right now, and I don't want God to tell me how to serve Him. I want to choose the place of my own sacrifice. And I want to have certain people watching me and saying, 'Well done.' "

It is one thing to follow God's way of service if you are regarded as a hero, but quite another thing if the road marked out for you by God requires becoming a "doormat" under other people's feet. God's purpose may be to teach you to say, "I know how to be abased . . ." (Philippians 4:12). Are you ready to be sacrificed like that? Are you ready to be less than a mere drop in the bucket—to be so totally insignificant that no one remembers you even if they think of those you served? Are you willing to give and be poured out until you are used up and exhausted—not seeking to be ministered to, but to minister? Some saints cannot do menial work while maintaining a saintly attitude, because they feel such service is beneath their dignity.

ARE YOU READY TO BE POURED OUT AS AN OFFERING?

"I am already being poured out as a drink offering . . ." (2 Timothy 4:6).

Are you ready to be poured out as an offering? It is an act of your will, not your emotions. *Tell* God you are ready to be offered as a sacrifice for Him. Then accept the consequences as they come, without any complaints, in spite of what God may send your way. God sends you through a crisis in private, where no other person can help you. From the outside your life may appear to be the same, but the difference is taking place in your will. Once you have experienced the crisis in your will, you will take no thought of the cost when it begins to affect you externally. If you don't deal with God on the level of your will first, the result will be only to arouse sympathy for yourself.

"Bind the sacrifice with cords to the horns of the altar" (Psalm 118:27). You must be willing to be placed on the altar and go through the fire; willing to experience what the altar represents—burning, purification, and separation for only one purpose—the elimination of every desire and affection not grounded in or directed toward God. But *you* don't eliminate it, God does. You "bind the sacrifice . . . to the horns of the altar" and see to it that you don't wallow in self-pity once the fire begins. After you have gone through the fire, there will be nothing that will be able to trouble or depress you. When another crisis arises, you will realize that things cannot touch you as they used to do. What fire lies ahead in your life?

Tell God you are ready to be poured out as an offering, and God will prove Himself to be all you ever dreamed He would be.

SPIRITUAL DEJECTION

> "We were hoping that it was He who was going to redeem Israel. Indeed, besides all this, today is the third day since these things happened" (Luke 24:21).

Every fact that the disciples stated was right, but the conclusions they drew from those facts were wrong. Anything that has even a hint of dejection spiritually is always wrong. If I am depressed or burdened, I am to blame, not God or anyone else. Dejection stems from one of two sources—I have either satisfied a lust or I have not had it satisfied. In either case, dejection is the result. *Lust* means "I must have it at once." Spiritual lust causes me to demand an answer from God, instead of seeking God Himself who gives the answer. What have I been hoping or trusting God would do? Is today "the third day" and He has still not done what I expected? Am I therefore justified in being dejected and in blaming God? Whenever we insist that God should give us an answer to prayer we are off track. The purpose of prayer is that we get ahold of God, not of the answer. It is impossible to be well physically and to be dejected, because dejection is a sign of sickness. This is also true spiritually. Dejection spiritually is wrong, and we are always to blame for it.

We look for visions from heaven and for earth-shaking events to see God's power. Even the fact that we are dejected is proof that we do this. Yet we never realize that all the time God is at work in our everyday events and in the people around us. If we will only obey, and do the task that He has placed closest to us, we will see Him. One of the most amazing revelations of God comes to us when we learn that it is in the everyday things of life that we realize the magnificent deity of Jesus Christ.

THE COST OF SANCTIFICATION

"May the God of peace Himself sanctify you completely . . ." (1 Thessalonians 5:23).

When we pray, asking God to sanctify us, are we prepared to measure up to what that really means? We take the word *sanctification* much too lightly. Are we prepared to pay the cost of sanctification? The cost will be a deep restriction of all our earthly concerns, and an extensive cultivation of all our godly concerns. Sanctification means to be intensely focused on God's point of view. It means to secure and to keep all the strength of our body, soul, and spirit for God's purpose alone. Are we really prepared for God to perform in us everything for which He separated us? And after He has done His work, are we then prepared to separate ourselves to God just as Jesus did? "For their sakes I sanctify Myself . . ." (John 17:19). The reason some of us have not entered into the experience of sanctification is that we have not realized the meaning of sanctification from God's perspective. Sanctification means being made one with Jesus so that the nature that controlled Him will control us. Are we really prepared for what that will cost? It will cost absolutely everything in us which is not of God.

Are we prepared to be caught up into the full meaning of Paul's prayer in this verse? Are we prepared to say, "Lord, make me, a sinner saved by grace, as holy as You can"? Jesus prayed that we might be one with Him, just as He is one with the Father (see John 17:21–23). The resounding evidence of the Holy Spirit in a person's life is the unmistakable family likeness to Jesus Christ, and the freedom from everything which is not like Him. Are we prepared to set ourselves apart for the Holy Spirit's work in us?

ARE YOU EXHAUSTED SPIRITUALLY?

"The everlasting God . . . neither faints nor is weary" (Isaiah 40:28).

Exhaustion means that our vital energies are completely worn out and spent. Spiritual exhaustion is never the result of sin, but of service. Whether or not you experience exhaustion will depend on where you get your supplies. Jesus said to Peter, "Feed My sheep," but He gave him nothing with which to feed them (John 21:17). The process of being made broken bread and poured-out wine means that *you* have to be the nourishment for other people's souls until they learn to feed on God. They must drain you completely—to the very last drop. But be careful to replenish your supply, or you will quickly be utterly exhausted. Until others learn to draw on the life of the Lord Jesus directly, they will have to draw on His life through you. You must literally be their source of supply, until they learn to take their nourishment from God. We owe it to God to be our best for His lambs and sheep, as well as for Him.

Have you delivered yourself over to exhaustion because of the way you have been serving God? If so, then renew and rekindle your desires and affections. Examine your reasons for service. Is your source based on your own understanding or is it grounded on the redemption of Jesus Christ? Continually look back to the foundation of your love and affection and remember where your Source of power lies. You have no right to complain, "O Lord, I am so exhausted." He saved and sanctified you to exhaust you. Be exhausted for God, but remember that He is your supply. "All my springs are in you" (Psalm 87:7).

IS YOUR ABILITY TO SEE GOD BLINDED?

"Lift up your eyes on high, and see who has created these things . . ." (Isaiah 40:26).

The people of God in Isaiah's time had starved their imagination by looking on the face of idols. But Isaiah made them look up at the heavens; that is, he made them begin to use their imagination correctly. If we are children of God, we have a tremendous treasure in nature and will realize that it is holy and sacred. We will see God reaching out to us in every wind that blows, every sunrise and sunset, every cloud in the sky, every flower that blooms, and every leaf that fades, if we will only begin to use our starved imagination to visualize it.

The real test of spiritual focus is being able to bring your thoughts and imagination under control. Is your mind focused on the face of an idol? Is the idol yourself? Is it your work? Is it your idea of what a servant should be, or maybe your experience of salvation and sanctification? If so, then your ability to see God is blinded. You will be powerless when faced with difficulties and will be forced to endure in darkness. If your power to see has been blinded, don't look back on your own experiences, but look to God. It is God you need. Go beyond yourself and away from the faces of your idols and away from everything else that has been blinding your thinking, your imagination. Wake up and accept the ridicule that Isaiah gave to his people, and deliberately turn your thoughts and your eyes to God.

One of the reasons for our sense of futility in prayer is that we have lost our power to visualize. We can no longer even imagine putting ourselves deliberately before God. It is actually more important to be broken bread and poured-out wine in the area of intercession than in our personal contact with others. The power of imagination is what God gives a saint so that he can go beyond himself and be firmly placed into relationships he never before experienced.

IS YOUR MIND STAYED ON GOD?

"You will keep him in perfect peace, whose mind is stayed on You, because he trusts in You" (Isaiah 26:3).

Is your mind stayed on God or is it starved? Starvation of the mind, caused by neglect, is one of the chief sources of exhaustion and weakness in a servant's life. If you have never used your mind to place yourself before God, begin to do it now. There is no reason to wait for God to come to you. You must turn your thoughts and your eyes away from the face of idols and look to Him and be saved (see Isaiah 45:22).

Your creative mind is the greatest gift God has given you and it ought to be devoted entirely to Him. You should seek to be "bringing every thought into captivity to the obedience of Christ . . ." (2 Corinthians 10:5). This will be one of the greatest assets of your faith when a time of trial comes, because then your faith and the Spirit of God will work together. When you have thoughts and ideas that are worthy of credit to God, learn to compare and associate them with all that happens in nature—the rising and the setting of the sun, the shining of the moon and the stars, and the changing of the seasons. You will begin to see that your thoughts are from God as well, and your mind will no longer be at the mercy of your impulsive thinking, but will always be used in service to God.

"We have sinned with our fathers . . . [and] . . . did not remember . . ." (Psalm 106:6-7). Then prod your memory and wake up immediately. Don't say to yourself, "But God is not talking to me right now." He ought to be. Remember whose you are and whom you serve. Encourage yourself to remember, and your affection for God will increase tenfold. Your mind will no longer be starved, but will be quick and enthusiastic, and your hope will be inexpressibly bright.

ARE YOU LISTENING TO GOD?

"They said to Moses, 'You speak with us, and we will hear; but let not God speak with us, lest we die' " (Exodus 20:19).

We don't consciously and deliberately disobey God—we simply don't listen to Him. God has given His commands to us, but we pay no attention to them—not because of willful disobedience, but because we do not truly love and respect Him. "If you love Me, keep My commandments" (John 14:15). Once we realize we have constantly been showing disrespect to God, we will be filled with shame and humiliation for ignoring Him.

"You speak with us, . . . but let not God speak with us . . . ." We show how little love we have for God by preferring to listen to His servants rather than to Him. We like to listen to personal testimonies, but we don't want God Himself to speak to us. Why are we so terrified for God to speak to us? It is because we know that when God speaks we must either do what He asks or tell Him we will not obey. But if it is simply one of God's servants speaking to us, we feel obedience is optional, not imperative. We respond by saying, "Well, that's only your own idea, even though I don't deny that what you said is probably God's truth."

Am I constantly humiliating God by ignoring Him, while He lovingly continues to treat me as His child? Once I finally do hear Him, the humiliation I have heaped on Him returns to me. My response then becomes, "Lord, why was I so insensitive and obstinate?" This is always the result once we hear God. But our real delight in finally hearing Him is tempered with the shame we feel for having taken so long to do so.

THE DEVOTION OF HEARING

"Samuel answered, 'Speak, for Your servant hears' " (1 Samuel 3:10).

Just because I have listened carefully and intently to one thing from God does not mean that I will listen to everything He says. I show God my lack of love and respect for Him by the insensitivity of my heart and mind toward what He says. If I love my friend, I will instinctively understand what he wants. And Jesus said, "You are My friends . . ." (John 15:14). Have I disobeyed some command of my Lord's this week? If I had realized that it was a command of Jesus, I would not have deliberately disobeyed it. But most of us show incredible disrespect to God because we don't even hear Him. He might as well never have spoken to us.

The goal of my spiritual life is such close identification with Jesus Christ that I will always hear God and know that God always hears me (see John 11:41). If I am united with Jesus Christ, I hear God all the time through the devotion of hearing. A flower, a tree, or a servant of God may convey God's message to me. What hinders me from hearing is my attention to other things. It is not that I don't want to hear God, but I am not devoted in the right areas of my life. I am devoted to things and even to service and my own convictions. God may say whatever He wants, but I just don't hear Him. The attitude of a child of God should always be, "Speak, for Your servant hears." If I have not developed and nurtured this devotion of hearing, I can only hear God's voice at certain times. At other times I become deaf to Him because my attention is to other things—things which I think I must do. This is not living the life of a child of God. Have you heard God's voice today?

THE DISCIPLINE OF HEARING

"Whatever I tell you in the dark, speak in the light; and what you hear in the ear, preach on the housetops" (Matthew 10:27).

Sometimes God puts us through the experience and discipline of darkness to teach us to hear and obey Him. Song birds are taught to sing in the dark, and God puts us into "the shadow of His hand" until we learn to hear Him (Isaiah 49:2). "Whatever I tell you in the dark. . ."—pay attention when God puts you into darkness, and keep your mouth closed while you are there. Are you in the dark right now in your circumstances, or in your life with God? If so, then remain quiet. If you open your mouth in the dark, you will speak while in the wrong mood—darkness is the time to listen. Don't talk to other people about it; don't read books to find out the reason for the darkness; just listen and obey. If you talk to other people, you cannot hear what God is saying. When you are in the dark, listen, and God will give you a very precious message for someone else once you are back in the light.

After every time of darkness, we should experience a mixture of delight and humiliation. If there is only delight, I question whether we have really heard God at all. We should experience delight for having heard God speak, but mostly humiliation for having taken so long to hear Him! Then we will exclaim, "How slow I have been to listen and understand what God has been telling me!" And yet God has been saying it for days and even weeks. But once you hear Him, He gives you the gift of humiliation, which brings a softness of heart—a gift that will always cause you to listen to God *now*.

"AM I MY BROTHER'S KEEPER?"

"None of us lives to himself . . ." (Romans 14:7).

H as it ever dawned on you that you are responsible spiritually to God for other people? For instance, if I allow any turning away from God in my private life, everyone around me suffers. We "sit *together* in the heavenly places . . ." (Ephesians 2:6). "If one member suffers, all the members suffer with it . . ." (1 Corinthians 12:26). If you allow physical selfishness, mental carelessness, moral insensitivity, or spiritual weakness, everyone in contact with you will suffer. But you ask, "Who is sufficient to be able to live up to such a lofty standard?" "Our sufficiency is from God . . ." and God alone (2 Corinthians 3:5).

"You shall be witnesses to Me . . ." (Acts 1:8). How many of us are willing to spend every bit of our nervous, mental, moral, and spiritual energy for Jesus Christ? That is what God means when He uses the word *witness*. But it takes time, so be patient with yourself. Why has God left us on the earth? Is it simply to be saved and sanctified? No, it is to be at work in service to Him. Am I willing to be broken bread and poured-out wine for Him? Am I willing to be of no value to this age or this life except for one purpose and one alone—to be used to disciple men and women to the Lord Jesus Christ. My life of service to God is the way I say "thank you" to Him for His inexpressibly wonderful salvation. Remember, it is quite possible for God to set any of us aside if we refuse to be of service to Him—". . . lest, when I have preached to others, I myself should become disqualified" (1 Corinthians 9:27).

THE INSPIRATION OF
SPIRITUAL INITIATIVE

"Arise from the dead . . ." (Ephesians 5:14).

Not all initiative, the willingness to take the first step, is inspired by God. Someone may say to you, "Get up and get going! Take your reluctance by the throat and throw it overboard—just do what needs to be done!" That is what we mean by ordinary human initiative. But when the Spirit of God comes to us and says, in effect, "Get up and get going," suddenly we find that the initiative is inspired.

We all have many dreams and aspirations when we are young, but sooner or later we realize we have no power to accomplish them. We cannot do the things we long to do, so our tendency is to think of our dreams and aspirations as dead. But God comes and says to us, "Arise from the dead . . . ." When God sends His inspiration, it comes to us with such miraculous power that we are able to "arise from the dead" and do the impossible. The remarkable thing about spiritual initiative is that the life and power comes after we "get up and get going." God does not give us overcoming life—He gives us life *as we overcome*. When the inspiration of God comes, and He says, "Arise from the dead . . . ," we have to get ourselves up; God will not lift us up. Our Lord said to the man with the withered hand, "Stretch out your hand" (Matthew 12:13). As soon as the man did so, his hand was healed. But he had to take the initiative. If we will take the initiative to overcome, we will find that we have the inspiration of God, because He immediately gives us the power of life.

TAKING THE INITIATIVE AGAINST DEPRESSION

"Arise and eat" (1 Kings 19:5).

The angel in this passage did not give Elijah a vision, or explain the Scriptures to him, or do anything remarkable. He simply told Elijah to do a very ordinary thing, that is, to get up and eat. If we were never depressed, we would not be alive—only material things don't suffer depression. If human beings were not capable of depression, we would have no capacity for happiness and exaltation. There are things in life that are designed to depress us; for example, things that are associated with death. Whenever you examine yourself, always take into account your capacity for depression.

When the Spirit of God comes to us, He does not give us glorious visions, but He tells us to do the most ordinary things imaginable. Depression tends to turn us away from the everyday things of God's creation. But whenever God steps in, His inspiration is to do the most natural, simple things—things we would never have imagined God was in, but as we do them we find Him there. The inspiration that comes to us in this way is an initiative against depression. But we must take the first step and do it in the inspiration of God. If, however, we do something simply to overcome our depression, we will only deepen it. But when the Spirit of God leads us instinctively to do something, the moment we do it the depression is gone. As soon as we arise and obey, we enter a higher plane of life.

TAKING THE INITIATIVE
AGAINST DESPAIR

"Rise, let us be going" (Matthew 26:46).

In the Garden of Gethsemane, the disciples went to sleep when they should have stayed awake, and once they realized what they had done it produced despair. The sense of having done something irreversible tends to make us despair. We say, "Well, it's all over and ruined now; what's the point in trying anymore." If we think this kind of despair is an exception, we are mistaken. It is a very ordinary human experience. Whenever we realize we have not taken advantage of a magnificent opportunity, we are apt to sink into despair. But Jesus comes and lovingly says to us, in essence, "Sleep on now. That opportunity is lost forever and you can't change that. But get up, and let's go on to the next thing." In other words, let the past sleep, but let it sleep in the sweet embrace of Christ, and let us go on into the invincible future with Him.

There will be experiences like this in each of our lives. We will have times of despair caused by real events in our lives, and we will be unable to lift ourselves out of them. The disciples, in this instance, had done a downright unthinkable thing—they had gone to sleep instead of watching with Jesus. But our Lord came to them taking the spiritual initiative against their despair and said, in effect, "Get up, and do the next thing." If we are inspired by God, what is the next thing? It is to trust Him absolutely and to pray on the basis of His redemption.

Never let the sense of past failure defeat your next step.

TAKING THE INITIATIVE
AGAINST DRUDGERY

"Arise, shine . . ." (Isaiah 60:1).

When it comes to taking the initiative against drudgery, we have to take the first step as though there were no God. There is no point in waiting for God to help us—He will not. But once we arise, immediately we find He is there. Whenever God gives us His inspiration, suddenly taking the initiative becomes a moral issue—a matter of obedience. Then we must act to be obedient and not continue to lie down doing nothing. If we will arise and shine, drudgery will be divinely transformed.

Drudgery is one of the finest tests to determine the genuineness of our character. Drudgery is work that is far removed from anything we think of as ideal work. It is the utterly hard, menial, tiresome, and dirty work. And when we experience it, our spirituality is instantly tested and we will know whether or not we are spiritually genuine. Read John 13. In this chapter, we see the Incarnate God performing the greatest example of drudgery—washing fishermen's feet. He then says to them, "If I then, your Lord and Teacher, have washed your feet, you also ought to wash one another's feet" (John 13:14). The inspiration of God is required if drudgery is to shine with the light of God upon it. In some cases the way a person does a task makes that work sanctified and holy forever. It may be a very common everyday task, but after we have seen it done, it becomes different. When the Lord does something through us, He always transforms it. Our Lord takes our human flesh and transforms it, and now every believer's body has become "the temple of the Holy Spirit" (1 Corinthians 6:19).

TAKING THE INITIATIVE
AGAINST DAYDREAMING

"Arise, let us go from here" (John 14:31).

Daydreaming about something in order to do it properly is right, but daydreaming about it when we should be doing it is wrong. In this passage, after having said these wonderful things to His disciples, we might have expected our Lord to tell them to go away and meditate over them all. But Jesus never allowed idle daydreaming. When our purpose is to seek God and to discover His will for us, daydreaming is right and acceptable. But when our inclination is to spend time daydreaming over what we have already been told to do, it is unacceptable and God's blessing is never on it. God will take the initiative against this kind of daydreaming by prodding us to action. His instructions to us will be along the lines of this: "Don't sit or stand there, just go!"

If we are quietly waiting before God after He has said to us, "Come aside by yourselves . . ." then that is meditation before Him to seek His will (Mark 6:31). Beware, however, of giving in to mere daydreaming once God has spoken. Allow Him to be the source of all your dreams, joys, and delights, and be careful to go and obey what He has said. If you are in love with someone, you don't sit and daydream about that person all the time—you go and do something for him. That is what Jesus Christ expects us to do. Daydreaming after God has spoken is an indication that we do not trust Him.

DO YOU REALLY LOVE HIM?

"She has done a good work for Me" (Mark 14:6).

If what we call love doesn't take us beyond ourselves, it is not really love. If we have the idea that love is characterized as cautious, wise, sensible, shrewd, and never taken to extremes, we have missed the true meaning. This may describe affection and it may bring us a warm feeling, but it is not a true and accurate description of love.

Have you ever been driven to do something for God not because you felt that it was useful or your duty to do so, or that there was anything in it for you, but simply because you love Him? Have you ever realized that you can give things to God that are of value to Him? Or are you just sitting around daydreaming about the greatness of His redemption, while neglecting all the things you could be doing for Him? I'm not referring to works which could be regarded as divine and miraculous, but ordinary, simple human things—things which would be evidence to God that you are totally surrendered to Him. Have you ever created what Mary of Bethany created in the heart of the Lord Jesus? "She has done a good work for Me."

There are times when it seems as if God watches to see if we will give Him even small gifts of surrender, just to show how genuine our love is for Him. To be surrendered to God is of more value than our personal holiness. Concern over our personal holiness causes us to focus our eyes on ourselves, and we become overly concerned about the way we walk and talk and look, out of fear of offending God. ". . . but perfect love casts out fear . . ." once we are surrendered to God (1 John 4:18). We should quit asking ourselves, "Am I of any use?" and accept the truth that we really are not of much use to Him. The issue is never of being of use, but of being of value to God Himself. Once we are totally surrendered to God, He will work through us all the time.

THE DISCIPLINE OF
SPIRITUAL PERSEVERANCE

"Be still, and know that I am God . . ." (Psalm 46:10).

Perseverance is more than endurance. It is endurance combined with absolute assurance and certainty that what we are looking for is going to happen. Perseverance means more than just hanging on, which may be only exposing our fear of letting go and falling. Perseverance is our supreme effort of refusing to believe that our hero is going to be conquered. Our greatest fear is not that we will be damned, but that somehow Jesus Christ will be defeated. Also, our fear is that the very things our Lord stood for—love, justice, forgiveness, and kindness among men—will not win out in the end and will represent an unattainable goal for us. Then there is the call to spiritual perseverance. A call not to hang on and do nothing, but to work deliberately, knowing with certainty that God will never be defeated.

If our hopes seem to be experiencing disappointment right now, it simply means that they are being purified. Every hope or dream of the human mind will be fulfilled if it is noble and of God. But one of the greatest stresses in life is the stress of waiting for God. He brings fulfillment, "because you have kept My command to persevere . . ." (Revelation 3:10).

Continue to persevere spiritually.

THE DETERMINATION TO SERVE

"The Son of Man did not come to be served, but to serve . . ." (Matthew 20:28).

Jesus also said, "Yet I am among you as the One who serves" (Luke 22:27). Paul's idea of service was the same as our Lord's—". . . ourselves your bondservants for Jesus' sake" (2 Corinthians 4:5). We somehow have the idea that a person called to the ministry is called to be different and above other people. But according to Jesus Christ, he is called to be a "doormat" for others—called to be their spiritual leader, but never their superior. Paul said, "I know how to be abased . . ." (Philippians 4:12). Paul's idea of service was to pour his life out to the last drop for others. And whether he received praise or blame made no difference. As long as there was one human being who did not know Jesus, Paul felt a debt of service to that person until he did come to know Him. But the chief motivation behind Paul's service was not love for others but love for his Lord. If our devotion is to the cause of humanity, we will be quickly defeated and broken-hearted, since we will often be confronted with a great deal of ingratitude from other people. But if we are motivated by our love for God, no amount of ingratitude will be able to hinder us from serving one another.

Paul's understanding of how Christ had dealt with him is the secret behind his determination to serve others. "I was formerly a blasphemer, a persecutor, and an insolent man . . ." (1 Timothy 1:13). In other words, no matter how badly others may have treated Paul, they could never have treated him with the same degree of spite and hatred with which he had treated Jesus Christ. Once we realize that Jesus has served us even to the depths of our meagerness, our selfishness, and our sin, nothing we encounter from others will be able to exhaust our determination to serve others for His sake.

THE DELIGHT OF SACRIFICE

"I will very gladly spend and be spent for your souls . . ." (2 Corinthians 12:15).

Once "the love of God has been poured out in our hearts by the Holy Spirit," we deliberately begin to identify ourselves with Jesus Christ's interests and purposes in others' lives (Romans 5:5). And Jesus has an interest in every individual person. We have no right in Christian service to be guided by our own interests and desires. In fact, this is one of the greatest tests of our relationship with Jesus Christ. The delight of sacrifice is that I lay down my life for my Friend, Jesus (see John 15:13). I don't throw my life away, but I willingly and deliberately lay it down for Him and His interests in other people. And I do this for no cause or purpose of my own. Paul spent his life for only one purpose—that he might win people to Jesus Christ. Paul always attracted people to his Lord, but never to himself. He said, "I have become all things to all men, that I might by all means save some" (1 Corinthians 9:22).

When someone thinks that to develop a holy life he must always be alone with God, he is no longer of any use to others. This is like putting himself on a pedestal and isolating himself from the rest of society. Paul was a holy person, but wherever he went Jesus Christ was always allowed to help Himself to his life. Many of us are interested only in our own goals, and Jesus cannot help Himself to our lives. But if we are totally surrendered to Him, we have no goals of our own to serve. Paul said that he knew how to be a "doormat" without resenting it, because the motivation of his life was devotion to Jesus. We tend to be devoted, not to Jesus Christ, but to the things which allow us more spiritual freedom than total surrender to Him would allow. Freedom was not Paul's motive at all. In fact, he stated, "I could wish that I myself were accursed from Christ for my brethren . . ." (Romans 9:3). Had Paul lost his ability to reason? Not at all! For someone who is in love, this is not an overstatement. And Paul was in love with Jesus Christ.

THE DESTITUTION OF SERVICE

". . . though the more abundantly I love you, the less I am loved" (2 Corinthians 12:15).

Natural human love expects something in return. But Paul is saying, "It doesn't really matter to me whether you love me or not. I am willing to be completely destitute anyway; willing to be poverty-stricken, not just for your sakes, but also that I may be able to get you to God." "For you know the grace of our Lord Jesus Christ, that though He was rich, yet for your sakes He became poor . . ." (2 Corinthians 8:9). And Paul's idea of service was the same as our Lord's. He did not care how high the cost was to himself—he would gladly pay it. It was a joyful thing to Paul.

The institutional church's idea of a servant of God is not at all like Jesus Christ's idea. His idea is that we serve Him by being the servants of others. Jesus Christ actually "out-socialized" the socialists. He said that in His kingdom the greatest one would be the servant of all (see Matthew 23:11). The real test of a saint is not one's willingness to preach the gospel, but one's willingness to do something like washing the disciples' feet—that is, being willing to do those things that seem unimportant in human estimation but count as everything to God. It was Paul's delight to spend his life for God's interests in other people, and he did not care what it cost. But before we will serve, we stop to ponder our personal and financial concerns—"What if God wants me to go over there? And what about my salary? What is the climate like there? Who will take care of me? A person must consider all these things." All that is an indication that we have reservations about serving God. But the apostle Paul had no conditions or reservations. Paul focused his life on Jesus Christ's idea of a New Testament saint; that is, not one who merely proclaims the gospel, but one who becomes broken bread and poured-out wine in the hands of Jesus Christ for the sake of others.

OUR MISGIVINGS ABOUT JESUS

**"The woman said to Him, 'Sir, You have nothing to draw [water] with, and the well is deep'"
(John 4:11).**

Have you ever said to yourself, "I am impressed with the wonderful truths of God's Word, but He can't really expect me to live up to that and work all those details into my life!" When it comes to confronting Jesus Christ on the basis of His qualities and abilities, our attitudes reflect religious superiority. We think His ideals are lofty and they impress us, but we believe He is not in touch with reality—that what He says cannot actually be done. Each of us thinks this about Jesus in one area of our life or another. These doubts or misgivings about Jesus begin as we consider questions that divert our focus away from God. While we talk of our dealings with Him, others ask us, "Where are you going to get enough money to live? How will you live and who will take care of you?" Or our misgivings begin within ourselves when we tell Jesus that our circumstances are just a little too difficult for Him. We say, "It's easy to say, 'Trust in the Lord,' but a person has to live; and besides, Jesus has nothing with which to draw water—no means to be able to give us these things." And beware of exhibiting religious deceit by saying, "Oh, I have no misgivings about Jesus, only misgivings about myself." If we are honest, we will admit that we never have misgivings or doubts about ourselves, because we know exactly what we are capable or incapable of doing. But we do have misgivings about Jesus. And our pride is hurt even at the thought that He can do what we can't.

My misgivings arise from the fact that I search within to find how He will do what He says. My doubts spring from the depths of my own inferiority. If I detect these misgivings in myself, I should bring them into the light and confess them openly—"Lord, I have had misgivings about You. I have not believed in Your abilities, but only my own. And I have not believed in Your almighty power apart from my finite understanding of it."

THE IMPOVERISHED
MINISTRY OF JESUS

**"Where then do You get that living water?"
(John 4:11).**

T he well is deep"—and even a great deal deeper than the Samaritan woman knew! (4:11). Think of the depths of human nature and human life; think of the depth of the "wells" in you. Have you been limiting, or impoverishing, the ministry of Jesus to the point that He is unable to work in your life? Suppose that you have a deep "well" of hurt and trouble inside your heart, and Jesus comes and says to you, "Let not your heart be troubled . . ." (John 14:1). Would your response be to shrug your shoulders and say, "But, Lord, the well is too deep, and even You can't draw up quietness and comfort out of it." Actually, that is correct. Jesus doesn't bring anything up from the wells of human nature—He brings them down from above. We limit the Holy One of Israel by remembering only what we have allowed Him to do for us in the past, and also by saying, "Of course, I cannot expect God to do this particular thing." The thing that approaches the very limits of His power is the very thing we as disciples of Jesus ought to believe He will do. We impoverish and weaken His ministry in us the moment we forget He is almighty. The impoverishment is in us, not in Him. We will come to Jesus for Him to be our comforter or our sympathizer, but we refrain from approaching Him as our Almighty God.

The reason some of us are such poor examples of Christianity is that we have failed to recognize that Christ is almighty. We have Christian attributes and experiences, but there is no abandonment or surrender to Jesus Christ. When we get into difficult circumstances, we impoverish His ministry by saying, "Of course, He can't do anything about this." We struggle to reach the bottom of our own well, trying to get water for ourselves. Beware of sitting back, and saying, "It can't be done." You will know it can be done if you will look to Jesus. The well of your incompleteness runs deep, but make the effort to look away from yourself and to look toward Him.

"Do You Now Believe?"

" 'By this we believe . . . .' Jesus answered them, 'Do you now believe?' " (John 16:30-31).

Now we believe. . . ." But Jesus asks, "Do you . . . ? Indeed the hour is coming . . . that you . . . will leave Me alone" (16:31-32). Many Christian workers have left Jesus Christ alone and yet tried to serve Him out of a sense of duty, or because they sense a need as a result of their own discernment. The reason for this is actually the absence of the resurrection life of Jesus. Our soul has gotten out of intimate contact with God by leaning on our own religious understanding (see Proverbs 3:5-6). This is not deliberate sin and there is no punishment attached to it. But once a person realizes how he has hindered his understanding of Jesus Christ, and caused uncertainties, sorrows, and difficulties for himself, it is with shame and remorse that he has to return.

We need to rely on the resurrection life of Jesus on a much deeper level than we do now. We should get in the habit of continually seeking His counsel on everything, instead of making our own commonsense decisions and then asking Him to bless them. He cannot bless them; it is not in His realm to do so, and those decisions are severed from reality. If we do something simply out of a sense of duty, we are trying to live up to a standard that competes with Jesus Christ. We become a prideful, arrogant person, thinking we know what to do in every situation. We have put our sense of duty on the throne of our life, instead of enthroning the resurrection life of Jesus. We are not told to "walk in the light" of our conscience or in the light of a sense of duty, but to "walk in the light *as He is in the light* . . ." (1 John 1:7). When we do something out of a sense of duty, it is easy to explain the reasons for our actions to others. But when we do something out of obedience to the Lord, there can be no other explanation—just obedience. That is why a saint can be so easily ridiculed and misunderstood.

WHAT DO YOU WANT THE LORD TO DO FOR YOU?

" 'What do you want Me to do for you?' He said, 'Lord, that I may receive my sight' " (Luke 18:41).

I s there something in your life that not only disturbs you, but makes you a disturbance to others? If so, it is always something you cannot handle yourself. "Then those who went before warned him that he should be quiet; but he cried out all the more . . ." (18:39). Be persistent with your disturbance until you get face to face with the Lord Himself. Don't deify common sense. To sit calmly by, instead of creating a disturbance, serves only to deify our common sense. When Jesus asks what we want Him to do for us about the incredible problem that is confronting us, remember that He doesn't work in commonsense ways, but only in supernatural ways.

Look at how we limit the Lord by only remembering what we have allowed Him to do for us in the past. We say, "I always failed there, and I always will." Consequently, we don't ask for what we want. Instead, we think, "It is ridiculous to ask God to do this." If it is an impossibility, it is the very thing for which we have to ask. If it is not an impossible thing, it is not a real disturbance. And God will do what is absolutely impossible.

This man received his sight. But the most impossible thing for you is to be so closely identified with the Lord that there is literally nothing of your old life remaining. God will do it if you will ask Him. But you have to come to the point of believing Him to be almighty. We find faith by not only believing what Jesus says, but, even more, by trusting Jesus Himself. If we only look at what He says, we will never believe. Once we see Jesus, the impossible things He does in our lives become as natural as breathing. The agony we suffer is only the result of the deliberate shallowness of our own heart. We *won't* believe; we *won't* let go by severing the line that secures the boat to the shore—we prefer to worry.

THE PIERCING QUESTION

"Do you love Me?" (John 21:17).

P eter's response to this piercing question is considerably different from the bold defiance he exhibited only a few days before when he declared, "Even if I have to die with You, I will not deny You!" (Matthew 26:35; also see verses 33–34). Our natural individuality, or our natural self, boldly speaks out and declares its feelings. But the true love within our inner spiritual self can be discovered only by experiencing the hurt of this question of Jesus Christ. Peter loved Jesus in the way any natural man loves a good person. Yet that is nothing but emotional love. It may reach deeply into our natural self, but it never penetrates to the spirit of a person. True love never simply declares itself. Jesus said, "Whoever *confesses* Me before men [that is, confesses his love by everything he does, not merely by his words], him the Son of Man also will confess before the angels of God" (Luke 12:8).

Unless we are experiencing the hurt of facing every deception about ourselves, we have hindered the work of the Word of God in our lives. The Word of God inflicts hurt on us more than sin ever could, because sin dulls our senses. But this question of the Lord intensifies our sensitivities to the point that this hurt produced by Jesus is the most exquisite pain conceivable. It hurts not only on the natural level, but also on the deeper spiritual level. "For the Word of God is living and powerful . . . , piercing even to the division of soul and spirit . . ."—to the point that no deception can remain (Hebrews 4:12). When the Lord asks us this question, it is impossible to think and respond properly, because when the Lord speaks directly to us, the pain is too intense. It causes such a tremendous hurt that any part of our life which may be out of line with His will can feel the pain. There is never any mistaking the pain of the Lord's Word by His children, but the moment that pain is felt is the very moment at which God reveals His truth to us.

HAVE YOU FELT THE PAIN INFLICTED BY THE LORD?

"He said to him the third time, '. . . do you love Me?'" (John 21:17).

Have you ever felt the pain, inflicted by the Lord, at the very center of your being, deep down in the most sensitive area of your life? The devil never inflicts pain there, and neither can sin nor human emotions. Nothing can cut through to that part of our being but the Word of God. "Peter was grieved because He said to him the third time, 'Do you love Me?' " Yet he was awakened to the fact that at the center of his personal life he was devoted to Jesus. And then he began to see what Jesus' patient questioning meant. There was not the slightest bit of doubt left in Peter's mind; he could never be deceived again. And there was no need for an impassioned response; no need for immediate action or an emotional display. It was a revelation to him to realize how much he did love the Lord, and with amazement he simply said, "Lord, You know all things . . . ." Peter began to see how very much he did love Jesus, and there was no need to say, "Look at this or that as proof of my love." Peter was beginning to discover within himself just how much he really did love the Lord. He discovered that his eyes were so fixed on Jesus Christ that he saw no one else in heaven above or on the earth below. But he did not know it until the probing, hurting questions of the Lord were asked. The Lord's questions always reveal the true me to myself.

Oh, the wonder of the patient directness and skill of Jesus Christ with Peter! Our Lord never asks questions until the perfect time. Rarely, but probably once in each of our lives, He will back us into a corner where He will hurt us with His piercing questions. Then we will realize that we do love Him far more deeply than our words can ever say.

HIS COMMISSION TO US

"Feed My sheep" (John 21:17).

This is love in the making. The love of God is not created—it is His nature. When we receive the life of Christ through the Holy Spirit, He unites us with God so that His love is demonstrated in us. The goal of the indwelling Holy Spirit is not just to unite us with God, but to do it in such a way that we will be one with the Father in exactly the same way Jesus was. And what kind of oneness did Jesus Christ have with the Father? He had such a oneness with the Father that He was obedient when His Father sent Him down here to be poured out for us. And He says to us, "As the Father has sent Me, I also send you" (John 20:21).

Peter now realizes that he does love Him, due to the revelation that came with the Lord's piercing question. The Lord's next point is—"Pour yourself out. Don't testify about how much you love Me and don't talk about the wonderful revelation you have had, just 'Feed My sheep.'" Jesus has some extraordinarily peculiar sheep: some that are unkempt and dirty, some that are awkward or pushy, and some that have gone astray! But it is impossible to exhaust God's love, and it is impossible to exhaust my love if it flows from the Spirit of God within me. The love of God pays no attention to my prejudices caused by my natural individuality. If I love my Lord, I have no business being guided by natural emotions—I have to feed His sheep. We will not be delivered or released from His commission to us. Beware of counterfeiting the love of God by following your own natural human emotions, sympathies, or understandings. That will only serve to revile and abuse the true love of God.

IS THIS TRUE OF ME?

"None of these things move me; nor do I count my life dear to myself . . ." (Acts 20:24).

It is easier to serve or work for God without a vision and without a call, because then you are not bothered by what He requires. Common sense, covered with a layer of Christian emotion, becomes your guide. You may be more prosperous and successful from the world's perspective, and will have more leisure time, if you never acknowledge the call of God. But once you receive a commission from Jesus Christ, the memory of what God asks of you will always be there to prod you on to do His will. You will no longer be able to work for Him on the basis of common sense.

What do I count in my life as "dear to myself"? If I have not been seized by Jesus Christ and have not surrendered myself to Him, I will consider the time I decide to give God and my own ideas of service as dear. I will also consider my own life as "dear to myself." But Paul said he considered his life dear so that he might fulfill the ministry he had received, and he refused to use his energy on anything else. This verse shows an almost noble annoyance by Paul at being asked to consider himself. He was absolutely indifferent to any consideration other than that of fulfilling the ministry he had received. Our ordinary and reasonable service to God may actually compete against our total surrender to Him. Our reasonable work is based on the following argument which we say to ourselves, "Remember how useful you are here, and think how much value you would be in that particular type of work." That attitude chooses our own judgment, instead of Jesus Christ, to be our guide as to where we should go and where we could be used the most. Never consider whether or not you are of use—but always consider that "you are not your own" (1 Corinthians 6:19). You are His.

Is He Really My Lord?

"... so that I may finish my race with joy, and the ministry which I received from the Lord Jesus ..." (Acts 20:24).

Joy comes from seeing the complete fulfillment of the specific purpose for which I was created and born again, not from successfully doing something of my own choosing. The joy our Lord experienced came from doing what the Father sent Him to do. And He says to us, "As the Father has sent Me, I also send you" (John 20:21). Have you received a ministry from the Lord? If so, you must be faithful to it—to consider your life valuable only for the purpose of fulfilling that ministry. Knowing that you have done what Jesus sent you to do, think how satisfying it will be to hear Him say to you, "Well done, good and faithful servant" (Matthew 25:21). We each have to find a niche in life, and spiritually we find it when we receive a ministry from the Lord. To do this we must have close fellowship with Jesus and must know Him as more than our personal Savior. And we must be willing to experience the full impact of Acts 9:16—"I will show him how many things he must suffer *for My name's sake.*"

"Do you love Me?" Then, "Feed My sheep" (John 21:17). He is not offering us a choice of how we can serve Him; He is asking for absolute loyalty to His commission, a faithfulness to what we discern when we are in the closest possible fellowship with God. If you have received a ministry from the Lord Jesus, you will know that the need is not the same as the call—the need is the opportunity to exercise the call. The call is to be faithful to the ministry you received when you were in true fellowship with Him. This does not imply that there is a whole series of differing ministries marked out for you. It does mean that you must be sensitive to what God has called you to do, and this may sometimes require ignoring demands for service in other areas.

TAKING THE NEXT STEP

". . . in much patience, in tribulations, in needs, in distresses" (2 Corinthians 6:4).

When you have no vision from God, no enthusiasm left in your life, and no one watching and encouraging you, it requires the grace of Almighty God to take the next step in your devotion to Him, in the reading and studying of His Word, in your family life, or in your duty to Him. It takes much more of the grace of God, and a much greater awareness of drawing upon Him, to take that next step, than it does to preach the gospel.

Every Christian must experience the essence of the incarnation by bringing the next step down into flesh-and-blood reality and by working it out with his hands. We lose interest and give up when we have no vision, no encouragement, and no improvement, but only experience our everyday life with its trivial tasks. The thing that really testifies for God and for the people of God in the long run is steady perseverance, even when the work cannot be seen by others. And the only way to live an undefeated life is to live looking to God. Ask God to keep the eyes of your spirit open to the risen Christ, and it will be impossible for drudgery to discourage you. Never allow yourself to think that some tasks are beneath your dignity or too insignificant for you to do, and remind yourself of the example of Christ in John 13:1–17.

THE SOURCE OF ABUNDANT JOY

> "In all these things we are more than conquerors through Him who loved us" (Romans 8:37).

Paul was speaking here of the things that might seem likely to separate a saint from the love of God. But the remarkable thing is that nothing *can* come between the love of God and a saint. The things Paul mentioned in this passage can and do disrupt the close fellowship of our soul with God and separate our natural life from Him. But none of them is able to come between the love of God and the soul of a saint on the spiritual level. The underlying foundation of the Christian faith is the undeserved, limitless miracle of the love of God that was exhibited on the Cross of Calvary; a love that is not earned and can never be. Paul said this is the reason that "in all these things we are more than conquerors." We are super-victors with a joy that comes from experiencing the very things which look as if they are going to overwhelm us.

Huge waves that would frighten an ordinary swimmer produce a tremendous thrill for the surfer who has ridden them. Let's apply that to our own circumstances. The things we try to avoid and fight against—tribulation, suffering, and persecution—are the very things that produce abundant joy in us. "We are more than conquerors through Him" "*in* all these things"; not in spite of them, but in the midst of them. A saint doesn't know the joy of the Lord in spite of tribulation, but *because* of it. Paul said, "I am exceedingly joyful in all our tribulation" (2 Corinthians 7:4).

The undiminished radiance, which is the result of abundant joy, is not built on anything passing, but on the love of God that nothing can change. And the experiences of life, whether they are everyday events or terrifying ones, are powerless to "separate us from the love of God which is in Christ Jesus our Lord" (Romans 8:39).

THE SURRENDERED LIFE

"I have been crucified with Christ . . ."
(Galatians 2:20).

To become one with Jesus Christ, a person must be willing not only to give up sin, but also to surrender his whole way of looking at things. Being born again by the Spirit of God means that we must first be willing to let go before we can grasp something else. The first thing we must surrender is all of our pretense or deceit. What our Lord wants us to present to Him is not our goodness, honesty, or our efforts to do better, but real solid sin. Actually, that is all He can take from us. And what He gives us in exchange for our sin is real solid righteousness. But we must surrender all pretense that we are anything, and give up all our claims of even being worthy of God's consideration.

Once we have done that, the Spirit of God will show us what we need to surrender next. Along each step of this process, we will have to give up our claims to our rights to ourselves. Are we willing to surrender our grasp on all that we possess, our desires, and everything else in our lives? Are we ready to be identified with the death of Jesus Christ?

We will suffer a sharp painful disillusionment before we fully surrender. When people really see themselves as the Lord sees them, it is not the terribly offensive sins of the flesh that shock them, but the awful nature of the pride of their own hearts opposing Jesus Christ. When they see themselves in the light of the Lord, the shame, horror, and desperate conviction hit home for them.

If you are faced with the question of whether or not to surrender, make a determination to go on through the crisis, surrendering all that you have and all that you are to Him. And God will then equip you to do all that He requires of you.

TURNING BACK OR WALKING WITH JESUS?

"Do you also want to go away?" (John 6:67).

What a penetrating question! Our Lord's words often hit home for us when He speaks in the simplest way. In spite of the fact that we know who Jesus is, He asks, "Do you also want to go away?" We must continually maintain an adventurous attitude toward Him, despite any potential personal risk.

"From that time many of His disciples went back and walked with Him no more" (6:66). They turned back from walking with Jesus; not into sin, but away from Him. Many people today are pouring their lives out and working for Jesus Christ, but are not really walking with Him. One thing God constantly requires of us is a oneness with Jesus Christ. After being set apart through sanctification, we should discipline our lives spiritually to maintain this intimate oneness. When God gives you a clear determination of His will for you, all your striving to maintain that relationship by some particular method is completely unnecessary. All that is required is to live a natural life of absolute dependence on Jesus Christ. Never try to live your life with God in any other way than His way. And His way means absolute devotion to Him. Showing no concern for the uncertainties that lie ahead is the secret of walking with Jesus.

Peter saw in Jesus only someone who could minister salvation to him and to the world. But our Lord wants us to be fellow laborers with Him.

In verse 70 Jesus lovingly reminded Peter that he was chosen to go with Him. And each of us must answer this question for ourselves and no one else: "Do you also want to go away?"

BEING AN EXAMPLE
OF HIS MESSAGE

"Preach the word!" (2 Timothy 4:2).

We are not saved only to be instruments for God, but to be His sons and daughters. He does not turn us into spiritual agents but into spiritual messengers, and the message must be a part of us. The Son of God was His own message—"The words that I speak to you are spirit, and they are life" (John 6:63). As His disciples, our lives must be a holy example of the reality of our message. Even the natural heart of the unsaved will serve if called upon to do so, but it takes a heart broken by conviction of sin, baptized by the Holy Spirit, and crushed into submission to God's purpose to make a person's life a holy example of God's message.

There is a difference between giving a testimony and preaching. A preacher is someone who has received the call of God and is determined to use all his energy to proclaim God's truth. God takes us beyond our own aspirations and ideas for our lives, and molds and shapes us for His purpose, just as He worked in the disciples' lives after Pentecost. The purpose of Pentecost was not to teach the disciples something, but to make them the incarnation of what they preached so that they would literally become God's message in the flesh. ". . . you shall be witnesses to Me . . ." (Acts 1:8).

Allow God to have complete liberty in your life when you speak. Before God's message can liberate other people, His liberation must first be real in you. Gather your material carefully, and then allow God to "set your words on fire" for His glory.

OBEDIENCE TO THE "HEAVENLY VISION"

**"I was not disobedient to the heavenly vision"
(Acts 26:19).**

If we lose "the heavenly vision" God has given us, we alone are responsible—not God. We lose the vision because of our own lack of spiritual growth. If we do not apply our beliefs about God to the issues of everyday life, the vision God has given us will never be fulfilled. The only way to be obedient to "the heavenly vision" is to give our utmost for His highest—our best for His glory. This can be accomplished only when we make a determination to continually remember God's vision. But the acid test is obedience to the vision in the details of our everyday life—sixty seconds out of every minute, and sixty minutes out of every hour, not just during times of personal prayer or public meetings.

"Though it tarries, wait for it . . ." (Habakkuk 2:3). We cannot bring the vision to fulfillment through our own efforts, but must live under its inspiration until it fulfills itself. We try to be so practical that we forget the vision. At the very beginning we saw the vision but did not wait for it. We rushed off to do our practical work, and once the vision was fulfilled we could no longer even see it. Waiting for a vision that "tarries" is the true test of our faithfulness to God. It is at the risk of our own soul's welfare that we get caught up in practical busy-work, only to miss the fulfillment of the vision.

Watch for the storms of God. The only way God plants His saints is through the whirlwind of His storms. Will you be proven to be an empty pod with no seed inside? That will depend on whether or not you are actually living in the light of the vision you have seen. Let God send you out through His storm, and don't go until He does. If you select your own spot to be planted, you will prove yourself to be an unproductive, empty pod. However, if you allow God to plant you, you will "bear much fruit" (John 15:8).

It is essential that we live and "walk in the light" of God's vision for us (1 John 1:7).

MARCH 11

TOTAL SURRENDER

"Peter began to say to Him, 'See, we have left all and followed You' " (Mark 10:28).

Our Lord replies to this statement of Peter by saying that this surrender is "for My sake and the gospel's" (10:29). It was not for the purpose of what the disciples themselves would get out of it. Beware of surrender that is motivated by personal benefits that may result. For example, "I'm going to give myself to God because I want to be delivered from sin, because I want to be made holy." Being delivered from sin and being made holy are the result of being right with God, but surrender resulting from this kind of thinking is certainly not the true nature of Christianity. Our motive for surrender should not be *for* any personal gain at all. We have become so self-centered that we go to God only for something from Him, and not for God Himself. It is like saying, "No, Lord, I don't want you; I want myself. But I do want You to clean me and fill me with Your Holy Spirit. I want to be on display in Your showcase so I can say, 'This is what God has done for me.' " Gaining heaven, being delivered from sin, and being made useful to God are things that should never even be a consideration in real surrender. Genuine total surrender is a personal sovereign preference for Jesus Christ Himself.

Where does Jesus Christ figure in when we have a concern about our natural relationships? Most of us will desert Him with this excuse—"Yes, Lord, I heard you call me, but my family needs me and I have my own interests. I just can't go any further" (see Luke 9:57-62). "Then," Jesus says, "you 'cannot be My disciple' " (see Luke 14:26-33).

True surrender will always go beyond natural devotion. If we will only give up, God will surrender Himself to embrace all those around us and will meet their needs, which were created by our surrender. Beware of stopping anywhere short of total surrender to God. Most of us have only a vision of what this really means, but have never truly experienced it.

MARCH 12

GOD'S TOTAL SURRENDER TO US

"For God so loved the world that He gave . . ." (John 3:16).

Salvation does not mean merely deliverance from sin or the experience of personal holiness. The salvation which comes from God means being completely delivered from myself, and being placed into perfect union with Him. When I think of my salvation experience, I think of being delivered from sin and gaining personal holiness. But salvation is so much more! It means that the Spirit of God has brought me into intimate contact with the true Person of God Himself. And as I am caught up into total surrender to God, I become thrilled with something infinitely greater than myself.

To say that we are called to preach holiness or sanctification is to miss the main point. We are called to proclaim Jesus Christ (see 1 Corinthians 2:2). The fact that He saves from sin and makes us holy is actually part of the effect of His wonderful and total surrender to us.

If we are truly surrendered, we will never be aware of our own efforts to remain surrendered. Our entire life will be consumed with the One to whom we surrender. Beware of talking about surrender if you know nothing about it. In fact, you will never know anything about it until you understand that John 3:16 means that God completely and absolutely gave Himself to us. In our surrender, we must give ourselves to God in the same way He gave Himself for us—totally, unconditionally, and without reservation. The consequences and circumstances resulting from our surrender will never even enter our mind, because our life will be totally consumed with Him.

YIELDING

". . . you are that one's slaves whom you obey . . ." (Romans 6:16).

The first thing I must be willing to admit when I begin to examine what controls and dominates me is that I am the one responsible for having yielded myself to whatever it may be. If I am a slave to myself, I am to blame because somewhere in the past I yielded to myself. Likewise, if I obey God I do so because at some point in my life I yielded myself to Him.

If a child gives in to selfishness, he will find it to be the most enslaving tyranny on earth. There is no power within the human soul itself that is capable of breaking the bondage of the nature created by yielding. For example, yield for one second to anything in the nature of lust, and although you may hate yourself for having yielded, you become enslaved to that thing. (Remember what lust is—"I must have it now," whether it is the lust of the flesh or the lust of the mind.) No release or escape from it will ever come from any human power, but only through the power of redemption. You must yield yourself in utter humiliation to the only One who can break the dominating power in your life, namely, the Lord Jesus Christ. ". . . He has anointed Me . . . to proclaim liberty to the captives . . ." (Luke 4:18 and Isaiah 61:1).

When you yield to something, you will soon realize the tremendous control it has over you. Even though you say, "Oh, I can give up that habit whenever I like," you will know you can't. You will find that the habit absolutely dominates you because you willingly yielded to it. It is easy to sing, "He will break every fetter," while at the same time living a life of obvious slavery to yourself. But yielding to Jesus will break every kind of slavery in any person's life.

THE DISCIPLINE OF DISMAY

"As they followed they were afraid" (Mark 10:32).

At the beginning of our life with Jesus Christ, we were sure we knew all there was to know about following Him. It was a delight to forsake everything else and to throw ourselves before Him in a fearless statement of love. But now we are not quite so sure. Jesus is far ahead of us and is beginning to seem different and unfamiliar—"Jesus was going before them; and they were amazed" (10:32).

There is an aspect of Jesus that chills even a disciple's heart to its depth and makes his entire spiritual life gasp for air. This unusual Person with His face set "like a flint" (Isaiah 50:7) is walking with great determination ahead of me, and He strikes terror right through me. He no longer seems to be my Counselor and Friend and has a point of view about which I know nothing. All I can do is stand and stare at Him in amazement. At first I was confident that I understood Him, but now I am not so sure. I begin to realize that there is a distance between Jesus and me and I can no longer be intimate with Him. I have no idea where He is going, and the goal has become strangely distant.

Jesus Christ had to understand fully every sin and sorrow that human beings could experience, and that is what makes Him seem unfamiliar. When we see this aspect of Him, we realize we really don't know Him. We don't recognize even one characteristic of His life, and we don't know how to begin to follow Him. He is far ahead of us, a Leader who seems totally unfamiliar, and we have no friendship with Him.

The discipline of dismay is an essential lesson which a disciple must learn. The danger is that we tend to look back on our times of obedience and on our past sacrifices to God in an effort to keep our enthusiasm for Him strong (see Isaiah 50:10-11). But when the darkness of dismay comes, endure until it is over, because out of it will come the ability to follow Jesus truly, which brings inexpressibly wonderful joy.

THE MASTER WILL JUDGE

"We must all appear before the judgment seat of Christ . . ." (2 Corinthians 5:10).

Paul says that we must all, preachers and other people alike, "appear before the judgment seat of Christ." But if you will learn here and now to live under the scrutiny of Christ's pure light, your final judgment will bring you only delight in seeing the work God has done in you. Live constantly reminding yourself of the judgment seat of Christ, and walk in the knowledge of the holiness He has given you. Tolerating a wrong attitude toward another person causes you to follow the spirit of the devil, no matter how saintly you are. One carnal judgment of another person only serves the purposes of hell in you. Bring it immediately into the light and confess, "Oh, Lord, I have been guilty there." If you don't, your heart will become hardened through and through. One of the penalties of sin is our acceptance of it. It is not only God who punishes for sin, but sin establishes itself in the sinner and takes its toll. No struggling or praying will enable you to stop doing certain things, and the penalty of sin is that you gradually get used to it, until you finally come to the place where you no longer even realize that it is sin. No power, except the power that comes from being filled with the Holy Spirit, can change or prevent the inherent consequences of sin.

"If we walk in the light *as He is in the light* . . ." (1 John 1:7). For many of us, walking in the light means walking according to the standard we have set up for another person. The deadliest attitude of the Pharisees that we exhibit today is not hypocrisy but that which comes from unconsciously living a lie.

THE SERVANT'S PRIMARY GOAL

"We make it our aim . . . to be well pleasing to Him" (2 Corinthians 5:9).

We make it our aim. . . ." It requires a conscious decision and effort to keep our primary goal constantly in front of us. It means holding ourselves to the highest priority year in and year out; not making our first priority to win souls, or to establish churches, or to have revivals, but seeking only "to be well pleasing to Him." It is not a lack of spiritual experience that leads to failure, but a lack of working to keep our eyes focused and on the right goal. At least once a week examine yourself before God to see if your life is measuring up to the standard He has for you. Paul was like a musician who gives no thought to audience approval, if he can only catch a look of approval from his Conductor.

Any goal we have that diverts us even to the slightest degree from the central goal of being "approved to God" (2 Timothy 2:15) may result in our rejection from further service for Him. When you discern where the goal leads, you will understand why it is so necessary to keep "looking unto Jesus" (Hebrews 12:2). Paul spoke of the importance of controlling his own body so that it would not take him in the wrong direction. He said, "I discipline my body and bring it into subjection, lest . . . I myself should become disqualified" (1 Corinthians 9:27).

I must learn to relate everything to the primary goal, maintaining it without interruption. My worth to God publicly is measured by what I really am in my private life. Is my primary goal in life to please Him and to be acceptable to Him, or is it something less, no matter how lofty it may sound?

WILL I BRING MYSELF UP TO THIS LEVEL?

**". . . perfecting holiness in the fear of God"
(2 Corinthians 7:1).**

Therefore, having these promises. . . ." I claim God's promises for my life and look to their fulfillment, and rightly so, but that shows only the human perspective on them. God's perspective is that through His promises I will come to recognize His claim of ownership on me. For example, do I realize that my "body is the temple of the Holy Spirit," or am I condoning some habit in my body which clearly could not withstand the light of God on it? (1 Corinthians 6:19). God formed His Son in me through sanctification, setting me apart from sin and making me holy in His sight (see Galatians 4:19). But I must begin to transform my natural life into spiritual life by obedience to Him. God instructs us even in the smallest details of life. And when He brings you conviction of sin, do not "confer with flesh and blood," but cleanse yourself from it at once (Galatians 1:16). Keep yourself cleansed in your daily walk.

I must cleanse myself from all filthiness in my flesh and my spirit until both are in harmony with the nature of God. Is the mind of my spirit in perfect agreement with the life of the Son of God in me, or am I mentally rebellious and defiant? Am I allowing the mind of Christ to be formed in me? (see Philippians 2:5). Christ never spoke of His right to Himself, but always maintained an inner vigilance to submit His spirit continually to His Father. I also have the responsibility to keep my spirit in agreement with His Spirit. And when I do, Jesus gradually lifts me up to the level where He lived—a level of perfect submission to His Father's will—where I pay no attention to anything else. Am I perfecting this kind of holiness in the fear of God? Is God having His way with me, and are people beginning to see God in my life more and more?

Be serious in your commitment to God and gladly leave everything else alone. Literally put God first in your life.

MARCH 18

ABRAHAM'S LIFE OF FAITH

"He went out, not knowing where he was going" (Hebrews 11:8).

In the Old Testament, a person's relationship with God was seen by the degree of separation in that person's life. This separation is exhibited in the life of Abraham by his separation from his country and his family. When we think of separation today, we do not mean to be literally separated from those family members who do not have a personal relationship with God, but to be separated mentally and morally from their viewpoints. This is what Jesus Christ was referring to in Luke 14:26.

Living a life of faith means never knowing where you are being led. But it does mean loving and knowing the One who is leading. It is literally a life of *faith*, not of understanding and reason—a life of knowing Him who calls us to go. Faith is rooted in the knowledge of a Person, and one of the biggest traps we fall into is the belief that if we have faith, God will surely lead us to success in the world.

The final stage in the life of faith is the attainment of character, and we encounter many changes in the process. We feel the presence of God around us when we pray, yet we are only momentarily changed. We tend to keep going back to our everyday ways and the glory vanishes. A life of faith is not a life of one glorious mountaintop experience after another, like soaring on eagles' wings, but is a life of day-in and day-out consistency; a life of walking without fainting (see Isaiah 40:31). It is not even a question of the holiness of sanctification, but of something which comes much farther down the road. It is a faith that has been tried and proved and has withstood the test. Abraham is not a type or an example of the holiness of sanctification, but a type of the life of faith—a faith, tested and true, built on the true God. *"Abraham believed God . . ."* (Romans 4:3).

FRIENDSHIP WITH GOD

"Shall I hide from Abraham what I am doing . . . ?" (Genesis 18:17).

The Delights of His Friendship. Genesis 18 brings out the delight of true friendship with God, as compared with simply feeling His presence occasionally in prayer. This friendship means being so intimately in touch with God that you never even need to ask Him to show you His will. It is evidence of a level of intimacy which confirms that you are nearing the final stage of your discipline in the life of faith. When you have a right-standing relationship with God, you have a life of freedom, liberty, and delight; you *are* God's will. And all of your commonsense decisions are actually His will for you, unless you sense a feeling of restraint brought on by a check in your spirit. You are free to make decisions in the light of a perfect and delightful friendship with God, knowing that if your decisions are wrong He will lovingly produce that sense of restraint. Once he does, you must stop immediately.

The Difficulties of His Friendship. Why did Abraham stop praying when he did? He stopped because he still was lacking the level of intimacy in his relationship with God, which would enable him boldly to continue on with the Lord in prayer until his desire was granted. Whenever we stop short of our true desire in prayer and say, "Well, I don't know, maybe this is not God's will," then we still have another level to go. It shows that we are not as intimately acquainted with God as Jesus was, and as Jesus would have us to be—". . . that they may be one just as We are one . . ." (John 17:22). Think of the last thing you prayed about—were you devoted to your desire or to God? Was your determination to get some gift of the Spirit for yourself or to get to God? "For your Father knows the things you have need of before you ask Him" (Matthew 6:8). The reason for asking is so you may get to know God better. "Delight yourself also in the LORD, and He shall give you the desires of your heart" (Psalm 37:4). We should keep praying to get a perfect understanding of God Himself.

IDENTIFIED OR SIMPLY INTERESTED?

**"I have been crucified with Christ . . . ."
(Galatians 2:20).**

The inescapable spiritual need each of us has is the need to sign the death certificate of our sin nature. I must take my emotional opinions and intellectual beliefs and be willing to turn them into a moral verdict against the nature of sin; that is, against any claim I have to my right to myself. Paul said, "I have been crucified with Christ . . . ." He did not say, "I have made a determination to imitate Jesus Christ," or, "I will really make an effort to follow Him"—but—"I have been *identified* with Him in His death." Once I reach this moral decision and act on it, all that Christ accomplished *for* me on the Cross is accomplished *in* me. My unrestrained commitment of myself to God gives the Holy Spirit the opportunity to grant to me the holiness of Jesus Christ.

". . . it is no longer I who live . . . ." My individuality remains, but my primary motivation for living and the nature that rules me are radically changed. I have the same human body, but the old satanic right to myself has been destroyed.

". . . and the life which I now live in the flesh," not the life which I long to live or even pray that I live, but the life I now live in my mortal flesh—the life which others can see, "I live by faith in the Son of God . . . ." This faith was not Paul's own faith in Jesus Christ, but the faith the Son of God had given to him (see Ephesians 2:8). It is no longer a faith in faith, but a faith that transcends all imaginable limits—a faith that comes only from the Son of God.

THE BURNING HEART

"Did not our heart burn within us . . . ?"
(Luke 24:32).

We need to learn this secret of the burning heart. Suddenly Jesus appears to us, fires are set ablaze, and we are given wonderful visions; but then we must learn to maintain the secret of the burning heart—a heart that can go through anything. It is the simple, dreary day, with its commonplace duties and people, that smothers the burning heart—unless we have learned the secret of abiding in Jesus.

Much of the distress we experience as Christians comes not as the result of sin, but because we are ignorant of the laws of our own nature. For instance, the only test we should use to determine whether or not to allow a particular emotion to run its course in our lives is to examine what the final outcome of that emotion will be. Think it through to its logical conclusion, and if the outcome is something that God would condemn, put a stop to it immediately. But if it is an emotion that has been kindled by the Spirit of God and you don't allow it to have its way in your life, it will cause a reaction on a lower level than God intended. That is the way unrealistic and overly emotional people are made. And the higher the emotion, the deeper the level of corruption, if it is not exercised on its intended level. If the Spirit of God has stirred you, make as many of your decisions as possible irrevocable, and let the consequences be what they will. We cannot stay forever on the "mount of transfiguration," basking in the light of our mountaintop experience (see Mark 9:1–9). But we must obey the light we received there; we must put it into action. When God gives us a vision, we must transact business with Him at that point, no matter what the cost.

> We cannot kindle when we will
>   The fire which in the heart resides,
> The spirit bloweth and is still,
>   In mystery our soul abides;
> But tasks in hours of insight willed
>   Can be through hours of gloom fulfilled.

MARCH 22

AM I CARNALLY MINDED?

> "Where there are envy, strife, and divisions among you, are you not carnal . . . ?"
> (1 Corinthians 3:3).

The natural man, or unbeliever, knows nothing about carnality. The desires of the flesh warring against the Spirit, and the Spirit warring against the flesh, which began at rebirth, are what produce carnality and the awareness of it. But Paul said, "Walk in the Spirit, and you shall not fulfill the lust of the flesh" (Galatians 5:16). In other words, carnality will disappear.

Are you quarrelsome and easily upset over small things? Do you think that no one who is a Christian is ever like that? Paul said they are, and he connected these attitudes with carnality. Is there a truth in the Bible that instantly awakens a spirit of malice or resentment in you? If so, that is proof that you are still carnal. If the process of sanctification is continuing in your life, there will be no trace of that kind of spirit remaining.

If the Spirit of God detects anything in you that is wrong, He doesn't ask you to make it right; He only asks you to accept the light of truth, and then He will make it right. A child of the light will confess sin instantly and stand completely open before God. But a child of the darkness will say, "Oh, I can explain that." When the light shines and the Spirit brings conviction of sin, be a child of the light. Confess your wrongdoing, and God will deal with it. If, however, you try to vindicate yourself, you prove yourself to be a child of the darkness.

What is the proof that carnality has gone? Never deceive yourself; when carnality is gone you will know it—it is the most real thing you can imagine. And God will see to it that you have a number of opportunities to prove to yourself the miracle of His grace. The proof is in a very practical test. You will find yourself saying, "If this had happened before, I would have had the spirit of resentment!" And you will never cease to be the most amazed person on earth at what God has done for you on the inside.

DECREASING FOR HIS PURPOSE

"He must increase, but I must decrease" (John 3:30).

I f you become a necessity to someone else's life, you are out of God's will. As a servant, your primary responsibility is to be a "friend of the bridegroom" (3:29). When you see a person who is close to grasping the claims of Jesus Christ, you know that your influence has been used in the right direction. And when you begin to see that person in the middle of a difficult and painful struggle, don't try to prevent it, but pray that his difficulty will grow even ten times stronger, until no power on earth or in hell could hold him away from Jesus Christ. Over and over again, we try to be amateur providences in someone's life. We are indeed amateurs, coming in and actually preventing God's will and saying, "This person should not have to experience this difficulty." Instead of being friends of the Bridegroom, our sympathy gets in the way. One day that person will say to us, "You are a thief; you stole my desire to follow Jesus, and because of you I lost sight of Him."

Beware of rejoicing with someone over the wrong thing, but always look to rejoice over the right thing. ". . . the friend of the bridegroom . . . rejoices greatly because of the bridegroom's voice. Therefore this joy of mine is fulfilled. He must increase, but I must decrease" (3:29-30). This was spoken with joy, not with sadness—at last they were to see the Bridegroom! And John said this was his joy. It represents a stepping aside, an absolute removal of the servant, never to be thought of again.

Listen intently with your entire being until you hear the Bridegroom's voice in the life of another person. And never give any thought to what devastation, difficulties, or sickness it will bring. Just rejoice with godly excitement that His voice has been heard. You may often have to watch Jesus Christ wreck a life before He saves it (see Matthew 10:34).

MAINTAINING THE PROPER RELATIONSHIP

"... the friend of the bridegroom ..." (John 3:29).

Goodness and purity should never be traits that draw attention to themselves, but should simply be magnets that draw people to Jesus Christ. If my holiness is not drawing others to Him, it is not the right kind of holiness; it is only an influence which awakens undue emotions and evil desires in people and diverts them from heading in the right direction. A person who is a beautiful saint can be a hindrance in leading people to the Lord by presenting only what Christ has done for him, instead of presenting Jesus Christ Himself. Others will be left with this thought—"What a fine person that man is!" That is not being a true "friend of the bridegroom"—*I* am increasing all the time; *He* is not.

To maintain this friendship and faithfulness to the Bridegroom, we have to be more careful to have the moral and vital relationship to Him above everything else, including obedience. Sometimes there is nothing to obey and our only task is to maintain a vital connection with Jesus Christ, seeing that nothing interferes with it. Only occasionally is it a matter of obedience. At those times when a crisis arises, we have to find out what God's will is. Yet most of our life is not spent in trying to be consciously obedient, but in maintaining this relationship—being the "friend of the bridegroom." Christian work can actually be a means of diverting a person's focus away from Jesus Christ. Instead of being friends "of the bridegroom," we may become amateur providences of God to someone else, working against Him while we use His weapons.

Spiritual Vision Through Personal Purity

"Blessed are the pure in heart, for they shall see God" (Matthew 5:8).

Purity is not innocence—it is much more than that. Purity is the result of continued spiritual harmony with God. We have to grow in purity. Our life with God may be right and our inner purity unblemished, yet occasionally our outer life may become spotted and stained. God intentionally does not protect us from this possibility, because this is the way we recognize the necessity of maintaining our spiritual vision through personal purity. If the outer level of our spiritual life with God is impaired to the slightest degree, we must put everything else aside until we make it right. Remember that spiritual vision depends on our character—it is *"the pure in heart"* who "see" God.

God makes us pure by an act of His sovereign grace, but we still have something that we must carefully watch. It is through our bodily life coming in contact with other people and other points of view that we tend to become tarnished. Not only must our "inner sanctuary" be kept right with God, but also the "outer courts" must be brought into perfect harmony with the purity God gives us through His grace. Our spiritual vision and understanding is immediately blurred when our "outer court" is stained. If we want to maintain personal intimacy with the Lord Jesus Christ, it will mean refusing to do or even think certain things. And some things that are acceptable for others will become unacceptable for us.

A practical help in keeping your personal purity unblemished in your relations with other people is to begin to see them as God does. Say to yourself, "That man or that woman is *perfect in Christ Jesus!* That friend or that relative is *perfect in Christ Jesus!*"

SPIRITUAL VISION THROUGH PERSONAL CHARACTER

"Come up here, and I will show you things which must take place . . ." (Revelation 4:1).

A higher state of mind and spiritual vision can only be achieved through the higher practice of personal character. If you live up to the highest and best that you know in the outer level of your life, God will continually say to you, "Friend, come up even higher." There is also a continuing rule in temptation which calls you to go higher; but when you do, you only encounter other temptations and character traits. Both God and Satan use the strategy of elevation, but Satan uses it in temptation, and the effect is quite different. When the devil elevates you to a certain place, he causes you to fasten your idea of what holiness is far beyond what flesh and blood could ever bear or achieve. Your life becomes a spiritual acrobatic performance high atop a steeple. You cling to it, trying to maintain your balance and daring not to move. But when God elevates you by His grace into heavenly places, you find a vast plateau where you can move about with ease.

Compare this week in your spiritual life with the same week last year to see how God has called you to a higher level. We have all been brought to see from a higher viewpoint. Never allow God to show you a truth which you do not instantly begin to live up to, applying it to your life. Always work through it, staying in its light.

Your growth in grace is not measured by the fact that you haven't turned back, but that you have an insight and understanding into where you are spiritually. Have you heard God say, "Come up higher," not audibly on the outer level, but to the innermost part of your character?

"Shall I hide from Abraham what I am doing . . . ?" (Genesis 18:17). God has to hide from us what He does, until, due to the growth of our personal character, we get to the level where He is then able to reveal it.

ISN'T THERE SOME MISUNDERSTANDING?

" 'Let us go to Judea again.' The disciples said
to Him, '. . . are You going there again?' "
(John 11:7–8).

Just because I don't understand what Jesus Christ says,
I have no right to determine that He must be mistaken in what He says. That is a dangerous view, and it
is never right to think that my obedience to God's directive will bring dishonor to Jesus. The only thing that will
bring dishonor is not obeying Him. To put my view of
His honor ahead of what He is plainly guiding me to do
is never right, even though it may come from a real desire
to prevent Him from being put to an open shame. I know
when the instructions have come from God because of
their quiet persistence. But when I begin to weigh the
pros and *cons*, and doubt and debate enter into my mind,
I am bringing in an element that is not of God. This will
only result in my concluding that His instructions to me
were not right. Many of us are faithful to our ideas about
Jesus Christ, but how many of us are faithful to Jesus
Himself? Faithfulness to Jesus means that I must step out
even when and where I can't see anything (see Matthew
14:29). But faithfulness to my own ideas means that I
first clear the way mentally. Faith, however, is not intellectual understanding; faith is a deliberate commitment
to the Person of Jesus Christ, even when I can't see the
way ahead.

Are you debating whether you should take a step of
faith in Jesus, or whether you should wait until you can
clearly see how to do what He has asked? Simply obey
Him with unrestrained joy. When He tells you something and you begin to debate, it is because you have a
misunderstanding of what honors Him and what doesn't.
Are you faithful to Jesus, or faithful to your ideas about
Him? Are you faithful to what He says, or are you trying
to compromise His words with thoughts that never came
from Him? "Whatever He says to you, *do it*" (John 2:5).

OUR LORD'S SURPRISE VISITS

"You also be ready . . ." (Luke 12:40).

A Christian worker's greatest need is a readiness to face Jesus Christ at any and every turn. This is not easy, no matter what our experience has been. This battle is not against sin, difficulties, or circumstances, but against being so absorbed in our service to Jesus Christ that we are not ready to face Jesus Himself at every turn. The greatest need is not facing our beliefs or doctrines, or even facing the question of whether or not we are of any use to Him, but the need is to face *Him*.

Jesus rarely comes where we expect Him; He appears where we least expect Him, and always in the most illogical situations. The only way a servant can remain true to God is to be ready for the Lord's surprise visits. This readiness will not be brought about by service, but through intense spiritual reality, expecting Jesus Christ at every turn. This sense of expectation will give our life the attitude of childlike wonder He wants it to have. If we are going to be ready for Jesus Christ, we have to stop being religious. In other words, we must stop using religion as if it were some kind of a lofty lifestyle—we must be spiritually real.

If you are avoiding the call of the religious thinking of today's world, and instead are "looking unto Jesus" (Hebrews 12:2), setting your heart on what He wants, and thinking His thoughts, you will be considered impractical and a daydreamer. But when He suddenly appears in the work of the heat of the day, you will be the only one who is ready. You should trust no one, and even ignore the finest saint on earth if he blocks your sight of Jesus Christ.

HOLINESS OR HARDNESS
TOWARD GOD?

"He . . . wondered that there was no intercessor . . ." (Isaiah 59:16).

The reason many of us stop praying and become hard toward God is that we only have an emotional interest in prayer. It sounds good to say that we pray, and we read books on prayer which tell us that prayer is beneficial—that our minds are quieted and our souls are uplifted when we pray. But Isaiah implied in this verse that God is amazed at such thoughts about prayer.

Worship and intercession must go together; one is impossible without the other. Intercession means raising ourselves up to the point of getting the mind of Christ regarding the person for whom we are praying (see Philippians 2:5). Instead of worshiping God, we recite speeches to God about how prayer is supposed to work. Are we worshiping God or disputing Him when we say, "But God, I just don't see how you are going to do this"? This is a sure sign that we are not worshiping. When we lose sight of God, we become hard and dogmatic. We throw our petitions at His throne and dictate to Him what we want Him to do. We don't worship God, nor do we seek to conform our minds to the mind of Christ. And if we are hard toward God, we will become hard toward other people.

Are we worshiping God in a way that will raise us up to where we can take hold of Him, having such intimate contact with Him that we know His mind about the ones for whom we pray? Are we living in a holy relationship with God, or have we become hard and dogmatic?

Do you find yourself thinking that there is no one interceding properly? Then be that person yourself. Be a person who worships God and lives in a holy relationship with Him. Get involved in the real work of intercession, remembering that it truly is work—work that demands all your energy, but work which has no hidden pitfalls. Preaching the gospel has its share of pitfalls, but intercessory prayer has none whatsoever.

HEEDFULNESS OR HYPOCRISY IN OURSELVES?

"If anyone sees his brother sinning a sin which does not lead to death, he will ask, and He will give him life for those who commit sin not leading to death" (1 John 5:16).

If we are not heedful and pay no attention to the way the Spirit of God works in us, we will become spiritual hypocrites. We see where other people are failing, and then we take our discernment and turn it into comments of ridicule and criticism, instead of turning it into intercession on their behalf. God reveals this truth about others to us not through the sharpness of our minds but through the direct penetration of His Spirit. If we are not attentive, we will be completely unaware of the source of the discernment God has given us, becoming critical of others and forgetting that God says, ". . . he will ask, and He will give him life for those who commit sin not leading to death." Be careful that you don't become a hypocrite by spending all your time trying to get others right with God before you worship Him yourself.

One of the most subtle and illusive burdens God ever places on us as saints is this burden of discernment concerning others. He gives us discernment so that we may accept the responsibility for those souls before Him and form the mind of Christ about them (see Philippians 2:5). We should intercede in accordance with what God says He will give us, namely, "life for those who commit sin not leading to death." It is not that we are able to bring God into contact with our minds, but that we awaken ourselves to the point where God is able to convey His mind to us regarding the people for whom we intercede.

Can Jesus Christ see the agony of His soul in us? He can't unless we are so closely identified with Him that we have His view concerning the people for whom we pray. May we learn to intercede so wholeheartedly that Jesus Christ will be completely and overwhelmingly satisfied with us as intercessors.

MARCH 31

HELPFUL OR HEARTLESS TOWARD OTHERS?

> "It is Christ . . . who also makes intercession for us. . . . the Spirit . . . makes intercession for the saints . . ." (Romans 8:34, 27).

Do we need any more arguments than these to become intercessors—that Christ "always lives to make intercession" (Hebrews 7:25), and that the Holy Spirit "makes intercession for the saints"? Are we living in such a relationship with others that we do the work of intercession as a result of being the children of God who are taught by His Spirit? We should take a look at our current circumstances. Do crises which affect us or others in our home, business, country, or elsewhere, seem to be crushing in on us? Are we being pushed out of the presence of God and left with no time for worship? If so, we must put a stop to such distractions and get into such a living relationship with God that our relationship with others is maintained through the work of intercession, where God works His miracles.

Beware of getting ahead of God by your very desire to do His will. We run ahead of Him in a thousand and one activities, becoming so burdened with people and problems that we don't worship God, and we fail to intercede. If a burden and its resulting pressure come upon us while we are not in an attitude of worship, it will only produce a hardness toward God and despair in our own souls. God continually introduces us to people in whom we have no interest, and unless we are worshiping God the natural tendency is to be heartless toward them. We give them a quick verse of Scripture, like jabbing them with a spear, or leave them with a hurried, uncaring word of counsel before we go. A heartless Christian must be a terrible grief to our Lord.

Are our lives in the proper place so that we may participate in the intercession of our Lord and the Holy Spirit?

THE GLORY THAT'S UNSURPASSED

". . . the Lord Jesus . . . has sent me that you may receive your sight . . ." (Acts 9:17).

When Paul received his sight, he also received spiritual insight into the Person of Jesus Christ. His entire life and preaching from that point on were totally consumed with nothing but Jesus Christ—"For I determined not to know anything among you except Jesus Christ and Him crucified" (1 Corinthians 2:2). Paul never again allowed anything to attract and hold the attention of his mind and soul except the face of Jesus Christ.

We must learn to maintain a strong degree of character in our lives, even to the level that has been revealed in our vision of Jesus Christ.

The lasting characteristic of a spiritual man is the ability to understand correctly the meaning of the Lord Jesus Christ in his life, and the ability to explain the purposes of God to others. The overruling passion of his life is Jesus Christ. Whenever you see this quality in a person, you get the feeling that he is truly a man after God's own heart (see Acts 13:22).

Never allow anything to divert you from your insight into Jesus Christ. It is the true test of whether you are spiritual or not. To be unspiritual means that other things have a growing fascination for you.

> Since mine eyes have looked on Jesus,
> I've lost sight of all beside,
> So enchained my spirit's vision,
> Gazing on the Crucified.

"If You Had Known!"

> "If you had known . . . in this your day, the
> things that make for your peace! But now they
> are hidden from your eyes" (Luke 19:42).

Jesus entered Jerusalem triumphantly and the city was
stirred to its very foundations, but a strange god was
there—the pride of the Pharisees. It was a god that
seemed religious and upright, but Jesus compared it to
"whitewashed tombs which indeed appear beautiful out-
wardly, but inside are full of dead men's bones and all
uncleanness" (Matthew 23:27).

What is it that blinds you to the peace of God "in
this *your* day"? Do you have a strange god—not a disgust-
ing monster but perhaps an unholy nature that controls
your life? More than once God has brought me face to
face with a strange god in my life, and I knew that I
should have given it up, but I didn't do it. I got through
the crisis "by the skin of my teeth," only to find myself
still under the control of that strange god. I am blind to
the very things that make for my own peace. It is a shock-
ing thing that we can be in the exact place where the
Spirit of God should be having His completely unhindered way with us, and yet we only make matters worse,
increasing our blame in God's eyes.

"If you had known . . . ." God's words here cut directly to the heart, with the tears of Jesus behind them. These
words imply responsibility for our own faults. God holds
us accountable for what we refuse to see or are unable to
see because of our sin. And "now they are hidden from
your eyes" because you have never completely yielded your
nature to Him. Oh, the deep, unending sadness for what
might have been! God never again opens the doors that
have been closed. He opens other doors, but He reminds
us that there are doors which we have shut—doors which
had no need to be shut. Never be afraid when God brings
back your past. Let your memory have its way with you.
It is a minister of God bringing its rebuke and sorrow to
you. God will turn what might have been into a wonderful lesson of growth for the future.

THE WAY TO PERMANENT FAITH

"Indeed the hour is coming . . . that you will
be scattered . . ." (John 16:32).

Jesus was not rebuking the disciples in this passage.
Their faith was real, but it was disordered and unfocused, and was not at work in the important realities
of life. The disciples were scattered to their own concerns
and they had interests apart from Jesus Christ. After
we have the perfect relationship with God, through the
sanctifying work of the Holy Spirit, our faith must be
exercised in the realities of everyday life. We will be scattered, not into service but into the emptiness of our lives
where we will see ruin and barrenness, to know what
internal death to God's blessings means. Are we prepared
for this? It is certainly not of our own choosing, but God
engineers our circumstances to take us there. Until we
have been through that experience, our faith is sustained
only by feelings and by blessings. But once we get there,
no matter where God may place us or what inner emptiness we experience, we can praise God that all is well.
That is what is meant by faith being exercised in the realities of life.

". . . you . . . will leave Me alone." Have we been
scattered and have we left Jesus alone by not seeing His
providential care for us? Do we not see God at work in
our circumstances? Dark times are allowed and come
to us through the sovereignty of God. Are we prepared to
let God do what He wants with us? Are we prepared to
be separated from the outward, evident blessings of God?
Until Jesus Christ is truly our Lord, we each have goals
of our own which we serve. Our faith is real, but it is not
yet permanent. And God is never in a hurry. If we are
willing to wait, we will see God pointing out that we have
been interested only in His blessings, instead of in God
Himself. The sense of God's blessings is fundamental.

". . . be of good cheer, I have overcome the world"
(16:33). Unyielding spiritual fortitude is what we need.

HIS AGONY AND OUR ACCESS

> "Jesus came with them to a place called Gethsemane, and said to the disciples . . . . 'Stay here and watch with Me' " (Matthew 26:36, 38).

We can never fully comprehend Christ's agony in the Garden of Gethsemane, but at least we don't have to misunderstand it. It is the agony of God and man in one Person, coming face to face with sin. We cannot learn about Gethsemane through personal experience. Gethsemane and Calvary represent something totally unique—they are the gateway into life for us.

It was not death on the cross that Jesus agonized over in Gethsemane. In fact, He stated very emphatically that He came with the purpose of dying. His concern here was that He might not get through this struggle as the Son of Man. He was confident of getting through it as the Son of God—Satan could not touch Him there. But Satan's assault was that our Lord would come through for us on His own solely as the Son of Man. If Jesus had done that, He could not have been our Savior (see Hebrews 9:11-15). Read the record of His agony in Gethsemane in light of His earlier wilderness temptation—". . . the devil . . . departed from Him until an opportune time" (Luke 4:13). In Gethsemane, Satan came back and was overthrown again. Satan's final assault against our Lord as the *Son of Man* was in Gethsemane.

The agony in Gethsemane was the agony of the Son of God in fulfilling His destiny as the Savior of the world. The veil is pulled back here to reveal all that it cost Him to make it possible for us to become sons of God. His agony was the basis for the simplicity of our salvation. The Cross of Christ was a triumph for the *Son of Man*. It was not only a sign that our Lord had triumphed, but that He had triumphed to save the human race. Because of what the Son of Man went through, every human being has been provided with a way of access into the very presence of God.

THE COLLISION OF GOD AND SIN

> ". . . who Himself bore our sins in His own body on the tree . . ." (1 Peter 2:24).

The Cross of Christ is the revealed truth of God's judgment on sin. Never associate the idea of martyrdom with the Cross of Christ. It was the supreme triumph, and it shook the very foundations of hell. There is nothing in time or eternity more absolutely certain and irrefutable than what Jesus Christ accomplished on the Cross—He made it possible for the entire human race to be brought back into a right-standing relationship with God. He made redemption the foundation of human life; that is, He made a way for every person to have fellowship with God.

The Cross was not something that *happened* to Jesus—He came to die; the Cross was His purpose in coming. He is "the Lamb slain from the foundation of the world" (Revelation 13:8). The incarnation of Christ would have no meaning without the Cross. Beware of separating "*God was manifested in the flesh . . .*" from "*. . . He made Him . . . to be sin for us . . .*" (1 Timothy 3:16; 2 Corinthians 5:21). The purpose of the incarnation was redemption. God came in the flesh to take sin away, not to accomplish something for Himself. The Cross is the central event in time and eternity, and the answer to all the problems of both.

The Cross is not the cross of a man, but the Cross of God, and it can never be fully comprehended through human experience. The Cross is God exhibiting His nature. It is the gate through which any and every individual can enter into oneness with God. But it is not a gate we pass right through; it is one where we abide in the life that is found there.

The heart of salvation is the Cross of Christ. The reason salvation is so easy to obtain is that it cost God so much. The Cross was the place where God and sinful man merged with a tremendous collision and where the way to life was opened. But all the cost and pain of the collision was absorbed by the heart of God.

WHY WE LACK UNDERSTANDING

"He commanded them that they should tell no one the things they had seen, till the Son of Man had risen from the dead" (Mark 9:9).

As the disciples were commanded, you should also say nothing until the Son of Man has risen in you—until the life of the risen Christ so dominates you that you truly understand what He taught while here on earth. When you grow and develop the right condition inwardly, the words Jesus spoke become so clear that you are amazed you did not grasp them before. In fact, you were not able to understand them before because you had not yet developed the proper spiritual condition to deal with them.

Our Lord doesn't hide these things from us, but we are not prepared to receive them until we are in the right condition in our spiritual life. Jesus said, "I still have many things to say to you, but you cannot bear them now" (John 16:12). We must have a oneness with His risen life before we are prepared to bear any particular truth from Him. Do we really know anything about the indwelling of the risen life of Jesus? The evidence that we do is that His Word is becoming understandable to us. God cannot reveal anything to us if we don't have His Spirit. And our own unyielding and headstrong opinions will effectively prevent God from revealing anything to us. But our insensible thinking will end immediately once His resurrection life has its way with us.

". . . tell no one . . . ." But so many people do tell what they saw on the Mount of Transfiguration—their mountaintop experience. They have seen a vision and they testify to it, but there is no connection between what they say and how they live. Their lives don't add up because the Son of Man has not yet risen in them. How long will it be before His resurrection life is formed and evident in you and in me?

HIS RESURRECTION DESTINY

"Ought not the Christ to have suffered these things and to enter into His glory?" (Luke 24:26).

Our Lord's Cross is the gateway into His life. His resurrection means that He has the power to convey His life to me. When I was born again, I received the very life of the risen Lord from Jesus Himself.

Christ's resurrection destiny—His foreordained purpose—was to bring "many sons to glory" (Hebrews 2:10). The fulfilling of His destiny gives Him the right to make us sons and daughters of God. We never have exactly the same relationship to God that the Son of God has, but we are brought by the Son into the relation of sonship. When our Lord rose from the dead, He rose to an absolutely new life—a life He had never lived before He was God Incarnate. He rose to a life that had never been before. And what His resurrection means for us is that we are raised to His risen life, not to our old life. One day we will have a body like His glorious body, but we can know here and now the power and effectiveness of His resurrection and can "walk in newness of life" (Romans 6:4). Paul's determined purpose was to "know Him *and the power of His resurrection*" (Philippians 3:10).

Jesus prayed, ". . . as You have given Him authority over all flesh that He should give eternal life to as many as You have given Him" (John 17:2). The term *Holy Spirit* is actually another name for the experience of eternal life working in human beings here and now. The Holy Spirit is the deity of God who continues to apply the power of the atonement by the Cross of Christ to our lives. Thank God for the glorious and majestic truth that His Spirit can work the very nature of Jesus into us, if we will only obey Him.

HAVE YOU SEEN JESUS?

"After that, He appeared in another form to two of them . . ." (Mark 16:12).

Being saved and seeing Jesus are not the same thing. Many people who have never seen Jesus have received and share in God's grace. But once you have seen Him, you can never be the same. Other things will not have the appeal they did before.

You should always recognize the difference between what you see Jesus to be and what He has done for you. If you see only what He has done for you, your God is not big enough. But if you have had a vision, seeing Jesus as He really is, experiences can come and go, yet you will endure "as seeing Him who is invisible" (Hebrews 11:27). The man who was blind from birth did not know who Jesus was until Christ appeared and revealed Himself to him (see John 9). Jesus appears to those for whom He has done something, but we cannot order or predict when He will come. He may appear suddenly, at any turn. Then you can exclaim, "Now I see Him!" (see John 9:25).

Jesus must appear to you and to your friend individually; no one can see Jesus with your eyes. And division takes place when one has seen Him and the other has not. You cannot bring your friend to the point of seeing; God must do it. Have you seen Jesus? If so, you will want others to see Him too. "And they went and told it to the rest, but they did not believe them either" (Mark 16:13). When you see Him, you must tell, even if they don't believe.

> O could I tell, you surely would believe it!
>   O could I only say what I have seen!
> How should I tell or how can you receive it,
>   How, till He bringeth you where I have been?

COMPLETE AND EFFECTIVE
DECISION ABOUT SIN

"... our old man was crucified with Him, that
the body of sin might be done away with, that
we should no longer be slaves of sin" (Romans
6:6).

Co-Crucifixion. Have you made the following decision about sin—that it must be completely killed
in you? It takes a long time to come to the point
of making this complete and effective decision about sin.
It is, however, the greatest moment in your life once you
decide that sin must die in you—not simply be restrained,
suppressed, or counteracted, but crucified—just as Jesus
Christ died for the sin of the world. No one can bring
anyone else to this decision. We may be mentally and
spiritually convinced, but what we need to do is actually
make the decision that Paul urged us to do in this passage.

Pull yourself up, take some time alone with God,
and make this important decision, saying, "Lord, identify
me with Your death until I know that sin is dead in me."
Make the moral decision that sin in you must be put to
death.

This was not some divine future expectation on the
part of Paul, but was a very radical and definite experience in his life. Are you prepared to let the Spirit of God
search you until you know what the level and nature of
sin is in your life—to see the very things that struggle
against God's Spirit in you? If so, will you then agree
with God's verdict on the nature of sin—that it should be
identified with the death of Jesus? You cannot "reckon
yourselves to be dead indeed to sin" (6:11) unless you
have radically dealt with the issue of your will before
God.

Have you entered into the glorious privilege of
being crucified with Christ, until all that remains in
your flesh and blood is His life? "I have been crucified
with Christ; it is no longer I who live, but Christ lives in
me ..." (Galatians 2:20).

COMPLETE AND EFFECTIVE DIVINITY

"If we have been united together in the likeness of His death, certainly we also shall be in the likeness of His resurrection . . ." (Romans 6:5).

Co-Resurrection. The proof that I have experienced crucifixion with Jesus is that I have a definite likeness to Him. The Spirit of Jesus entering me rearranges my personal life before God. The resurrection of Jesus has given Him the authority to give the life of God to me, and the experiences of my life must now be built on the foundation of His life. I can have the resurrection life of Jesus here and now, and it will exhibit itself through holiness.

The idea all through the apostle Paul's writings is that after the decision to be identified with Jesus in His death has been made, the resurrection life of Jesus penetrates every bit of my human nature. It takes the omnipotence of God—His complete and effective divinity—to live the life of the Son of God in human flesh. The Holy Spirit cannot be accepted as a guest in merely one room of the house—He invades all of it. And once I decide that my "old man" (that is, my heredity of sin) should be identified with the death of Jesus, the Holy Spirit invades me. He takes charge of everything. My part is to walk in the light and to obey all that He reveals to me. Once I have made that important decision about sin, it is easy to "reckon" that I am actually "dead indeed to sin," because I find the life of Jesus in me all the time (Romans 6:11). Just as there is only one kind of humanity, there is only one kind of holiness—the holiness of Jesus. And it is His holiness that has been given to me. God puts the holiness of His Son into me, and I belong to a new spiritual order.

COMPLETE AND EFFECTIVE DOMINION

> "Death no longer has dominion over Him. . . . the life that He lives, He lives to God. Likewise you also, reckon yourselves to be dead indeed to sin, but alive to God . . ." (Romans 6:9–11).

Co-Eternal Life. Eternal life is the life which Jesus Christ exhibited on the human level. And it is this same life, not simply a copy of it, which is made evident in our mortal flesh when we are born again. Eternal life is not a gift from God; eternal life is the gift *of* God. The energy and the power which was so very evident in Jesus will be exhibited in us by an act of the absolute sovereign grace of God, once we have made that complete and effective decision about sin.

"You shall receive power when the Holy Spirit has come upon you . . ." (Acts 1:8)—not power as a gift from the Holy Spirit; the power *is* the Holy Spirit, not something that He gives us. The life that was in Jesus becomes ours because of His Cross, once we make the decision to be identified with Him. If it is difficult to get right with God, it is because we refuse to make this moral decision about sin. But once we do decide, the full life of God comes in immediately. Jesus came to give us an endless supply of life—". . . that you may be filled with all the fullness of God" (Ephesians 3:19). Eternal life has nothing to do with time. It is the life which Jesus lived when He was down here, and the only Source of life is the Lord Jesus Christ.

Even the weakest saint can experience the power of the deity of the Son of God, when he is willing to "let go." But any effort to "hang on" to the least bit of our own power will only diminish the life of Jesus in us. We have to keep letting go, and slowly, but surely, the great full life of God will invade us, penetrating every part. Then Jesus will have complete and effective dominion in us, and people will take notice that we have been with Him.

WHAT TO DO WHEN YOUR
BURDEN IS OVERWHELMING

"Cast your burden on the LORD . . ." (Psalm 55:22).

We must recognize the difference between burdens that are right for us to bear and burdens that are wrong. We should never bear the burdens of sin or doubt, but there are some burdens placed on us by God which He does not intend to lift off. God wants us to roll them back on Him—to literally "cast your burden," which He has given you, "on the LORD . . . ." If we set out to serve God and do His work but get out of touch with Him, the sense of responsibility we feel will be overwhelming and defeating. But if we will only roll back on God the burdens He has placed on us, He will take away that immense feeling of responsibility, replacing it with an awareness and understanding of Himself and His presence.

Many servants set out to serve God with great courage and with the right motives. But with no intimate fellowship with Jesus Christ, they are soon defeated. They do not know what to do with their burden, and it produces weariness in their lives. Others will see this and say, "What a sad end to something that had such a great beginning!"

"Cast your burden on the LORD . . . ." You have been bearing it all, but you need to deliberately place one end on God's shoulder. ". . . the government will be upon His shoulder" (Isaiah 9:6). Commit to God whatever burden He has placed on you. Don't just cast it aside, but put it over onto Him and place yourself there with it. You will see that your burden is then lightened by the sense of companionship. But you should never try to separate yourself from your burden.

INNER INVINCIBILITY

**"Take My yoke upon you and learn from Me . . ."
(Matthew 11:29).**

Whom the LORD loves He chastens . . ." (Hebrews 12:6). How petty our complaining is! Our Lord begins to bring us to the point where we can have fellowship with Him, only to hear us moan and groan, saying, "Oh Lord, just let me be like other people!" Jesus is asking us to get beside Him and take one end of the yoke, so that we can pull together. That's why Jesus says to us, "My yoke is easy and My burden is light" (Matthew 11:30). Are you closely identified with the Lord Jesus like that? If so, you will thank God when you feel the pressure of His hand upon you.

". . . to those who have no might He increases strength" (Isaiah 40:29). God comes and takes us out of our emotionalism, and then our complaining turns into a hymn of praise. The only way to know the strength of God is to take the yoke of Jesus upon us and to learn from Him.

". . . the joy of the LORD is your strength" (Nehemiah 8:10). Where do the saints get their joy? If we did not know some Christians well, we might think from just observing them that they have no burdens at all to bear. But we must lift the veil from our eyes. The fact that the peace, light, and joy of God is in them is proof that a burden is there as well. The burden that God places on us squeezes the grapes in our lives and produces the wine, but most of us see only the wine and not the burden. No power on earth or in hell can conquer the Spirit of God living within the human spirit; it creates an inner invincibility.

If your life is producing only a whine, instead of the wine, then ruthlessly kick it out. It is definitely a crime for a Christian to be weak in God's strength.

THE FAILURE TO PAY CLOSE ATTENTION

"The high places were not removed from Israel. Nevertheless the heart of Asa was loyal all his days" (2 Chronicles 15:17).

Asa was not completely obedient in the outward, visible areas of his life. He was obedient in what he considered the most important areas, but he was not entirely right. Beware of ever thinking, "Oh, that thing in my life doesn't matter much." The fact that it doesn't matter much to you may mean that it matters a great deal to God. Nothing should be considered a trivial matter by a child of God. How much longer are we going to prevent God from teaching us even one thing? But He keeps trying to teach us and He never loses patience. You say, "I know I am right with God"—yet the "high places" still remain in your life. There is still an area of disobedience. Do you protest that your heart is right with God, and yet there is something in your life He causes you to doubt? Whenever God causes a doubt about something, stop it immediately, no matter what it may be. Nothing in our lives is a mere insignificant detail to God.

Are there some things regarding your physical or intellectual life to which you have been paying no attention at all? If so, you may think you are all correct in the important areas, but you are careless—you are failing to concentrate or to focus properly. You no more need a day off from spiritual concentration on matters in your life than your heart needs a day off from beating. As you cannot take a day off morally and remain moral, neither can you take a day off spiritually and remain spiritual. God wants you to be entirely His, and it requires paying close attention to keep yourself fit. It also takes a tremendous amount of time. Yet some of us expect to rise above all of our problems, going from one mountaintop experience to another, with only a few minutes' effort.

CAN YOU COME DOWN FROM THE MOUNTAIN?

"While you have the light, believe in the light . . ." (John 12:36).

We all have moments when we feel better than ever before, and we say, "I feel fit for anything; if only I could always be like this!" We are not meant to be. Those moments are moments of insight which we have to live up to even when we do not feel like it. Many of us are no good for the everyday world when we are not on the mountaintop. Yet we must bring our everyday life up to the standard revealed to us on the mountaintop when we were there.

Never allow a feeling that was awakened in you on the mountaintop to evaporate. Don't place yourself on the shelf by thinking, "How great to be in such a wonderful state of mind!" Act immediately—do something, even if your only reason to act is that you would rather not. If, during a prayer meeting, God shows you something to do, don't say, "I'll do it"—just *do it*! Pick yourself up by the back of the neck and shake off your fleshly laziness. Laziness can always be seen in our cravings for a mountaintop experience; all we talk about is our planning for our time on the mountain. We must learn to live in the ordinary "gray" day according to what we saw on the mountain.

Don't give up because you have been blocked and confused once—go after it again. Burn your bridges behind you, and stand committed to God by an act of your own will. Never change your decisions, but be sure to make your decisions in the light of what you saw and learned on the mountain.

ALL OR NOTHING?

"When Simon Peter heard that it was the Lord, he put on his outer garment . . . and plunged into the sea" (John 21:7).

Have you ever had a crisis in your life in which you deliberately, earnestly, and recklessly abandoned everything? It is a crisis of the will. You may come to that point many times externally, but it will amount to nothing. The true deep crisis of abandonment, or total surrender, is reached internally, not externally. The giving up of only external things may actually be an indication of your being in total bondage.

Have you deliberately committed your will to Jesus Christ? It is a transaction of the will, not of emotion; any positive emotion that results is simply a superficial blessing arising out of the transaction. If you focus your attention on the emotion, you will never make the transaction. Do not ask God what the transaction is to be, but make the determination to surrender your will regarding whatever you see, whether it is in the shallow or the deep, profound places internally.

If you have heard Jesus Christ's voice on the waves of the sea, you can let your convictions and your consistency take care of themselves by concentrating on maintaining your intimate relationship to Him.

READINESS

"God called to him . . . . And he said, 'Here I am'" (Exodus 3:4).

When God speaks, many of us are like people in a fog, and we give no answer. Moses' reply to God revealed that he knew where he was and that he was ready. Readiness means having a right relationship to God and having the knowledge of where we are. We are so busy telling God where we would like to go. Yet the man or woman who is ready for God and His work is the one who receives the prize when the summons comes. We wait with the idea that some great opportunity or something sensational will be coming our way, and when it does come we are quick to cry out, "Here I am." Whenever we sense that Jesus Christ is rising up to take authority over some great task, we are there, but we are not ready for some obscure duty.

Readiness for God means that we are prepared to do the smallest thing or the largest thing—it makes no difference. It means we have no choice in what we want to do, but that whatever God's plans may be, we are there and ready. Whenever any duty presents itself, we hear God's voice as our Lord heard His Father's voice, and we are ready for it with the total readiness of our love for Him. Jesus Christ expects to do with us just as His Father did with Him. He can put us wherever He wants, in pleasant duties or in menial ones, because our union with Him is the same as His union with the Father. ". . . that they may be one just as We are one . . ." (John 17:22).

Be ready for the sudden surprise visits of God. A ready person never needs to *get* ready—he *is* ready. Think of the time we waste trying to get ready once God has called! The burning bush is a symbol of everything that surrounds the person who is ready, and it is on fire with the presence of God Himself.

BEWARE OF THE LEAST
LIKELY TEMPTATION

**"Joab had defected to Adonijah, though he had
not defected to Absalom" (1 Kings 2:28).**

Joab withstood the greatest test of his life, remaining
absolutely loyal to David by not turning to follow after
the fascinating and ambitious Absalom. Yet toward the
end of his life he turned to follow after the weak and cowardly Adonijah. Always remain alert to the fact that where
one person has turned back is exactly where anyone may
be tempted to turn back (see 1 Corinthians 10:11-13).
You may have just victoriously gone through a great crisis,
but now be alert about the things that may appear to be
the least likely to tempt you. Beware of thinking that the
areas of your life where you have experienced victory in
the past are now the least likely to cause you to stumble
and fall.

We are apt to say, "It is not at all likely that having
been through the greatest crisis of my life I would now
turn back to the things of the world." Do not try to
predict where the temptation will come; it is the least
likely thing that is the real danger. It is in the aftermath
of a great spiritual event that the least likely things begin
to have an effect. They may not be forceful and domi-
nant, but they are there. And if you are not careful to
be forewarned, they will trip you. You have remained
true to God under great and intense trials—now beware
of the undercurrent. Do not be abnormally examining
your inner self, looking forward with dread, but stay
alert; keep your memory sharp before God. Unguarded
strength is actually a double weakness, because that is
where the least likely temptations will be effective in sap-
ping strength. The Bible characters stumbled over their
strong points, never their weak ones.

". . . kept by the power of God . . ."—that is the only
safety (1 Peter 1:5).

CAN A SAINT
FALSELY ACCUSE GOD?

"All the promises of God in Him are Yes, and in Him Amen . . ." **(2 Corinthians 1:20).**

Jesus' parable of the talents recorded in Matthew 25:14-30 was a warning that it is possible for us to misjudge our capacities. This parable has nothing to do with natural gifts and abilities, but relates to the gift of the Holy Spirit as He was first given at Pentecost. We must never measure our spiritual capacity on the basis of our education or our intellect; our capacity in spiritual things is measured on the basis of the promises of God. If we get less than God wants us to have, we will falsely accuse Him as the servant falsely accused his master when he said, "You expect more of me than you gave me the power to do. You demand too much of me, and I cannot stand true to you here where you have placed me." When it is a question of God's Almighty Spirit, never say, "I can't." Never allow the limitation of your own natural ability to enter into the matter. If we have received the Holy Spirit, God expects the work of the Holy Spirit to be exhibited in us.

The servant justified himself, while condemning his lord on every point, as if to say, "Your demand on me is way out of proportion to what you gave to me." Have we been falsely accusing God by daring to worry after He has said, "But seek first the kingdom of God and His righteousness, and all these things shall be added to you"? (Matthew 6:33). Worrying means exactly what this servant implied—"I know your intent is to leave me unprotected and vulnerable." A person who is lazy in the natural realm is always critical, saying, "I haven't had a decent chance," and someone who is lazy in the spiritual realm is critical of God. Lazy people always strike out at others in an independent way.

Never forget that our capacity and capability in spiritual matters is measured by, and based on, the promises of God. Is God able to fulfill His promises? Our answer depends on whether or not we have received the Holy Spirit.

DON'T HURT THE LORD

"Have I been with you so long, and yet you have not known Me, Philip?" (John 14:9).

Our Lord must be repeatedly astounded at us—astounded at how "un-simple" we are. It is our own opinions that make us dense and slow to understand, but when we are simple we are never dense; we have discernment all the time. Philip expected the future revelation of a tremendous mystery, but not in Jesus, the Person he thought he already knew. The mystery of God is not in what is going to be—it is now, though we look for it to be revealed in the future in some overwhelming, momentous event. We have no reluctance to obey Jesus, but it is highly probable that we are hurting Him by what we ask—"Lord, show us the Father . . ." (14:8). His response immediately comes back to us as He says, "Can't you see Him? He is always right here or He is nowhere to be found." We look for God to exhibit Himself *to* His children, but God only exhibits Himself *in* His children. And while others see the evidence, the child of God does not. We want to be fully aware of what God is doing in us, but we cannot have complete awareness and expect to remain reasonable or balanced in our expectations of Him. If all we are asking God to give us is experiences, and the awareness of those experiences is blocking our way, we hurt the Lord. The very questions we ask hurt Jesus, because they are not the questions of a child.

"Let not your heart be troubled . . ." (14:1, 27). Am I then hurting Jesus by allowing my heart to be troubled? If I believe in Jesus and His attributes, am I living up to my belief? Am I allowing anything to disturb my heart, or am I allowing any questions to come in which are unsound or unbalanced? I have to get to the point of the absolute and unquestionable relationship that takes everything exactly as it comes from Him. God never guides us at some time in the future, but always here and now. Realize that the Lord is here *now*, and the freedom you receive is immediate.

APRIL 21

THE LIGHT THAT NEVER FAILS

"We all, with unveiled face, beholding . . . the glory of the Lord . . ." (2 Corinthians 3:18).

A servant of God must stand so very much alone that he never realizes he is alone. In the early stages of the Christian life, disappointments will come—people who used to be lights will flicker out, and those who used to stand with us will turn away. We have to get so used to it that we will not even realize we are standing alone. Paul said, ". . . no one stood with me, but all forsook me . . . . But the Lord stood with me and strengthened me . . ." (2 Timothy 4:16-17). We must build our faith not on fading lights but on the Light that never fails. When "important" individuals go away we are sad, until we see that they are meant to go, so that only one thing is left for us to do—to look into the face of God for ourselves.

Allow nothing to keep you from looking with strong determination into the face of God regarding yourself and your doctrine. And every time you preach make sure you look God in the face about the message first, then the glory will remain through all of it. A Christian servant is one who perpetually looks into the face of God and then goes forth to talk to others. The ministry of Christ is characterized by an abiding glory of which the servant is totally unaware—". . . Moses did not know that the skin of his face shone while he talked with Him" (Exodus 34:29).

We are never called on to display our doubts openly or to express the hidden joys and delights of our life with God. The secret of the servant's life is that he stays in tune with God all the time.

DO YOU WORSHIP THE WORK?

"We are God's fellow workers . . ."
(1 Corinthians 3:9).

Beware of any work for God that causes or allows you to avoid concentrating on Him. A great number of Christian workers worship their work. The only concern of Christian workers should be their concentration on God. This will mean that all the other boundaries of life, whether they are mental, moral, or spiritual limits, are completely free with the freedom God gives His child; that is, a worshiping child, not a wayward one. A worker who lacks this serious controlling emphasis of concentration on God is apt to become overly burdened by his work. He is a slave to his own limits, having no freedom of his body, mind, or spirit. Consequently, he becomes burned out and defeated. There is no freedom and no delight in life at all. His nerves, mind, and heart are so overwhelmed that God's blessing cannot rest on him.

But the opposite case is equally true—once our concentration is on God, all the limits of our life are free and under the control and mastery of God alone. There is no longer any responsibility on you for the work. The only responsibility you have is to stay in living constant touch with God, and to see that you allow nothing to hinder your cooperation with Him. The freedom that comes after sanctification is the freedom of a child, and the things that used to hold your life down are gone. But be careful to remember that you have been freed for only one thing—to be absolutely devoted to your co-Worker.

We have no right to decide where we should be placed, or to have preconceived ideas as to what God is preparing us to do. God engineers everything; and wherever He places us, our one supreme goal should be to pour out our lives in wholehearted devotion to Him in that particular work. "Whatever your hand finds to do, do it with your might . . ." (Ecclesiastes 9:10).

APRIL 23

THE WARNING AGAINST DESIRING SPIRITUAL SUCCESS

"Do not rejoice in this, that the spirits are subject to you . . ." (Luke 10:20).

Worldliness is not the trap that most endangers us as Christian workers; nor is it sin. The trap we fall into is extravagantly desiring spiritual success; that is, success measured by, and patterned after, the form set by this religious age in which we now live. Never seek after anything other than the approval of God, and always be willing to go "outside the camp, bearing His reproach" (Hebrews 13:13). In Luke 10:20, Jesus told the disciples not to rejoice in successful service, and yet this seems to be the one thing in which most of us do rejoice. We have a commercialized view—we count how many souls have been saved and sanctified, we thank God, and then we think everything is all right. Yet our work only begins where God's grace has laid the foundation. Our work is not to save souls, but to disciple them. Salvation and sanctification are the work of God's sovereign grace, and our work as His disciples is to disciple others' lives until they are totally yielded to God. One life totally devoted to God is of more value to Him than one hundred lives which have been simply awakened by His Spirit. As workers for God, we must reproduce our own kind spiritually, and those lives will be God's testimony to us as His workers. God brings us up to a standard of life through His grace, and we are responsible for reproducing that same standard in others.

Unless the worker lives a life that "is hidden with Christ in God" (Colossians 3:3), he is apt to become an irritating dictator to others, instead of an active, living disciple. Many of us are dictators, dictating our desires to individuals and to groups. But Jesus never dictates to us in that way. Whenever our Lord talked about discipleship, He always prefaced His words with an "if," never with the forceful or dogmatic statement—"You must." Discipleship carries with it an option.

"READY IN SEASON"

**"Be ready in season and out of season"
(2 Timothy 4:2).**

Many of us suffer from the unbalanced tendency to "be ready" only "out of season." The season does not refer to time; it refers to us. This verse says, "Preach the Word! Be ready in season and out of season." In other words, we should "be ready" whether we feel like it or not. If we do only what we feel inclined to do, some of us would never do anything. There are some people who are totally unemployable in the spiritual realm. They are spiritually feeble and weak, and they refuse to do anything unless they are supernaturally inspired. The proof that our relationship is right with God is that we do our best whether we feel inspired or not.

One of the worst traps a Christian worker can fall into is to become obsessed with his own exceptional moments of inspiration. When the Spirit of God gives you a time of inspiration and insight, you tend to say, "Now that I've experienced this moment, I will always be like this for God." No, you will not, and God will make sure of that. Those times are entirely the gift of God. You cannot give them to yourself when you choose. If you say you will only be at your best for God, as during those exceptional times, you actually become an intolerable burden on Him. You will never do anything unless God keeps you consciously aware of His inspiration to you at all times. If you make a god out of your best moments, you will find that God will fade out of your life, never to return until you are obedient in the work He has placed closest to you, and until you have learned not to be obsessed with those exceptional moments He has given you.

THE SUPREME CLIMB

"Take now your son . . . and offer him . . . as a burnt offering on one of the mountains of which I shall tell you" (Genesis 22:2).

Aperson's character determines how he interprets God's will (see Psalm 18:25-26). Abraham interpreted God's command to mean that he had to kill his son, and he could only leave this traditional belief behind through the pain of a tremendous ordeal. God could purify his faith in no other way. If we obey what God says according to our sincere belief, God will break us from those traditional beliefs that misrepresent Him. There are many such beliefs which must be removed—for example, that God removes a child because his mother loves him too much. That is the devil's lie and a travesty on the true nature of God! If the devil can hinder us from taking the supreme climb and getting rid of our wrong traditional beliefs about God, he will do so. But if we will stay true to God, God will take us through an ordeal that will serve to bring us into a better knowledge of Himself.

The great lesson to be learned from Abraham's faith in God is that he was prepared to do anything for God. He was there to obey God, no matter what contrary belief of his might be violated by his obedience. Abraham was not devoted to his own convictions or else he would have slain Isaac and said that the voice of the angel was actually the voice of the devil. That is the attitude of a fanatic. If you will remain true to God, God will lead you directly through every barrier and right into the inner chamber of the knowledge of Himself. But you must always be willing to come to the point of giving up your own convictions and traditional beliefs. Don't ask God to test you. Never declare as Peter did that you are willing to do anything, even "to go . . . both to prison and to death" (Luke 22:33). Abraham did not make any such statement—he simply remained true to God, and God purified his faith.

WHAT DO YOU WANT?

**"Do you seek great things for yourself?"
(Jeremiah 45:5).**

Are you seeking great things for yourself, instead of seeking to be a great person? God wants you to be in a much closer relationship with Himself than simply receiving His gifts—He wants you to get to know Him. Even some large thing we want is only incidental; it comes and it goes. But God never gives us anything incidental. There is nothing easier than getting into the right relationship with God, unless it is not God you seek, but only what He can give you.

If you have only come as far as asking God for things, you have never come to the point of understanding the least bit of what surrender really means. You have become a Christian based on your own terms. You protest, saying, "I asked God for the Holy Spirit, but He didn't give me the rest and the peace I expected." And instantly God puts His finger on the reason—you are not seeking the Lord at all; you are seeking something for yourself. Jesus said, "Ask, and it will be given to you . . ." (Matthew 7:7). Ask God for what you want and do not be concerned about asking for the wrong thing, because as you draw ever closer to Him, you will cease asking for things altogether. "Your Father knows the things you have need of before you ask Him" (Matthew 6:8). Then why should you ask? So that you may get to know Him.

Are you seeking great things for yourself? Have you said, "Oh, Lord, completely fill me with your Holy Spirit"? If God does not, it is because you are not totally surrendered to Him; there is something you still refuse to do. Are you prepared to ask yourself what it is you want from God and why you want it? God always ignores your present level of completeness in favor of your ultimate future completeness. He is not concerned about making you blessed and happy right now, but He's continually working out His ultimate perfection for you—". . . that they may be one just as We are one . . ." (John 17:22).

WHAT YOU WILL GET

"I will give your life to you as a prize in all places, wherever you go" (Jeremiah 45:5).

This is the firm and immovable secret of the Lord to those who trust Him—"I will give your life to you. . . ." What more does a man want than his life? It is the essential thing. ". . . your life . . . as a prize . . ." means that wherever you may go, even if it is into hell, you will come out with your life and nothing can harm it. So many of us are caught up in exhibiting things for others to see, not showing off property and possessions, but our blessings. All these things that we so proudly show have to go. But there is something greater that can never go—the life that "is hidden with Christ in God" (Colossians 3:3).

Are you prepared to let God take you into total one-ness with Himself, paying no more attention to what you call the great things of life? Are you prepared to surrender totally and let go? The true test of abandonment or surrender is in refusing to say, "Well, what about this?" Beware of your own ideas and speculations. The moment you allow yourself to think, "What about this?" you show that you have not surrendered and that you do not really trust God. But once you do surrender, you will no longer think about what God is going to do. Abandonment means to refuse yourself the luxury of asking any questions. If you totally abandon yourself to God, He immediately says to you, "I will give your life to you as a prize. . . ." The reason people are tired of life is that God has not given them anything—they have not been given their life "as a prize." The way to get out of that condition is to abandon yourself to God. And once you do get to the point of total surrender to Him, you will be the most surprised and delighted person on earth. God will have you absolutely, without any limitations, and He will have given you your life. If you are not there, it is either because of disobedience in your life or your refusal to be simple enough.

GRACIOUS UNCERTAINTY

". . . it has not yet been revealed what we shall be . . ." (1 John 3:2).

Our natural inclination is to be so precise—trying always to forecast accurately what will happen next—that we look upon uncertainty as a bad thing. We think that we must reach some predetermined goal, but that is not the nature of the spiritual life. The nature of the spiritual life is that we are certain in our uncertainty. Consequently, we do not put down roots. Our common sense says, "Well, what if I were in that circumstance?" We cannot presume to see ourselves in any circumstance in which we have never been.

Certainty is the mark of the commonsense life—gracious uncertainty is the mark of the spiritual life. To be certain of God means that we are uncertain in all our ways, not knowing what tomorrow may bring. This is generally expressed with a sigh of sadness, but it should be an expression of breathless expectation. We are uncertain of the next step, but we are certain of God. As soon as we abandon ourselves to God and do the task He has placed closest to us, He begins to fill our lives with surprises. When we become simply a promoter or a defender of a particular belief, something within us dies. That is not believing God—it is only believing our belief about Him. Jesus said, ". . . unless you . . . become as little children . . ." (Matthew 18:3). The spiritual life is the life of a child. We are not uncertain of God, just uncertain of what He is going to do next. If our certainty is only in our beliefs, we develop a sense of self-righteousness, become overly critical, and are limited by the view that our beliefs are complete and settled. But when we have the right relationship with God, life is full of spontaneous, joyful uncertainty and expectancy. Jesus said, ". . . believe also in Me" (John 14:1), not, "Believe certain things about Me." Leave everything to Him and it will be gloriously and graciously uncertain how He will come in—but you can be certain that He will come. Remain faithful to Him.

SPONTANEOUS LOVE

"Love suffers long and is kind . . ."
(1 Corinthians 13:4).

Love is not premeditated—it is spontaneous; that is, it bursts forth in extraordinary ways. There is nothing of precise certainty in Paul's description of love. We cannot predetermine our thoughts and actions by saying, "Now I will never think any evil thoughts, and I will believe everything that Jesus would have me to believe." No, the characteristic of love is spontaneity. We don't deliberately set the statements of Jesus before us as our standard, but when His Spirit is having His way with us, we live according to His standard without even realizing it. And when we look back, we are amazed at how unconcerned we have been over our emotions, which is the very evidence that real spontaneous love was there. The nature of everything involved in the life of God in us is only discerned when we have been through it and it is in our past.

The fountains from which love flows are in God, not in us. It is absurd to think that the love of God is naturally in our hearts, as a result of our own nature. His love is there only because it "has been poured out in our hearts by the Holy Spirit . . ." (Romans 5:5).

If we try to prove to God how much we love Him, it is a sure sign that we really don't love Him. The evidence of our love for Him is the absolute spontaneity of our love, which flows naturally from His nature within us. And when we look back, we will not be able to determine why we did certain things, but we can know that we did them according to the spontaneous nature of His love in us. The life of God exhibits itself in this spontaneous way because the fountains of His love are in the Holy Spirit.

FAITH—NOT EMOTION

"We walk by faith, not by sight" (2 Corinthians 5:7).

For a while, we are fully aware of God's concern for us. But then, when God begins to use us in His work, we begin to take on a pitiful look and talk only of our trials and difficulties. And all the while God is trying to make us do our work as hidden people who are not in the spotlight. None of us would be hidden spiritually if we could help it. Can we do our work when it seems that God has sealed up heaven? Some of us always want to be brightly illuminated saints with golden halos and with the continual glow of inspiration, and to have other saints of God dealing with us all the time. A self-assured saint is of no value to God. He is abnormal, unfit for daily life, and completely unlike God. We are here, not as immature angels, but as men and women, to do the work of this world. And we are to do it with an infinitely greater power to withstand the struggle because we have been born from above.

If we continually try to bring back those exceptional moments of inspiration, it is a sign that it is not God we want. We are becoming obsessed with the moments when God did come and speak with us, and we are insisting that He do it again. But what God wants us to do is to "walk by faith." How many of us have set ourselves aside as if to say, "I cannot do anything else until God appears to me"? He will never do it. We will have to get up on our own, without any inspiration and without any sudden touch from God. Then comes our surprise and we find ourselves exclaiming, "Why, He was there all the time, and I never knew it!" Never live for those exceptional moments—they are surprises. God will give us His touches of inspiration only when He sees that we are not in danger of being led away by them. We must never consider our moments of inspiration as the standard way of life—our work is our standard.

THE PATIENCE TO WAIT
FOR THE VISION

"Though it tarries, wait for it . . ." (Habakkuk 2:3).

Patience is not the same as indifference; patience conveys the idea of someone who is tremendously strong and able to withstand all assaults. Having the vision of God is the source of patience because it gives us God's true and proper inspiration. Moses endured, not because of his devotion to his principles of what was right, nor because of his sense of duty to God, but because he had a vision of God. ". . . he endured as seeing Him who is invisible" (Hebrews 11:27). A person who has the vision of God is not devoted to a cause or to any particular issue—he is devoted to God Himself. You always know when the vision is of God because of the inspiration that comes with it. Things come to you with greatness and add vitality to your life because everything is energized by God. He may give you a time spiritually, with no word from Himself at all, just as His Son experienced during His time of temptation in the wilderness. When God does that, simply endure, and the power to endure will be there because you see God.

"Though it tarries, wait for it . . . ." The proof that we have the vision is that we are reaching out for more than we have already grasped. It is a bad thing to be satisfied spiritually. The psalmist said, "What shall I render to the Lord . . . ? I will *take up* the cup of salvation . . ." (Psalm 116:12–13). We are apt to look for satisfaction within ourselves and say, "Now I've got it! Now I am completely sanctified. Now I can endure." Instantly we are on the road to ruin. Our reach must exceed our grasp. Paul said, "Not that I have already attained, or am already perfected; but I press on . . ." (Philippians 3:12). If we have only what we have experienced, we have nothing. But if we have the inspiration of the vision of God, we have more than we can experience. Beware of the danger of spiritual relaxation.

VITAL INTERCESSION

". . . praying always with all prayer and suppli-
cation in the Spirit . . ." (Ephesians 6:18).

As we continue on in our intercession for others,
we may find that our obedience to God in interceding is going to cost those for whom we intercede more than we ever thought. The danger in this is
that we begin to intercede in sympathy with those whom
God was gradually lifting up to a totally different level in
direct answer to our prayers. Whenever we step back from
our close identification with God's interest and concern
for others and step into having emotional sympathy with
them, the vital connection with God is gone. We have
then put our sympathy and concern for them in the way,
and this is a deliberate rebuke to God.

It is impossible for us to have living and vital intercession unless we are perfectly and completely sure of
God. And the greatest destroyer of that confident relationship to God, so necessary for intercession, is our own
personal sympathy and preconceived bias. Identification
with God is the key to intercession, and whenever we
stop being identified with Him it is because of our sympathy with others, not because of sin. It is not likely that
sin will interfere with our intercessory relationship with
God, but sympathy will. It is sympathy with ourselves or
with others that makes us say, "I will not allow that thing
to happen." And instantly we are out of that vital connection with God.

Vital intercession leaves you with neither the time
nor the inclination to pray for your own "sad and pitiful
self." You do not have to struggle to keep thoughts of
yourself out, because they are not even there to be kept
out of your thinking. You are completely and entirely
identified with God's interests and concerns in other
lives. God gives us discernment in the lives of others to
call us to intercession for them, never so that we may
find fault with them.

VICARIOUS INTERCESSION

". . . having boldness to enter the Holiest by
the blood of Jesus . . ." (Hebrews 10:19).

Beware of thinking that intercession means bringing
our own personal sympathies and concerns into
the presence of God, and then demanding that He
do whatever we ask. Our ability to approach God is due
entirely to the vicarious, or substitutionary, identification of our Lord with sin. We have "boldness to enter the
Holiest *by the blood of Jesus.*"

Spiritual stubbornness is the most effective hindrance to intercession, because it is based on a sympathetic "understanding" of things we see in ourselves and
others that we think needs no atonement. We have the
idea that there are certain good and virtuous things in
each of us that do not need to be based on the atonement by the Cross of Christ. Just the sluggishness and
lack of interest produced by this kind of thinking makes
us unable to intercede. We do not identify ourselves
with God's interests and concerns for others, and we get
irritated with Him. Yet we are always ready with our own
ideas, and our intercession becomes only the glorification of our own natural sympathies. We have to realize
that the identification of Jesus with sin means a radical
change of all of our sympathies and interests. Vicarious
intercession means that we deliberately substitute God's
interests in others for our natural sympathy with them.

Am I stubborn or substituted? Am I spoiled or complete in my relationship to God? Am I irritable or spiritual? Am I determined to have my own way or determined
to be identified with Him?

JUDGMENT AND
THE LOVE OF GOD

"The time has come for judgment to begin at the house of God . . ." (1 Peter 4:17).

The Christian servant must never forget that salvation is God's idea, not man's; therefore, it has an unfathomable depth. Salvation is the great thought of God, not an experience. Experience is simply the door through which salvation comes into the conscious level of our life so that we are aware of what has taken place on a much deeper level. Never preach the experience—preach the great thought of God behind the experience. When we preach, we are not simply proclaiming how people can be saved from hell and be made moral and pure; we are conveying good news about God.

In the teachings of Jesus Christ the element of judgment is always brought out—it is the sign of the love of God. Never sympathize with someone who finds it difficult to get to God; God is not to blame. It is not for us to figure out the reason for the difficulty, but only to present the truth of God so that the Spirit of God will reveal what is wrong. The greatest test of the quality of our preaching is whether or not it brings everyone to judgment. When the truth is preached, the Spirit of God brings each person face to face with God Himself.

If Jesus ever commanded us to do something that He was unable to equip us to accomplish, He would be a liar. And if we make our own inability a stumbling block or an excuse not to be obedient, it means that we are telling God that there is something which He has not yet taken into account. Every element of our own self-reliance must be put to death by the power of God. The moment we recognize our complete weakness and our dependence upon Him will be the very moment that the Spirit of God will exhibit His power.

LIBERTY AND THE
STANDARDS OF JESUS

**"Stand fast therefore in the liberty by which
Christ has made us free . . ." (Galatians 5:1).**

A spiritually-minded person will never come to you
with the demand—"Believe this and that"; a spiritually-minded person will demand that you align
your life with the standards of Jesus. We are not asked to
believe the Bible, but to believe the One whom the Bible
reveals (see John 5:39–40). We are called to present liberty for the conscience of others, not to bring them liberty
for their thoughts and opinions. And if we ourselves are
free with the liberty of Christ, others will be brought into
that same liberty—the liberty that comes from realizing
the absolute control and authority of Jesus Christ.

Always measure your life solely by the standards of
Jesus. Submit yourself to His yoke, and His alone; and
always be careful never to place a yoke on others that is
not of Jesus Christ. It takes God a long time to get us to
stop thinking that unless everyone sees things exactly as
we do, they must be wrong. That is never God's view.
There is only one true liberty—the liberty of Jesus at
work in our conscience enabling us to do what is right.

Don't get impatient with others. Remember how
God dealt with you—with patience and with gentleness.
But never water down the truth of God. Let it have its
way and never apologize for it. Jesus said, "Go . . . and
make *disciples* . . ." (Matthew 28:19), not, "Make converts to your own thoughts and opinions."

BUILDING FOR ETERNITY

"Which of you, intending to build a tower, does not sit down first and count the cost, whether he has enough to finish it . . ." (Luke 14:28).

Our Lord was not referring here to a cost which we have to count, but to a cost which He has already counted. The cost was those thirty years in Nazareth, those three years of popularity, scandal, and hatred, the unfathomable agony He experienced in Gethsemane, and the assault upon Him at Calvary—the central point upon which all of time and eternity turn. Jesus Christ has counted the cost. In the final analysis, people are not going to laugh at Him and say, "This man began to build and was not able to finish" (14:30).

The conditions of discipleship given to us by our Lord in verses 26, 27, and 33 mean that the men and women He is going to use in His mighty building enterprises are those in whom He has done everything. "If anyone comes to Me and does not hate his father and mother, wife and children, brothers and sisters, yes, and his own life also, *he cannot be My disciple*" (14:26). This verse teaches us that the only men and women our Lord will use in His building enterprises are those who love Him personally, passionately, and with great devotion— those who have a love for Him that goes far beyond any of the closest relationships on earth. The conditions are strict, but they are glorious.

All that we build is going to be inspected by God. When God inspects us with His searching and refining fire, will He detect that we have built enterprises of our own on the foundation of Jesus? (see 1 Corinthians 3:10-15). We are living in a time of tremendous enterprises, a time when we are trying to work for God, and that is where the trap is. Profoundly speaking, we can never work for God. Jesus, as the Master Builder, takes us over so that He may direct and control us completely for *His* enterprises and *His* building plans; and no one has any right to demand where he will be put to work.

THE FAITH TO PERSEVERE

"Because you have kept My command to persevere . . ." (Revelation 3:10).

Perseverance means more than endurance—more than simply holding on until the end. A saint's life is in the hands of God like a bow and arrow in the hands of an archer. God is aiming at something the saint cannot see, but our Lord continues to stretch and strain, and every once in a while the saint says, "I can't take any more." Yet God pays no attention; He goes on stretching until His purpose is in sight, and then He lets the arrow fly. Entrust yourself to God's hands. Is there something in your life for which you need perseverance right now? Maintain your intimate relationship with Jesus Christ through the perseverance of faith. Proclaim as Job did, "Though He slay me, yet will I trust Him" (Job 13:15).

Faith is not some weak and pitiful emotion, but is strong and vigorous confidence built on the fact that God is holy love. And even though you cannot see Him right now and cannot understand what He is doing, you know *Him*. Disaster occurs in your life when you lack the mental composure that comes from establishing yourself on the eternal truth that God is holy love. Faith is the supreme effort of your life—throwing yourself with abandon and total confidence upon God.

God ventured His all in Jesus Christ to save us, and now He wants us to venture our all with total abandoned confidence in Him. There are areas in our lives where that faith has not worked in us as yet—places still untouched by the life of God. There were none of those places in Jesus Christ's life, and there are to be none in ours. Jesus prayed, "This is eternal life, that they may know You . . ." (John 17:3). The real meaning of eternal life is a life that can face anything it has to face without wavering. If we will take this view, life will become one great romance—a glorious opportunity of seeing wonderful things all the time. God is disciplining us to get us into this central place of power.

REACHING BEYOND OUR GRASP

> "Where there is no revelation [or prophetic vision], the people cast off restraint . . ." (Proverbs 29:18).

There is a difference between holding on to a principle and having a vision. A principle does not come from moral inspiration, but a vision does. People who are totally consumed with idealistic principles rarely *do* anything. A person's own idea of God and His attributes may actually be used to justify and rationalize his deliberate neglect of his duty. Jonah tried to excuse his disobedience by saying to God, ". . . I know that You are a gracious and merciful God, slow to anger and abundant in lovingkindness, One who relents from doing harm" (Jonah 4:2). I too may have the right idea of God and His attributes, but that may be the very reason why I do not do my duty. But wherever there is vision, there is also a life of honesty and integrity, because the vision gives me the moral incentive.

Our own idealistic principles may actually lull us into ruin. Examine yourself spiritually to see if you have vision, or only principles.

Ah, but a man's reach should exceed his grasp,
Or what's a heaven for?

"Where there is no revelation [or prophetic vision] . . ." Once we lose sight of God, we begin to be reckless. We cast off certain restraints from activities we know are wrong. We set prayer aside as well and cease having God's vision in the little things of life. We simply begin to act on our own initiative. If we are eating only out of our own hand, and doing things solely on our own initiative without expecting God to come in, we are on a downward path. We have lost the vision. Is our attitude today an attitude that flows from our vision of God? Are we expecting God to do greater things than He has ever done before? Is there a freshness and a vitality in our spiritual outlook?

TAKE THE INITIATIVE

"... add to your faith virtue ..." (2 Peter 1:5).

*A*dd means that we have to do something. We are in danger of forgetting that we cannot do what God does, and that God will not do what we can do. We cannot save nor sanctify ourselves—God does that. But God will not give us good habits or character, and He will not force us to walk correctly before Him. We have to do all that ourselves. We must "work *out*" our "own salvation" which God has worked *in* us (Philippians 2:12). *Add* means that we must get into the habit of doing things, and in the initial stages that is difficult. To take the initiative is to make a beginning—to instruct yourself in the way you must go.

Beware of the tendency to ask the way when you know it perfectly well. Take the initiative—stop hesitating—take the first step. Be determined to act immediately in faith on what God says to you when He speaks, and never reconsider or change your initial decisions. If you hesitate when God tells you to do something, you are being careless, spurning the grace in which you stand. Take the initiative yourself, make a decision of your will right now, and make it impossible to go back. Burn your bridges behind you, saying, "I *will* write that letter," or "I *will* pay that debt"; and then do it! Make it irrevocable.

We have to get into the habit of carefully listening to God about everything, forming the habit of finding out what He says and heeding it. If, when a crisis comes, we instinctively turn to God, we will know that the habit has been formed in us. We have to take the initiative where we *are*, not where we have not yet been.

"Love One Another"

". . . add to your . . . brotherly kindness love"
(2 Peter 1:5, 7).

L ove is an indefinite thing to most of us; we don't
know what we mean when we talk about love. Love
is the loftiest preference of one person for another,
and spiritually Jesus demands that this sovereign preference be for Himself (see Luke 14:26). Initially, when "the
love of God has been poured out in our hearts by the
Holy Spirit" (Romans 5:5), it is easy to put Jesus first. But
then we must practice the things mentioned in 2 Peter 1
to see them worked out in our lives.

The first thing God does is forcibly remove any
insincerity, pride, and vanity from my life. And the Holy
Spirit reveals to me that God loved me not because I was
lovable, but because it was His nature to do so. Now He
commands me to show the same love to others by saying,
". . . love one another as I have loved you" (John 15:12).
He is saying, "I will bring a number of people around you
whom you cannot respect, but you must exhibit My love
to them, just as I have exhibited it to you." This kind of
love is not a patronizing love for the unlovable—it is His
love, and it will not be evidenced in us overnight. Some
of us may have tried to force it, but we were soon tired
and frustrated.

"The Lord . . . is longsuffering toward us, not willing
that any should perish . . ." (2 Peter 3:9). I should look
within and remember how wonderfully He has dealt
with me. The knowledge that God has loved me beyond
all limits will compel me to go into the world to love
others in the same way. I may get irritated because I have
to live with an unusually difficult person. But just think
how disagreeable I have been with God! Am I prepared
to be identified so closely with the Lord Jesus that His
life and His sweetness will be continually poured out
through Me? Neither natural love nor God's divine love
will remain and grow in me unless it is nurtured. Love
is spontaneous, but it has to be maintained through
discipline.

THE HABIT OF
HAVING NO HABITS

"If these things are yours and abound, you will be neither barren nor unfruitful . . ."
(2 Peter 1:8).

When we first begin to form a habit, we are fully aware of it. There are times when we are aware of becoming virtuous and godly, but this awareness should only be a stage we quickly pass through as we grow spiritually. If we stop at this stage, we will develop a sense of spiritual pride. The right thing to do with godly habits is to immerse them in the life of the Lord until they become such a spontaneous expression of our lives that we are no longer aware of them. Our spiritual life continually causes us to focus our attention inwardly for the determined purpose of self-examination, because each of us has some qualities we have not yet added to our lives.

Your god may be your little Christian habit—the habit of prayer or Bible reading at certain times of your day. Watch how your Father will upset your schedule if you begin to worship your habit instead of what the habit symbolizes. We say, "I can't do that right now; this is my time alone with God." No, this is your time alone with your habit. There is a quality that is still lacking in you. Identify your shortcoming and then look for opportunities to work into your life that missing quality.

Love means that there are no visible habits—that your habits are so immersed in the Lord that you practice them without realizing it. If you are consciously aware of your own holiness, you place limitations on yourself from doing certain things—things God is not restricting you from at all. This means there is a missing quality that needs to be added to your life. The only supernatural life is the life the Lord Jesus lived, and He was at home with God anywhere. Is there someplace where you are not at home with God? Then allow God to work through whatever that particular circumstance may be until you increase in Him, adding His qualities. Your life will then become the simple life of a child.

THE HABIT OF KEEPING
A CLEAR CONSCIENCE

"... strive to have a conscience without offense
toward God and men" (Acts 24:16).

God's commands to us are actually given to the life
of His Son in us. Consequently, to our human
nature in which God's Son has been formed (see
Galatians 4:19), His commands are difficult. But they
become divinely easy once we obey.

Conscience is that ability within me that attaches
itself to the highest standard I know, and then continually reminds me of what that standard demands that I
do. It is the eye of the soul which looks out either toward
God or toward what we regard as the highest standard.
This explains why conscience is different in different
people. If I am in the habit of continually holding God's
standard in front of me, my conscience will always direct
me to God's perfect law and indicate what I should do.
The question is, will I obey? I have to make an effort to
keep my conscience so sensitive that I can live without
any offense toward anyone. I should be living in such
perfect harmony with God's Son that the spirit of my
mind is being renewed through every circumstance of
life, and that I may be able to quickly "prove what is that
good and acceptable and perfect will of God" (Romans
12:2; also see Ephesians 4:23).

God always instructs us down to the last detail. Is
my ear sensitive enough to hear even the softest whisper
of the Spirit, so that I know what I should do? "Do not
grieve the Holy Spirit of God . . ." (Ephesians 4:30). He
does not speak with a voice like thunder—His voice is so
gentle that it is easy for us to ignore. And the only thing
that keeps our conscience sensitive to Him is the habit
of being open to God on the inside. When you begin
to debate, stop immediately. Don't ask, "Why can't I do
this?" You are on the wrong track. There is no debating possible once your conscience speaks. Whatever it
is—drop it, and see that you keep your inner vision clear.

THE HABIT OF
ENJOYING ADVERSITY

". . . that the life of Jesus also may be manifested in our body" (2 Corinthians 4:10).

We have to develop godly habits to express what God's grace has done in us. It is not just a question of being saved from hell, but of being saved so that "the life of Jesus also may be manifested in our body." And it is adversity that makes us exhibit His life in our mortal flesh. Is my life exhibiting the essence of the sweetness of the Son of God, or just the basic irritation of "myself" that I would have apart from Him? The only thing that will enable me to enjoy adversity is the acute sense of eagerness of allowing the life of the Son of God to evidence itself in me. No matter how difficult something may be, I must say, "Lord, I am delighted to obey You in this." Instantly, the Son of God will move to the forefront of my life, and will manifest in my body that which glorifies Him.

You must not debate. The moment you obey the light of God, His Son shines through you in that very adversity; but if you debate with God, you grieve His Spirit (see Ephesians 4:30). You must keep yourself in the proper condition to allow the life of the Son of God to be manifested in you, and you cannot keep yourself fit if you give way to self-pity. Our circumstances are the means God uses to exhibit just how wonderfully perfect and extraordinarily pure His Son is. Discovering a new way of manifesting the Son of God should make our heart beat with renewed excitement. It is one thing to choose adversity, and quite another to enter into adversity through the orchestrating of our circumstances by God's sovereignty. And if God puts you into adversity, He is adequately sufficient to "supply all your need" (Philippians 4:19).

Keep your soul properly conditioned to manifest the life of the Son of God. Never live on your memories of past experiences, but let the Word of God always be living and active in you.

THE HABIT OF RISING
TO THE OCCASION

"... that you may know what is the hope of His calling ... " (Ephesians 1:18).

Remember that you have been saved so that the life of Jesus may be manifested in your body (see 2 Corinthians 4:10). Direct the total energy of your powers so that you may achieve everything your election as a child of God provides; rise every time to whatever occasion may come your way.

You did not do anything to achieve your salvation, but you must do something to exhibit it. You must "work *out* your own salvation" which God has worked *in* you already (Philippians 2:12). Are your speech, your thinking, and your emotions evidence that you are working it "out"? If you are still the same miserable, grouchy person, set on having your own way, then it is a lie to say that God has saved and sanctified you.

God is the Master Designer, and He allows adversities into your life to see if you can jump over them properly—"By my God I can leap over a wall" (Psalm 18:29). God will never shield you from the requirements of being His son or daughter. First Peter 4:12 says, "Beloved, do not think it strange concerning the fiery trial which is to try you, as though some strange thing happened to you . . . ." Rise to the occasion—do what the trial demands of you. It does not matter how much it hurts as long as it gives God the opportunity to manifest the life of Jesus in your body.

May God not find complaints in us anymore, but spiritual vitality—a readiness to face anything He brings our way. The only proper goal of life is that we manifest the Son of God; and when this occurs, all of our dictating of our demands to God disappears. Our Lord never dictated demands to His Father, and neither are we to make demands on God. We are here to submit to His will so that He may work through us what He wants. Once we realize this, He will make us broken bread and poured-out wine with which to feed and nourish others.

THE HABIT OF RECOGNIZING GOD'S PROVISION

". . . you may be partakers of the divine nature . . ." (2 Peter 1:4).

We are made "partakers of the divine nature," receiving and sharing God's own nature through His promises. Then we have to work that divine nature into our human nature by developing godly habits. The first habit to develop is the habit of recognizing God's provision for us. We say, however, "Oh, I can't afford it." One of the worst lies is wrapped up in that statement. We talk as if our heavenly Father has cut us off without a penny! We think it is a sign of true humility to say at the end of the day, "Well, I just barely got by today, but it was a severe struggle." And yet all of Almighty God is ours in the Lord Jesus! And He will reach to the last grain of sand and the remotest star to bless us if we will only obey Him. Does it really matter that our circumstances are difficult? Why shouldn't they be! If we give way to self-pity and indulge in the luxury of misery, we remove God's riches from our lives and hinder others from entering into His provision. No sin is worse than the sin of self-pity, because it removes God from the throne of our lives, replacing Him with our own self-interests. It causes us to open our mouths only to complain, and we simply become spiritual sponges—always absorbing, never giving, and never being satisfied. And there is nothing lovely or generous about our lives.

Before God becomes satisfied with us, He will take everything of our so-called wealth, until we learn that He is our Source; as the psalmist said, "All my springs are in You" (Psalm 87:7). If the majesty, grace, and power of God are not being exhibited in us, God holds us responsible. "God is able to make all grace abound toward you, that you . . . may have an abundance . . ." (2 Corinthians 9:8)—then learn to lavish the grace of God on others, generously giving of yourself. Be marked and identified with God's nature, and His blessing will flow through you all the time.

HIS ASCENSION
AND OUR ACCESS

"It came to pass, while He blessed them, that He was parted from them and carried up into heaven" (Luke 24:51).

We have no experiences in our lives that correspond to the events in our Lord's life after the transfiguration. From that moment forward His life was altogether substitutionary. Up to the time of the transfiguration, He had exhibited the normal, perfect life of a man. But from the transfiguration forward—Gethsemane, the Cross, the resurrection—everything is unfamiliar to us. His Cross is the door by which every member of the human race can enter into the life of God; by His resurrection He has the right to give eternal life to anyone, and by His ascension our Lord entered heaven, keeping the door open for humanity.

The transfiguration was completed on the Mount of Ascension. If Jesus had gone to heaven directly from the Mount of Transfiguration, He would have gone alone. He would have been nothing more to us than a glorious Figure. But He turned His back on the glory, and came down from the mountain to identify Himself with fallen humanity.

The ascension is the complete fulfillment of the transfiguration. Our Lord returned to His original glory, but not simply as the Son of God—He returned to His father as the *Son of Man* as well. There is now freedom of access for anyone straight to the very throne of God because of the ascension of the Son of Man. As the Son of Man, Jesus Christ deliberately limited His omnipotence, omnipresence, and omniscience. But now they are His in absolute, full power. As the Son of Man, Jesus Christ now has all the power at the throne of God. From His ascension forward He is the King of kings and Lord of lords.

LIVING SIMPLY—YET FOCUSED

"Look at the birds of the air . . . . Consider the lilies of the field . . ." (Matthew 6:26, 28).

Consider the lilies of the field, how they grow: they neither toil nor spin"—they simply *are*! Think of the sea, the air, the sun, the stars, and the moon— all of these simply *are* as well—yet what a ministry and service they render on our behalf! So often we impair God's designed influence, which He desires to exhibit through us, because of our own conscious efforts to be consistent and useful. Jesus said there is only one way to develop and grow spiritually, and that is through focusing and concentrating on God. In essence, Jesus was saying, "Do not worry about being of use to others; simply believe on Me." In other words, pay attention to the Source, and out of you "will flow rivers of living water" (John 7:38). We cannot discover the source of our natural life through common sense and reasoning, and Jesus is teaching here that growth in our spiritual life comes not from focusing directly on it, but from concentrating on our Father in heaven. Our heavenly Father knows our circumstances, and if we will stay focused on Him, instead of our circumstances, we will grow spiritually—just as "the lilies of the field."

The people who influence us the most are not those who detain us with their continual talk, but those who live their lives like the stars in the sky and "the lilies of the field"—simply and unaffectedly. Those are the lives that mold and shape us.

If you want to be of use to God, maintain the proper relationship with Jesus Christ by staying focused on Him, and He will make use of you every minute you live—yet you will be unaware, on the conscious level of your life, that you are being used of Him.

"OUT OF THE WRECK I RISE"

"Who shall separate us from the love of Christ?" (Romans 8:35).

God does not keep His child immune from trouble; He promises, "I will be with him in trouble . . ." (Psalm 91:15). It doesn't matter how real or intense the adversities may be; nothing can ever separate him from his relationship to God. "*In* all these things we are more than conquerors . . ." (Romans 8:37). Paul was not referring here to imaginary things, but to things that are dangerously real. And he said we are "super-victors" in the midst of them, not because of our own ingenuity, nor because of our courage, but because none of them affects our essential relationship with God in Jesus Christ. I feel sorry for the Christian who doesn't have something in the circumstances of his life that he wishes were not there.

"Shall tribulation . . . ?" Tribulation is never a grand, highly welcomed event; but whatever it may be—whether exhausting, irritating, or simply causing some weakness—it is not able to "separate us from the love of Christ." Never allow tribulations or the "cares of this world" to separate you from remembering that God loves you (Matthew 13:22).

"Shall . . . distress . . . ?" Can God's love continue to hold fast, even when everyone and everything around us seems to be saying that His love is a lie, and that there is no such thing as justice?

"Shall . . . famine . . . ?" Can we not only believe in the love of God but also be "more than conquerors," even while we are being starved?

Either Jesus Christ is a deceiver, having deceived even Paul, or else some extraordinary thing happens to someone who holds on to the love of God when the odds are totally against him. Logic is silenced in the face of each of these things which come against him. Only one thing can account for it—the *love of God in Christ Jesus*. "Out of the wreck I rise" every time.

TAKING POSSESSION OF
OUR OWN SOUL

"By your patience possess your souls" (Luke 21:19).

When a person is born again, there is a period of time when he does not have the same vitality in his thinking or reasoning that he previously had. We must learn to express this new life within us, which comes by forming the mind of Christ (see Philippians 2:5). Luke 21:19 means that we take possession of our souls through patience. But many of us prefer to stay at the entrance to the Christian life, instead of going on to create and build our soul in accordance with the new life God has placed within us. We fail because we are ignorant of the way God has made us, and we blame things on the devil that are actually the result of our own undisciplined natures. Just think what we could be when we are awakened to the truth!

There are certain things in life that we need not pray about—moods, for instance. We will never get rid of moodiness by praying, but we will by kicking it out of our lives. Moods nearly always are rooted in some physical circumstance, not in our true inner self. It is a continual struggle not to listen to the moods which arise as a result of our physical condition, but we must never submit to them for a second. We have to pick ourselves up by the back of the neck and shake ourselves; then we will find that we can do what we believed we were unable to do. The problem that most of us are cursed with is simply that we *won't*. The Christian life is one of spiritual courage and determination lived out in our flesh.

HAVING GOD'S
"UNREASONABLE" FAITH

"Seek first the kingdom of God and His righteousness, and all these things shall be added to you" (Matthew 6:33).

When we look at these words of Jesus, we immediately find them to be the most revolutionary that human ears have ever heard. "Seek *first* the kingdom of God . . . ." Even the most spiritually-minded of us argue the exact opposite, saying, "But I *must* live; I *must* make a certain amount of money; I *must* be clothed; I *must* be fed." The great concern of our lives is not the kingdom of God but how we are going to take care of ourselves to live. Jesus reversed the order by telling us to get the right relationship with God first, maintaining it as the primary concern of our lives, and never to place our concern on taking care of the other things of life.

". . . *do not worry about your life* . . ." (6:25). Our Lord pointed out that from His standpoint it is absolutely unreasonable for us to be anxious, worrying about how we will live. Jesus did not say that the person who takes no thought for anything in his life is blessed—no, that person is a fool. But Jesus *did* teach that His disciple must make his relationship with God the dominating focus of his life, and to be cautiously carefree about everything else in comparison to that. In essence, Jesus was saying, "Don't make food and drink the controlling factor of your life, but be focused absolutely on God." Some people are careless about what they eat and drink, and they suffer for it; they are careless about what they wear, having no business looking the way they do; they are careless with their earthly matters, and God holds them responsible. Jesus is saying that the greatest concern of life is to place our relationship with God first, and everything else second.

It is one of the most difficult, yet critical, disciplines of the Christian life to allow the Holy Spirit to bring us into absolute harmony with the teaching of Jesus in these verses.

THE EXPLANATION FOR OUR DIFFICULTIES

". . . that they all may be one, as You, Father, are in Me, and I in You; that they also may be one in Us . . ." (John 17:21).

If you are going through a time of isolation, seemingly all alone, read John 17. It will explain exactly why you are where you are—because Jesus has prayed that you "may be one" with the Father as He is. Are you helping God to answer that prayer, or do you have some other goal for your life? Since you became a disciple, you cannot be as independent as you used to be.

God reveals in John 17 that His purpose is not just to answer our prayers, but that through prayer we might come to discern His mind. Yet there is one prayer which God must answer, and that is the prayer of Jesus— ". . . that they may be one just as We are one . . ." (17:22). Are we as close to Jesus Christ as that?

God is not concerned about our plans; He doesn't ask, "Do you want to go through this loss of a loved one, this difficulty, or this defeat?" No, He allows these things for His own purpose. The things we are going through are either making us sweeter, better, and nobler men and women, or they are making us more critical and fault-finding, and more insistent on our own way. The things that happen either make us evil, or they make us more saintly, depending entirely on our relationship with God and its level of intimacy. If we will pray, regarding our own lives, "Your will be done" (Matthew 26:42), then we will be encouraged and comforted by John 17, knowing that our Father is working according to His own wisdom, accomplishing what is best. When we understand God's purpose, we will not become small-minded and cynical. Jesus prayed nothing less for us than absolute oneness with Himself, just as He was one with the Father. Some of us are far from this oneness; yet God will not leave us alone until we *are* one with Him—because Jesus prayed, ". . . that they *all* may be one . . . ."

OUR CAREFUL UNBELIEF

"... do not worry about your life, what you
will eat or what you will drink; nor about your
body, what you will put on" (Matthew 6:25).

Jesus summed up commonsense carefulness in the life
of a disciple as *unbelief*. If we have received the Spirit
of God, He will squeeze right through our lives, as if
to ask, "Now where do I come into this relationship, this
vacation you have planned, or these new books you want
to read?" And He always presses the point until we learn
to make Him our first consideration. Whenever we put
other things first, there is confusion.

"... do not worry about your life ...." Don't take
the pressure of your provision upon yourself. It is not
only wrong to worry, it is unbelief; worrying means we
do not believe that God can look after the practical
details of our lives, and it is never anything but those
details that worry us. Have you ever noticed what Jesus
said would choke the Word He puts in us? Is it the devil?
No—"the cares of this world" (Matthew 13:22). It is
always our little worries. We say, "I will not trust when I
cannot see"—and that is where unbelief begins. The only
cure for unbelief is obedience to the Spirit.

The greatest word of Jesus to His disciples is
abandon.

THE DELIGHT OF DESPAIR

"When I saw Him, I fell at His feet as dead" (Revelation 1:17).

It may be that, like the apostle John, you know Jesus Christ intimately. Yet when He suddenly appears to you with totally unfamiliar characteristics, the only thing you can do is fall "at His feet as dead." There are times when God cannot reveal Himself in any other way than in His majesty, and it is the awesomeness of the vision which brings you to the delight of despair. You experience this joy in hopelessness, realizing that if you are ever to be raised up it must be by the hand of God.

"He laid His right hand on me . . ." (1:17). In the midst of the awesomeness, a touch comes, and you know it is the right hand of Jesus Christ. You know it is not the hand of restraint, correction, nor chastisement, but the right hand of the Everlasting Father. Whenever His hand is laid upon you, it gives inexpressible peace and comfort, and the sense that "underneath are the everlasting arms" (Deuteronomy 33:27), full of support, provision, comfort, and strength. And once His touch comes, nothing at all can throw you into fear again. In the midst of all His ascended glory, the Lord Jesus comes to speak to an insignificant disciple, saying, "Do not be afraid" (Revelation 1:17). His tenderness is inexpressibly sweet. Do I know Him like that?

Take a look at some of the things that cause despair. There is despair which has no delight, no limits whatsoever, and no hope of anything brighter. But the delight of despair comes when "I know that in me (that is, in my flesh) nothing good dwells . . ." (Romans 7:18). I delight in knowing that there is something in me which must fall prostrate before God when He reveals Himself to me, and also in knowing that if I am ever to be raised up it must be by the hand of God. God can do nothing for me until I recognize the limits of what is humanly possible, allowing Him to do the impossible.

THE GOOD OR THE BEST?

**"If you take the left, then I will go to the right;
or, if you go to the right, then I will go to the
left" (Genesis 13:9).**

As soon as you begin to live the life of faith in God,
fascinating and physically gratifying possibilities
will open up before you. These things are yours by
right, but if you are living the life of faith you will exercise
your right to waive your rights, and let God make your
choice for you. God sometimes allows you to get into
a place of testing where your own welfare would be the
appropriate thing to consider, if you were not living the
life of faith. But if you are, you will joyfully waive your
right and allow God to make your choice for you. This is
the discipline God uses to transform the natural into the
spiritual through obedience to His voice.

Whenever our *right* becomes the guiding factor
of our lives, it dulls our spiritual insight. The greatest
enemy of the life of faith in God is not sin, but good
choices which are not quite good enough. The good is
always the enemy of the best. In this passage, it would
seem that the wisest thing in the world for Abram to
do would be to choose. It was his right, and the people
around him would consider him to be a fool for not
choosing.

Many of us do not continue to grow spiritually
because we prefer to choose on the basis of our rights,
instead of relying on God to make the choice for us. We
have to learn to walk according to the standard which
has its eyes focused on God. And God says to us, as He
did to Abram, "... *walk before Me* ..." (Genesis 17:1).

THINKING OF PRAYER
AS JESUS TAUGHT

"Pray without ceasing . . ." (1 Thessalonians
5:17).

O ur thinking about prayer, whether right or wrong,
is based on our own mental conception of it. The
correct concept is to think of prayer as the breath
in our lungs and the blood from our hearts. Our blood
flows and our breathing continues "without ceasing"; we
are not even conscious of it, but it never stops. And we
are not always conscious of Jesus keeping us in perfect
oneness with God, but if we are obeying Him, He always
is. Prayer is not an exercise, it is the life of the saint.
Beware of anything that stops the offering up of prayer.
"Pray without ceasing . . ."—maintain the childlike habit
of offering up prayer in your heart to God all the time.

Jesus never mentioned unanswered prayer. He had
the unlimited certainty of knowing that prayer is always
answered. Do we have through the Spirit of God that
inexpressible certainty that Jesus had about prayer, or
do we think of the times when it seemed that God did
not answer our prayer? Jesus said, ". . . everyone who asks
receives . . ." (Matthew 7:8). Yet we say, "But . . . , but . . . ."
God answers prayer in the best way—not just sometimes,
but every time. However, the evidence of the answer in
the area we want it may not always immediately follow.
Do we expect God to answer prayer?

The danger we have is that we want to water down
what Jesus said to make it mean something that aligns
with our common sense. But if it were only common
sense, what He said would not even be worthwhile. The
things Jesus taught about prayer are supernatural truths
He reveals to us.

THE LIFE TO KNOW HIM

". . . tarry in the city of Jerusalem until you are endued with power from on high" (Luke 24:49).

The disciples had to tarry, staying in Jerusalem until the day of Pentecost, not only for their own preparation but because they had to wait until the Lord was actually glorified. And as soon as He was glorified, what happened? "Therefore being exalted to the right hand of God, and having received from the Father the promise of the Holy Spirit, He poured out this which you now see and hear" (Acts 2:33). The statement in John 7:39—". . . for the Holy Spirit was not yet given, because Jesus was not yet glorified"—does not pertain to us. The Holy Spirit *has been* given; the Lord *is* glorified—our waiting is not dependent on the providence of God, but on our own spiritual fitness.

The Holy Spirit's influence and power were at work before Pentecost, but *He* was not here. Once our Lord was glorified in His ascension, the Holy Spirit came into the world, and He has been here ever since. We have to receive the revealed truth that He is here. The attitude of receiving and welcoming the Holy Spirit into our lives is to be the continual attitude of a believer. When we receive the Holy Spirit, we receive reviving life from our ascended Lord.

It is not the baptism of the Holy Spirit that changes people, but the power of the ascended Christ coming into their lives through the Holy Spirit. We all too often separate things that the New Testament never separates. The baptism of the Holy Spirit is not an experience apart from Jesus Christ—it is the evidence of the ascended Christ.

The baptism of the Holy Spirit does not make you think of time or eternity—it is one amazing glorious *now*. "This is eternal life, that they may know You . . ." (John 17:3). Begin to know Him now, and never finish.

UNQUESTIONED REVELATION

"In that day you will ask Me nothing" (John 16:23).

When is "that day"? It is when the ascended Lord makes you one with the Father. "In that day" you will be one with the Father just as Jesus is, and He said, "In that day you will ask Me nothing." Until the resurrection life of Jesus is fully exhibited in you, you have questions about many things. Then after a while you find that all your questions are gone—you don't seem to have any left to ask. You have come to the point of total reliance on the resurrection life of Jesus, which brings you into complete oneness with the purpose of God. Are you living that life now? If not, why aren't you?

"In that day" there may be any number of things still hidden to your understanding, but they will not come between your heart and God. "In that day you will ask Me nothing"—you will not need to ask, because you will be certain that God will reveal things in accordance with His will. The faith and peace of John 14:1 has become the real attitude of your heart, and there are no more questions to be asked. If anything is a mystery to you and is coming between you and God, never look for the explanation in your mind, but look for it in your spirit, your true inner nature—that is where the problem is. Once your inner spiritual nature is willing to submit to the life of Jesus, your understanding will be perfectly clear, and you will come to the place where there is no distance between the Father and you, His child, because the Lord has made you one. "In that day you will ask Me nothing."

UNTROUBLED RELATIONSHIP

> "In that day you will ask in My name . . .
> for the Father Himself loves you . . ."
> (John 16:26–27).

In that day you will ask in My name . . . ," that is, in My nature. Not—"You will use My name as some magic word," but—"You will be so intimate with Me that you will be one with Me." "That day" is not a day in the next life, but a day meant for here and now. ". . . for the Father Himself loves you . . ."—the Father's love is evidence that our union with Jesus is complete and absolute. Our Lord does not mean that our lives will be free from external difficulties and uncertainties, but that just as He knew the Father's heart and mind, we too can be lifted by Him into heavenly places through the baptism of the Holy Spirit, so that He can reveal the teachings of God to us.

". . . whatever you ask the Father in My name . . ." (16:23). "That day" is a day of peace and an untroubled relationship between God and His saint. Just as Jesus stood unblemished and pure in the presence of His Father, we too by the mighty power and effectiveness of the baptism of the Holy Spirit can be lifted into that relationship—". . . that they may be one just as We are one . . ." (John 17:22).

". . . He will give you" (John 16:23). Jesus said that because of His name God will recognize and respond to our prayers. What a great challenge and invitation—to pray in His name! Through the resurrection and ascension power of Jesus, and through the Holy Spirit He has sent, we can be lifted into such a relationship. Once in that wonderful position, having been placed there by Jesus Christ, we can pray to God in Jesus' name—in His nature. This is a gift granted to us through the Holy Spirit, and Jesus said, ". . . whatever you ask the Father in My name He will give you." The sovereign character of Jesus Christ is tested and proved by His own statements.

"YES—BUT . . . !"

"Lord, I will follow You, but . . ." (Luke 9:61).

Suppose God tells you to do something that is an enormous test of your common sense, totally going against it. What will you do? Will you hold back? If you get into the habit of doing something physically, you will do it every time you are tested until you break the habit through sheer determination. And the same is true spiritually. Again and again you will come right up to what Jesus wants, but every time you will turn back at the true point of testing, until you are determined to abandon yourself to God in total surrender. Yet we tend to say, "Yes, but—suppose I do obey God in this matter, what about . . . ?" Or we say, "Yes, I will obey God if what He asks of me doesn't go against my common sense, but don't ask me to take a step in the dark."

Jesus Christ demands the same unrestrained, adventurous spirit in those who have placed their trust in Him that the natural man exhibits. If a person is ever going to do anything worthwhile, there will be times when he must risk everything by his leap in the dark. In the spiritual realm, Jesus Christ demands that you risk everything you hold on to or believe through common sense, and leap by faith into what He says. Once you obey, you will immediately find that what He says is as solidly consistent as common sense.

By the test of common sense, Jesus Christ's statements may seem mad, but when you test them by the trial of faith, your findings will fill your spirit with the awesome fact that they are the very words of God. Trust completely in God, and when He brings you to a new opportunity of adventure, offering it to you, see that you take it. We act like pagans in a crisis—only one out of an entire crowd is daring enough to invest his faith in the character of God.

PUT GOD FIRST

**"Jesus did not commit Himself to them . . .
for He knew what was in man" (John 2:24–25).**

Put Trust in God First. Our Lord never put His trust in any person. Yet He was never suspicious, never bitter, and never lost hope for anyone, because He put His trust in God first. He trusted absolutely in what God's grace could do for others. If I put my trust in human beings first, the end result will be my despair and hopelessness toward everyone. I will become bitter because I have insisted that people be what no person can ever be—absolutely perfect and right. Never trust anything in yourself or in anyone else, except the grace of God.

Put God's Will First. "Behold, I have come to do Your will, O God" (Hebrews 10:9).

A person's obedience is to what he sees to be a need—our Lord's obedience was to the will of His Father. The rallying cry today is, "We must get to work! The heathen are dying without God. We must go and tell them about Him." But we must first make sure that God's "needs" and His will in us personally are being met. Jesus said, ". . . tarry . . . until you are endued with power from on high" (Luke 24:49). The purpose of our Christian training is to get us into the right relationship to the "needs" of God and His will. Once God's "needs" in us have been met, He will open the way for us to accomplish His will, meeting His "needs" elsewhere.

Put God's Son First. "Whoever receives one little child like this in My name receives Me" (Matthew 18:5).

God came as a baby, giving and entrusting Himself to me. He expects my personal life to be a "Bethlehem." Am I allowing my natural life to be slowly transformed by the indwelling life of the Son of God? God's ultimate purpose is that His Son might be exhibited in me.

THE STAGGERING QUESTION

"He said to me, 'Son of man, can these bones live?'" (Ezekiel 37:3).

Can a sinner be turned into a saint? Can a twisted life be made right? There is only one appropriate answer—"O Lord GOD, You know" (37:3). Never forge ahead with your religious common sense and say, "Oh, yes, with just a little more Bible reading, devotional time, and prayer, I see how it can be done."

It is much easier to *do* something than to trust in God; we see the activity and mistake panic for inspiration. That is why we see so few fellow workers *with* God, yet so many people working *for* God. We would much rather work for God than believe in Him. Do I really believe that God will do in me what I cannot do? The degree of hopelessness I have for others comes from never realizing that God has done anything for me. Is my own personal experience such a wonderful realization of God's power and might that I can never have a sense of hopelessness for anyone else I see? Has any spiritual work been accomplished in me at all? The degree of panic activity in my life is equal to the degree of my lack of personal spiritual experience.

"Behold, O My people, I will open your graves . . ." (37:12). When God wants to show you what human nature is like separated from Himself, He shows it to you in yourself. If the Spirit of God has ever given you a vision of what you are apart from the grace of God (and He will only do this when His Spirit is at work in you), then you know that in reality there is no criminal half as bad as you yourself could be without His grace. My "grave" has been opened by God and "I know that in me (that is, in my flesh) nothing good dwells" (Romans 7:18). God's Spirit continually reveals to His children what human nature is like apart from His grace.

ARE YOU OBSESSED BY SOMETHING?

"Who is the man that fears the LORD?" (Psalm 25:12).

Are you obsessed by something? You will probably say, "No, by nothing," but all of us are obsessed by something—usually by ourselves, or, if we are Christians, by our own experience of the Christian life. But the psalmist says that we are to be obsessed by God. The abiding awareness of the Christian life is to be God Himself, not just thoughts about Him. The total being of our life inside and out is to be absolutely obsessed by the presence of God. A child's awareness is so absorbed in his mother that although he is not consciously thinking of her, when a problem arises, the abiding relationship is that with the mother. In that same way, we are to "live and move and have our being" in God (Acts 17:28), looking at everything in relation to Him, because our abiding awareness of Him continually pushes itself to the forefront of our lives.

If we are obsessed by God, nothing else can get into our lives—not concerns, nor tribulation, nor worries. And now we understand why our Lord so emphasized the sin of worrying. How can we dare to be so absolutely unbelieving when God totally surrounds us? To be obsessed by God is to have an effective barricade against all the assaults of the enemy.

"He himself shall dwell in prosperity . . ." (Psalm 25:13). God will cause us to "dwell in prosperity," keeping us at ease, even in the midst of tribulation, misunderstanding, and slander, if our "life is hidden with Christ in God" (Colossians 3:3). We rob ourselves of the miraculous, revealed truth of this abiding companionship with God. "God is our refuge . . ." (Psalm 46:1). Nothing can break through His shelter of protection.

"THE SECRET OF THE LORD"

"The secret of the LORD is with those who fear Him . . ." (Psalm 25:14).

What is the sign of a friend? Is it that he tells you his secret sorrows? No, it is that he tells you his secret joys. Many people will confide their secret sorrows to you, but the final mark of intimacy is when they share their secret joys with you. Have we ever let God tell us any of His joys? Or are we continually telling God our secrets, leaving Him no time to talk to us? At the beginning of our Christian life we are full of requests to God. But then we find that God wants to get us into an intimate relationship with Himself—to get us in touch with His purposes. Are we so intimately united to Jesus Christ's idea of prayer—"Your will be done" (Matthew 6:10)—that we catch the secrets of God? What makes God so dear to us is not so much His big blessings to us, but the tiny things, because they show His amazing intimacy with us—He knows every detail of each of our individual lives.

"Him shall He teach in the way He chooses" (Psalm 25:12). At first, we want the awareness of being guided by God. But then as we grow spiritually, we live so fully aware of God that we do not even need to ask what His will is, because the thought of choosing another way will never occur to us. If we are saved and sanctified, God guides us by our everyday choices. And if we are about to choose what He does not want, He will give us a sense of doubt or restraint, which we must heed. Whenever there is doubt, stop at once. Never try to reason it out, saying, "I wonder why I shouldn't do this?" God instructs us in what we choose; that is, He actually guides our common sense. And when we yield to His teachings and guidance, we no longer hinder His Spirit by continually asking, "Now, Lord, what is Your will?"

THE NEVER-FORSAKING GOD

"He Himself has said, 'I will never leave you nor forsake you' " (Hebrews 13:5).

What line of thinking do my thoughts take? Do I turn to what God says or to my own fears? Am I simply repeating what God says, or am I learning to truly hear Him and then to respond after I have heard what He says? "For He Himself has said, 'I will never leave you nor forsake you.' So we may boldly say: 'The Lord is my helper; I will not fear. What can man do to me?' " (13:5-6).

"I will never leave you . . ."—not for any reason; not my sin, selfishness, stubbornness, nor waywardness. Have I really let God say to me that He will never leave me? If I have not truly heard this assurance of God, then let me listen again.

"I will never . . . forsake you." Sometimes it is not the difficulty of life but the drudgery of it that makes me think God will forsake me. When there is no major difficulty to overcome, no vision from God, nothing wonderful or beautiful—just the everyday activities of life—do I hear God's assurance even in these?

We have the idea that God is going to do some exceptional thing—that He is preparing and equipping us for some extraordinary work in the future. But as we grow in His grace we find that God is glorifying Himself here and now, at this very moment. If we have God's assurance behind us, the most amazing strength becomes ours, and we learn to sing, glorifying Him even in the ordinary days and ways of life.

GOD'S ASSURANCE

"He Himself has said . . . . So we may boldly say . . ." (Hebrews 13:5–6).

My assurance is to be built upon God's assurance to me. God says, "I will never leave you," so that then I "may boldly say, 'The Lord is my helper; I will not fear' " (13:5–6). In other words, I will not be obsessed with apprehension. This does not mean that I will not be tempted to fear, but I will remember God's words of assurance. I will be full of courage, like a child who strives to reach the standard his father has set for him. The faith of many people begins to falter when apprehensions enter their thinking, and they forget the meaning of God's assurance—they forget to take a deep spiritual breath. The only way to remove the fear from our lives is to listen to God's assurance to us.

What are you fearing? Whatever it may be, you are not a coward about it—you are determined to face it, yet you still have a feeling of fear. When it seems that there is nothing and no one to help you, say to yourself, "But 'The Lord is my helper' this very moment, even in my present circumstance." Are you learning to listen to God before you speak, or are you saying things and then trying to make God's Word fit what you have said? Take hold of the Father's assurance, and then say with strong courage, "I will not fear." It does not matter what evil or wrong may be in our way, because "He Himself has said, 'I will never leave you . . . .' "

Human frailty is another thing that gets between God's words of assurance and our own words and thoughts. When we realize how feeble we are in facing difficulties, the difficulties become like giants, we become like grasshoppers, and God seems to be nonexistent. But remember God's assurance to us—*"I will never . . . forsake you."* Have we learned to sing after hearing God's keynote? Are we continually filled with enough courage to say, "The Lord is my helper," or are we yielding to fear?

"Work Out" What God "Works in" You

> ". . . work out your own salvation . . . for it is God who works in you . . ." (Philippians 2:12–13).

Your will agrees with God, but in your flesh there is a nature that renders you powerless to do what you know you ought to do. When the Lord initially comes in contact with our conscience, the first thing our conscience does is awaken our will, and our will always agrees with God. Yet you say, "But I don't know if my will is in agreement with God." Look to Jesus and you will find that your will and your conscience are in agreement with Him every time. What causes you to say "I will not obey" is something less deep and penetrating than your will. It is perversity or stubbornness, and they are never in agreement with God. The most profound thing in a person is his will, not sin.

The will is the essential element in God's creation of human beings—sin is a perverse nature which entered into people. In someone who has been born again, the source of the will is Almighty God. ". . . for it is God who works in you both to will and to do for His good pleasure." With focused attention and great care, you have to "work out" what God "works in" you—not *work* to accomplish or earn "your own salvation," but *work it out* so you will exhibit the evidence of a life based with determined, unshakable faith on the complete and perfect redemption of the Lord. As you do this, you do not bring an opposing will up against God's will—God's will *is* your will. Your natural choices will be in accordance with God's will, and living this life will be as natural as breathing. Stubbornness is an unintelligent barrier, refusing enlightenment and blocking its flow. The only thing to do with this barrier of stubbornness is to blow it up with "dynamite," and the "dynamite" is obedience to the Holy Spirit.

Do I believe that Almighty God is the Source of my will? God not only expects me to do His will, but He is in me to do it.

THE GREATEST
SOURCE OF POWER

"Whatever you ask in My name, that I will do . . ." (John 14:13).

A m I fulfilling this ministry of intercession deep within the hidden recesses of my life? There is no trap nor any danger at all of being deceived or of showing pride in true intercession. It is a hidden ministry that brings forth fruit through which the Father is glorified. Am I allowing my spiritual life to waste away, or am I focused, bringing everything to one central point—the atonement of my Lord? Is Jesus Christ more and more dominating every interest of my life? If the central point, or the most powerful influence, of my life is the atonement of the Lord, then every aspect of my life will bear fruit for Him.

However, I must take the time to realize what this central point of power is. Am I willing to give one minute out of every hour to concentrate on it? "If you abide in Me . . . "—that is, if you continue to act, and think, and work from that central point—"you will ask what you desire, and it shall be done for you" (John 15:7). Am I abiding? Am I taking the time to abide? What is the greatest source of power in my life? Is it my work, service, and sacrifice for others, or is it my striving to work for God? It should be none of these—what ought to exert the greatest power in my life is the atonement of the Lord. It is not on what we spend the greatest amount of time that molds us the most, but whatever exerts the most power over us. We must make a determination to limit and concentrate our desires and interests on the atonement by the Cross of Christ.

"Whatever you ask in My name, that I will do . . . ." The disciple who abides in Jesus *is* the will of God, and what appears to be his free choices are actually God's foreordained decrees. Is this mysterious? Does it appear to contradict sound logic or seem totally absurd? Yes, but what a glorious truth it is to a saint of God.

WHAT'S NEXT TO DO?

"If you know these things, blessed are you if
you do them" (John 13:17).

Be determined to know more than others. If you
yourself do not cut the lines that tie you to the
dock, God will have to use a storm to sever them
and to send you out to sea. Put everything in your life
afloat upon God, going out to sea on the great swelling
tide of His purpose, and your eyes will be opened. If you
believe in Jesus, you are not to spend all your time in the
calm waters just inside the harbor, full of joy, but always
tied to the dock. You have to get out past the harbor into
the great depths of God, and begin to know things for
yourself—begin to have spiritual discernment.

When you know that you should do something and
you do it, immediately you know more. Examine where
you have become sluggish, where you began losing
interest spiritually, and you will find that it goes back to
a point where you did not do something you knew you
should do. You did not do it because there seemed to be
no immediate call to do it. But now you have no insight
or discernment, and at a time of crisis you are spiritually distracted instead of spiritually self-controlled. It is
a dangerous thing to refuse to continue learning and
knowing more.

The counterfeit of obedience is a state of mind in
which you create your own opportunities to sacrifice
yourself, and your zeal and enthusiasm are mistaken
for discernment. It is easier to sacrifice yourself than to
fulfill your spiritual destiny, which is stated in Romans
12:1-2. It is much better to fulfill the purpose of God in
your life by discerning His will than it is to perform great
acts of self-sacrifice. "Behold, to obey is better than sacrifice . . ." (1 Samuel 15:22). Beware of paying attention or
going back to what you once were, when God wants you
to be something that you have never been. "If anyone
wills to do His will, he shall know . . ." (John 7:17).

THEN WHAT'S NEXT TO DO?

"Everyone who asks receives . . ." (Luke 11:10).

A sk if you have not received. There is nothing more difficult than asking. We will have yearnings and desires for certain things, and even suffer as a result of their going unfulfilled, but not until we are at the limit of desperation will we *ask*. It is the sense of not being spiritually real that causes us to ask. Have you ever asked out of the depths of your total insufficiency and poverty? "If any of you lacks wisdom, let him ask of God . . . " (James 1:5), but be sure that you do lack wisdom before you ask. You cannot bring yourself to the point of spiritual reality anytime you choose. The best thing to do, once you realize you are not spiritually real, is to ask God for the Holy Spirit, basing your request on the promise of Jesus Christ (see Luke 11:13). The Holy Spirit is the one who makes everything that Jesus did for you real in your life.

"Everyone who asks receives . . . ." This does not mean that you will not *get* if you do not ask, but it means that until you come to the point of asking, you will not *receive* from God (see Matthew 5:45). To be able to receive means that you have to come into the relationship of a child of God, and then you comprehend and appreciate mentally, morally, and with spiritual understanding, that these things come from God.

"If any of you lacks wisdom . . . ." If you realize that you are lacking, it is because you have come in contact with spiritual reality—do not put the blinders of reason on again. The word *ask* actually means "beg." Some people are poor enough to be interested in their poverty, and some of us are poor enough spiritually to show our interest. Yet we will never receive if we ask with a certain result in mind, because we are asking out of our lust, not out of our poverty. A pauper does not ask out of any reason other than the completely hopeless and painful condition of his poverty. He is not ashamed to beg—blessed are the *paupers* in spirit (see Matthew 5:3).

AND AFTER THAT
WHAT'S NEXT TO DO?

". . . seek, and you will find . . ." (Luke 11:9).

Seek if you have not found. "You ask and do not receive, because you ask amiss . . ." (James 4:3). If you ask for things from life instead of from God, "you ask amiss"; that is, you ask out of your desire for self-fulfillment. The more you fulfill yourself the less you will seek God. ". . . seek, and you will find . . . ." Get to work—narrow your focus and interests to this one thing. Have you ever sought God with your whole heart, or have you simply given Him a feeble cry after some emotionally painful experience? ". . . seek, [focus,] and you will find . . . ."

"Ho! Everyone who thirsts, come to the waters. . ." (Isaiah 55:1). Are you thirsty, or complacent and indifferent—so satisfied with your own experience that you want nothing more of God? Experience is a doorway, not a final goal. Beware of building your faith on experience, or your life will not ring true and will only sound the note of a critical spirit. Remember that you can never give another person what you have found, but you can cause him to have a desire for it.

". . . knock, and it will be opened to you" (Luke 11:9). "Draw near to God . . ." (James 4:8). Knock—the door is closed, and your heartbeat races as you knock. "Cleanse your hands . . ." (4:8). Knock a bit louder—you begin to find that you are dirty. ". . . purify your hearts . . ." (4:8). It is becoming even more personal—you are desperate and serious now—you will do anything. "Lament . . . " (4:9). Have you ever lamented, expressing your sorrow before God for the condition of your inner life? There is no thread of self-pity left, only the heart-rending difficulty and amazement which comes from seeing what kind of person you really are. "Humble yourselves . . . " (4:10). It is a humbling experience to knock at God's door—you have to knock with the crucified thief. ". . . to him who knocks *it will be opened*" (Luke 11:10).

GETTING THERE

"Come to Me . . ." (Matthew 11:28).

Where sin and sorrow stops, and the song of the saint starts. Do I really want to get there? I can right now. The questions that truly matter in life are remarkably few, and they are all answered by these words—"Come to Me." Our Lord's words are not, "Do this, or don't do that," but—"Come to me." If I will simply come to Jesus, my real life will be brought into harmony with my real desires. I will actually cease from sin, and will find the song of the Lord beginning in my life.

Have you ever come to Jesus? Look at the stubbornness of your heart. You would rather do anything than this one simple childlike thing—"Come to Me." If you really want to experience ceasing from sin, you must come to Jesus.

Jesus Christ makes Himself the test to determine your genuineness. Look how He used the word *come*. At the most unexpected moments in your life there is this whisper of the Lord—"Come to Me," and you are immediately drawn to Him. Personal contact with Jesus changes everything. Be "foolish" enough to come and commit yourself to what He says. The attitude necessary for you to come to Him is one where your will has made the determination to let go of everything and deliberately commit it all to Him.

". . . and I will give you rest"—that is, "I will sustain you, causing you to stand firm." He is not saying, "I will put you to bed, hold your hand, and sing you to sleep." But, in essence, He is saying, "I will get you out of bed—out of your listlessness and exhaustion, and out of your condition of being half dead while you are still alive. I will penetrate you with the spirit of life, and you will be sustained by the perfection of vital activity." Yet we become so weak and pitiful and talk about "suffering" the will of the Lord! Where is the majestic vitality and the power of the Son of God in that?

GETTING THERE

"They said to Him, 'Rabbi . . . where are You staying?' He said to them, 'Come and see' " (John 1:38–39).

Where our self-interest sleeps and the real interest is awakened. "They . . . remained with Him that day . . . ." That is about all some of us ever do. We stay with Him a short time, only to wake up to our own realities of life. Our self-interest rises up and our abiding with Him is past. Yet there is no circumstance of life in which we cannot abide in Jesus.

"You are Simon . . . . You shall be called Cephas" (1:42). God writes our new name only on those places in our lives where He has erased our pride, self-sufficiency, and self-interest. Some of us have our new name written only in certain spots, like spiritual measles. And in those areas of our lives we look all right. When we are in our best spiritual mood, you would think we were the highest quality saints. But don't dare look at us when we are not in that mood. A true disciple is one who has his new name written all over him—self-interest, pride, and self-sufficiency have been completely erased.

Pride is the sin of making "self" our god. And some of us today do this, not like the Pharisee, but like the tax collector (see Luke 18:9–14). For you to say, "Oh, I'm no saint," is acceptable by human standards of pride, but it is unconscious blasphemy against God. You defy God to make you a saint, as if to say, "I am too weak and hopeless and outside the reach of the atonement by the Cross of Christ." Why aren't you a saint? It is either that you do not want to be a saint, or that you do not believe that God can make you into one. You say it would be all right if God saved you and took you straight to heaven. That is exactly what He will do! And not only do we make our home with Him, but Jesus said of His Father and Himself, ". . . We will come to him and make Our home with him" (John 14:23). Put no conditions on your life—let Jesus be everything to you, and He will take you home with Him not only for a day, but for eternity.

GETTING THERE

Where our individual desire dies and sanctified surrender lives. One of the greatest hindrances in coming to Jesus is the excuse of our own individual temperament. We make our temperament and our natural desires barriers to coming to Jesus. Yet the first thing we realize when we do come to Jesus is that He pays no attention whatsoever to our natural desires. We have the idea that we can dedicate our gifts to God. However, you cannot dedicate what is not yours. There is actually only one thing you can dedicate to God, and that is your right to yourself (see Romans 12:1). If you will give God your right to yourself, He will make a holy experiment out of you—and His experiments always succeed. The one true mark of a saint of God is the inner creativity that flows from being totally surrendered to Jesus Christ. In the life of a saint there is this amazing Well, which is a continual Source of original life. The Spirit of God is a Well of water springing up perpetually fresh. A saint realizes that it is God who engineers his circumstances; consequently there are no complaints, only unrestrained surrender to Jesus. Never try to make your experience a principle for others, but allow God to be as creative and original with others as He is with you.

If you abandon everything to Jesus, and come when He says, "Come," then He will continue to say, "Come," through you. You will go out into the world reproducing the echo of Christ's "Come." That is the result in every soul who has abandoned all and come to Jesus.

Have I come to Him? Will I come *now*?

GET MOVING!

"Abide in Me . . ." (John 15:4).

I n the matter of determination. The Spirit of Jesus is put into me by way of the atonement by the Cross of Christ. I then have to build my thinking patiently to bring it into perfect harmony with my Lord. God will not make me think like Jesus—I have to do it myself. I have to bring "every thought into captivity to the obedience of Christ" (2 Corinthians 10:5). "Abide in Me"—in intellectual matters, in money matters, in every one of the matters that make human life what it is. Our lives are not made up of only one neatly confined area.

Am I preventing God from doing things in my circumstances by saying that it will only serve to hinder my fellowship with Him? How irrelevant and disrespectful that is! It does not matter what my circumstances are. I can be as much assured of abiding in Jesus in any one of them as I am in any prayer meeting. It is unnecessary to change and arrange my circumstances myself. Our Lord's inner abiding was pure and unblemished. He was at home with God wherever His body was. He never chose His own circumstances, but was meek, submitting to His Father's plans and directions for Him. Just think of how amazingly relaxed our Lord's life was! But we tend to keep God at a fever pitch in our lives. We have none of the serenity of the life which is "hidden with Christ in God" (Colossians 3:3).

Think of the things that take you out of the position of abiding in Christ. You say, "Yes, Lord, just a minute—I still have this to do. Yes, I will abide as soon as this is finished, or as soon as this week is over. It will be all right, Lord. I will abide then." *Get moving*—begin to abide *now*. In the initial stages it will be a continual effort to abide, but as you continue, it will become so much a part of your life that you will abide in Him without any conscious effort. Make the determination to abide in Jesus wherever you are now or wherever you may be placed in the future.

GET MOVING!

"Also . . . add to your faith . . ." (2 Peter 1:5).

In the matter of drudgery. Peter said in this passage that we have become "partakers of the divine nature" and that we should now be "giving all diligence," concentrating on forming godly habits (1:4-5). We are to "add" to our lives all that character means. No one is born either naturally or supernaturally with character; it must be developed. Nor are we born with habits—we have to form godly habits on the basis of the new life God has placed within us. We are not meant to be seen as God's perfect, bright-shining examples, but to be seen as the everyday essence of ordinary life exhibiting the miracle of His grace. Drudgery is the test of genuine character. The greatest hindrance in our spiritual life is that we will only look for big things to do. Yet, "Jesus . . . took a towel and . . . began to wash the disciples' feet . . ." (John 13:3-5).

We all have those times when there are no flashes of light and no apparent thrill to life, where we experience nothing but the daily routine with its common everyday tasks. The routine of life is actually God's way of saving us between our times of great inspiration which come from Him. Don't always expect God to give you His thrilling moments, but learn to live in those common times of the drudgery of life by the power of God.

It is difficult for us to do the "adding" that Peter mentioned here. We say we do not expect God to take us to heaven on flowery beds of ease, and yet we act as if we do! I must realize that my obedience even in the smallest detail of life has all of the omnipotent power of the grace of God behind it. If I will do my duty, not for duty's sake but because I believe God is engineering my circumstances, then at the very point of my obedience all of the magnificent grace of God is mine through the glorious atonement by the Cross of Christ.

"WILL YOU LAY DOWN YOUR LIFE?"

"Greater love has no one than this, than to lay down one's life for his friends. . . . I have called you friends . . ." (John 15:13, 15).

Jesus does not ask me to die for Him, but to lay down my life for Him. Peter said to the Lord, "I will lay down my life for Your sake," and he meant it (John 13:37). He had a magnificent sense of the heroic. For us to be incapable of making this same statement Peter made would be a bad thing—our sense of duty is only fully realized through our sense of heroism. Has the Lord ever asked you, "Will you lay down your life for My sake?" (John 13:38). It is much easier to die than to lay down your life day in and day out with the sense of the high calling of God. We are not made for the bright-shining moments of life, but we have to walk in the light of them in our everyday ways. There was only one bright-shining moment in the life of Jesus, and that was on the Mount of Transfiguration. It was there that He emptied Himself of His glory for the second time, and then came down into the demon-possessed valley (see Mark 9:1–29). For thirty-three years Jesus laid down His life to do the will of His Father. "By this we know love, because He laid down His life for us. And we also ought to lay down our lives for the brethren" (1 John 3:16). Yet it is contrary to our human nature to do so.

If I am a friend of Jesus, I must deliberately and carefully lay down my life for Him. It is a difficult thing to do, and thank God that it is. Salvation is easy for us, because it cost God so much. But the exhibiting of salvation in my life is difficult. God saves a person, fills him with the Holy Spirit, and then says, in effect, "Now you work it out in your life, and be faithful to Me, even though the nature of everything around you is to cause you to be unfaithful." And Jesus says to us, ". . . I have called you friends. . . ." Remain faithful to your Friend, and remember that His honor is at stake in your bodily life.

BEWARE OF CRITICIZING OTHERS

"Judge not, that you be not judged" (Matthew 7:1).

Jesus' instructions with regard to judging others is very simply put; He says, *"Don't."* The average Christian is the most piercingly critical individual known. Criticism is one of the ordinary activities of people, but in the spiritual realm nothing is accomplished by it. The effect of criticism is the dividing up of the strengths of the one being criticized. The Holy Spirit is the only one in the proper position to criticize, and He alone is able to show what is wrong without hurting and wounding. It is impossible to enter into fellowship with God when you are in a critical mood. Criticism serves to make you harsh, vindictive, and cruel, and leaves you with the soothing and flattering idea that you are somehow superior to others. Jesus says that as His disciple you should cultivate a temperament that is never critical. This will not happen quickly but must be developed over a span of time. You must constantly beware of anything that causes you to think of yourself as a superior person.

There is no escaping the penetrating search of my life by Jesus. If I see the little speck in your eye, it means that I have a plank of timber in my own (see 7:3-5). Every wrong thing that I see in you, God finds in me. Every time I judge, I condemn myself (see Romans 2:17-24). Stop having a measuring stick for other people. There is always at least one more fact, which we know nothing about, in every person's situation. The first thing God does is to give us a thorough spiritual cleaning. After that, there is no possibility of pride remaining in us. I have never met a person I could despair of, or lose all hope for, after discerning what lies in me apart from the grace of God.

KEEP RECOGNIZING JESUS

"... Peter ... walked on the water to go to Jesus. But when he saw that the wind was boisterous, he was afraid ..." (Matthew 14:29–30).

The wind really was boisterous and the waves really were high, but Peter didn't see them at first. He didn't consider them at all; he simply recognized his Lord, stepped out in recognition of Him, and "walked on the water." Then he began to take those things around him into account, and instantly, down he went. Why couldn't our Lord have enabled him to walk at the bottom of the waves, as well as on top of them? He could have, yet neither could be done without Peter's continuing recognition of the Lord Jesus.

We step right out with recognition of God in some things, then self-consideration enters our lives and down we go. If you are truly recognizing your Lord, you have no business being concerned about how and where He engineers your circumstances. The things surrounding you *are* real, but when you look at them you are immediately overwhelmed, and even unable to recognize Jesus. Then comes His rebuke, "... why did you doubt?" (14:31). Let your actual circumstances be what they may, but keep recognizing Jesus, maintaining complete reliance upon Him.

If you debate for even one second when God has spoken, it is all over for you. Never start to say, "Well, I wonder if He really did speak to me?" Be reckless immediately—totally unrestrained and willing to risk everything—by casting your all upon Him. You do not know when His voice will come to you, but whenever the realization of God comes, even in the faintest way imaginable, be determined to recklessly abandon yourself, surrendering everything to Him. It is only through abandonment of yourself and your circumstances that you will recognize Him. You will only recognize His voice more clearly through recklessness—being willing to risk your all.

THE SERVICE OF
PASSIONATE DEVOTION

". . . do you love Me? . . . Tend My sheep"
(John 21:16).

J esus did not say to make converts to your way of thinking, but He said to look after His sheep, to see that
they get nourished in the knowledge of Him. We consider what we do in the way of Christian work as service,
yet Jesus Christ calls service to be what we *are* to Him, not
what we *do* for Him. Discipleship is based solely on devotion to Jesus Christ, not on following after a particular
belief or doctrine. "If anyone comes to Me and does not
hate . . . , he cannot be My disciple" (Luke 14:26). In this
verse, there is no argument and no pressure from Jesus to
follow Him; He is simply saying, in effect, "If you want
to be My disciple, you must be devoted solely to Me." A
person touched by the Spirit of God suddenly says, "Now
I see who Jesus is!"—that is the source of devotion.

Today we have substituted doctrinal belief for personal belief, and that is why so many people are devoted
to causes and so few are devoted to Jesus Christ. People
do not really want to be devoted to Jesus, but only to the
cause He started. Jesus Christ is deeply offensive to the
educated minds of today, to those who only want Him to
be their Friend, and who are unwilling to accept Him in
any other way. Our Lord's primary obedience was to the
will of His Father, not to the needs of people—the saving
of people was the natural outcome of His obedience to
the Father. If I am devoted solely to the cause of humanity, I will soon be exhausted and come to the point where
my love will waver and stumble. But if I love Jesus Christ
personally and passionately, I can serve humanity, even
though people may treat me like a "doormat." The secret
of a disciple's life is devotion to Jesus Christ, and the
characteristic of that life is its seeming insignificance and
its meekness. Yet it is like a grain of wheat that "falls into
the ground and dies"—it will spring up and change the
entire landscape (John 12:24).

HAVE YOU COME TO "WHEN" YET?

"The LORD restored Job's losses when he prayed for his friends" (Job 42:10).

A pitiful, sickly, and self-centered kind of prayer and a determined effort and selfish desire to be right with God are never found in the New Testament. The fact that I am trying to be right with God is actually a sign that I am rebelling against the atonement by the Cross of Christ. I pray, "Lord, I will purify my heart if You will answer my prayer—I will walk rightly before You if You will help me." But I *cannot* make myself right with God; I *cannot* make my life perfect. I can only be right with God if I accept the atonement of the Lord Jesus Christ as an absolute gift. Am I humble enough to accept it? I have to surrender all my rights and demands, and cease from every self-effort. I must leave myself completely alone in His hands, and then I can begin to pour my life out in the priestly work of intercession. There is a great deal of prayer that comes from actual disbelief in the atonement. Jesus is not just beginning to save us—He has already saved us completely. It is an accomplished fact, and it is an insult to Him for us to ask Him to do what He has already done.

If you are not now receiving the "hundredfold" which Jesus promised (see Matthew 19:29), and not getting insight into God's Word, then start praying for your friends—enter into the ministry of the inner life. "The LORD restored Job's losses *when he prayed for his friends.*" As a saved soul, the real business of your life is intercessory prayer. Whatever circumstances God may place you in, always pray immediately that His atonement may be recognized and as fully understood in the lives of others as it has been in yours. Pray for your friends *now*, and pray for those with whom you come in contact *now*.

THE MINISTRY OF THE INNER LIFE

"You are . . . a royal priesthood . . ." (1 Peter 2:9).

By what right have we become "a royal priesthood"? It is by the right of the atonement by the Cross of Christ that this has been accomplished. Are we prepared to purposely disregard ourselves and to launch out into the priestly work of prayer? The continual inner-searching we do in an effort to see if we are what we ought to be generates a self-centered, sickly type of Christianity, not the vigorous and simple life of a child of God. Until we get into this right and proper relationship with God, it is simply a case of our "hanging on by the skin of our teeth," although we say, "What a wonderful victory I have!" Yet there is nothing at all in that which indicates the miracle of redemption. Launch out in reckless, unrestrained belief that the redemption is complete. Then don't worry anymore about yourself, but begin to do as Jesus Christ has said, in essence, "Pray for the friend who comes to you at midnight, pray for the saints of God, and pray for all men." Pray with the realization that you are perfect only in Christ Jesus, not on the basis of this argument: "Oh, Lord, I have done my best; please hear me now."

How long is it going to take God to free us from the unhealthy habit of thinking only about ourselves? We must get to the point of being sick to death of ourselves, until there is no longer any surprise at anything God might tell us about ourselves. We cannot reach and understand the depths of our own meagerness. There is only one place where we are right with God, and that is in Christ Jesus. Once we are there, we have to pour out our lives for all we are worth in this ministry of the inner life.

THE UNCHANGING
LAW OF JUDGMENT

"With what judgment you judge, you will be judged; and with the measure you use, it will be measured back to you" (Matthew 7:2).

This statement is not some haphazard theory, but it is an eternal law of God. Whatever judgment you give will be the very way you are judged. There is a difference between retaliation and retribution. Jesus said that the basis of life is retribution—"with the measure you use, it will be measured back to you." If you have been shrewd in finding out the shortcomings of others, remember that will be exactly how you will be measured. The way you pay is the way life will pay you back. This eternal law works from God's throne down to us (see Psalm 18:25-26).

Romans 2:1 applies it in even a more definite way by saying that the one who criticizes another is guilty of the very same thing. God looks not only at the act itself, but also at the possibility of committing it, which He sees by looking at our hearts. To begin with, we do not believe the statements of the Bible. For instance, do we really believe the statement that says we criticize in others the very things we are guilty of ourselves? The reason we see hypocrisy, deceit, and a lack of genuineness in others is that they are all in our own hearts. The greatest characteristic of a saint is humility, as evidenced by being able to say honestly and humbly, "Yes, all those, as well as other evils, would have been exhibited in me if it were not for the grace of God. Therefore, I have no right to judge."

Jesus said, "Judge not, that you be not judged" (Matthew 7:1). He went on to say, in effect, "If you do judge, you will be judged in exactly the same way." Who of us would dare to stand before God and say, "My God, judge me as I have judged others"? We have judged others as sinners—if God should judge us in the same way, we would be condemned to hell. Yet God judges us on the basis of the miraculous atonement by the Cross of Christ.

"ACQUAINTED WITH GRIEF"

"He is . . . a Man of sorrows and acquainted with grief" (Isaiah 53:3).

We are not "acquainted with grief" in the same way our Lord was acquainted with it. We endure it and live through it, but we do not become intimate with it. At the beginning of our lives we do not bring ourselves to the point of dealing with the reality of sin. We look at life through the eyes of reason and say that if a person will control his instincts, and educate himself, he can produce a life that will slowly evolve into the life of God. But as we continue on through life, we find the presence of something which we have not yet taken into account, namely, sin—and it upsets all of our thinking and our plans. Sin has made the foundation of our thinking unpredictable, uncontrollable, and irrational.

We have to recognize that sin is a fact of life, not just a shortcoming. Sin is blatant mutiny against God, and either sin or God must die in my life. The New Testament brings us right down to this one issue—if sin rules in me, God's life in me will be killed; if God rules in me, sin in me will be killed. There is nothing more fundamental than that. The culmination of sin was the crucifixion of Jesus Christ, and what was true in the history of God on earth will also be true in your history and in mine—that is, sin will kill the life of God in us. We must mentally bring ourselves to terms with this fact of sin. It is the only explanation why Jesus Christ came to earth, and it is the explanation of the grief and sorrow of life.

RECONCILING YOURSELF
TO THE FACT OF SIN

**"This is your hour, and the power of darkness"
(Luke 22:53).**

Not being reconciled to the fact of sin—not recognizing it and refusing to deal with it—produces all the disasters in life. You may talk about the lofty virtues of human nature, but there is something in human nature that will mockingly laugh in the face of every principle you have. If you refuse to agree with the fact that there is wickedness and selfishness, something downright hateful and wrong, in human beings, when it attacks your life, instead of reconciling yourself to it, you will compromise with it and say that it is of no use to battle against it. Have you taken this "hour, and the power of darkness" into account, or do you have a view of yourself which includes no recognition of sin whatsoever? In your human relationships and friendships, have you reconciled yourself to the fact of sin? If not, just around the next corner you will find yourself trapped and you will compromise with it. But if you will reconcile yourself to the fact of sin, you will realize the danger immediately and say, "Yes, I see what this sin would mean." The recognition of sin does not destroy the basis of friendship—it simply establishes a mutual respect for the fact that the basis of sinful life is disastrous. Always beware of any assessment of life which does not recognize the fact that there is sin.

Jesus Christ never trusted human nature, yet He was never cynical nor suspicious, because He had absolute trust in what He could do for human nature. The pure man or woman is the one who is shielded from harm, not the innocent person. The so-called innocent man or woman is never safe. Men and women have no business trying to be innocent; God demands that they be pure and virtuous. Innocence is the characteristic of a child. Any person is deserving of blame if he is unwilling to reconcile himself to the fact of sin.

RECEIVING YOURSELF IN
THE FIRES OF SORROW

". . . what shall I say? 'Father, save Me from
this hour'? But for this purpose I came to
this hour. 'Father, glorify Your name' " (John
12:27–28).

As a saint of God, my attitude toward sorrow and
difficulty should not be to ask that they be prevented, but to ask that God protect me so that I
may remain what He created me to be, in spite of all my
fires of sorrow. Our Lord received Himself, accepting His
position and realizing His purpose, in the midst of the
fire of sorrow. He was saved not *from* the hour, but *out of*
the hour.

We say that there ought to be no sorrow, but there *is*
sorrow, and we have to accept and receive ourselves in its
fires. If we try to evade sorrow, refusing to deal with it,
we are foolish. Sorrow is one of the biggest facts in life,
and there is no use in saying it should not be. Sin, sorrow, and suffering *are*, and it is not for us to say that God
has made a mistake in allowing them.

Sorrow removes a great deal of a person's shallowness, but it does not always make that person better.
Suffering either gives me to myself or it destroys me. You
cannot find or receive yourself through success, because
you lose your head over pride. And you cannot receive
yourself through the monotony of your daily life, because
you give in to complaining. The only way to find yourself
is in the fires of sorrow. Why it should be this way is
immaterial. The fact is that it is true in the Scriptures
and in human experience. You can always recognize
who has been through the fires of sorrow and received
himself, and you know that you can go to him in your
moment of trouble and find that he has plenty of time
for you. But if a person has not been through the fires of
sorrow, he is apt to be contemptuous, having no respect
or time for you, only turning you away. If you will receive
yourself in the fires of sorrow, God will make you nourishment for other people.

DRAWING ON THE
GRACE OF GOD—NOW

"We . . . plead with you not to receive the grace of God in vain" (2 Corinthians 6:1).

The grace you had yesterday will not be sufficient for today. Grace is the overflowing favor of God, and you can always count on it being available to draw upon as needed. ". . . in much patience, in tribulations, in needs, in distresses"—that is where our patience is tested (6:4). Are you failing to rely on the grace of God there? Are you saying to yourself, "Oh well, I won't count this time"? It is not a question of praying and asking God to help you—it is taking the grace of God *now*. We tend to make prayer the preparation for our service, yet it is never that in the Bible. Prayer is the practice of drawing on the grace of God. Don't say, "I will endure this until I can get away and pray." Pray now—draw on the grace of God in your moment of need. Prayer is the most normal and useful thing; it is not simply a reflex action of your devotion to God. We are very slow to learn to draw on God's grace through prayer.

". . . in stripes, in imprisonments, in tumults, in labors . . ." (6:5)—in all these things, display in your life a drawing on the grace of God, which will show evidence to yourself and to others that you are a miracle of His. Draw on His grace now, not later. The primary word in the spiritual vocabulary is *now*. Let circumstances take you where they will, but keep drawing on the grace of God in whatever condition you may find yourself. One of the greatest proofs that you are drawing on the grace of God is that you can be totally humiliated before others without displaying even the slightest trace of anything but His grace.

". . . having nothing . . . ." Never hold anything in reserve. Pour yourself out, giving the best that you have, and always be poor. Never be diplomatic and careful with the treasure God gives you. ". . . and yet possessing all things"—this is poverty triumphant (6:10).

THE OVERSHADOWING OF GOD'S PERSONAL DELIVERANCE

" '. . . I am with you to deliver you,' says the LORD" (Jeremiah 1:8).

God promised Jeremiah that He would deliver him personally—". . . your life shall be as a prize to you . . ." (Jeremiah 39:18). That is all God promises His children. Wherever God sends us, He will guard our lives. Our personal property and possessions are to be a matter of indifference to us, and our hold on these things should be very loose. If this is not the case, we will have panic, heartache, and distress. Having the proper outlook is evidence of the deeply rooted belief in the overshadowing of God's personal deliverance.

The Sermon on the Mount indicates that when we are on a mission for Jesus Christ, there is no time to stand up for ourselves. Jesus says, in effect, "Don't worry about whether or not you are being treated justly." Looking for justice is actually a sign that we have been diverted from our devotion to Him. Never look for justice in this world, but never cease to give it. If we look for justice, we will only begin to complain and to indulge ourselves in the discontent of self-pity, as if to say, "Why should I be treated like this?" If we are devoted to Jesus Christ, we have nothing to do with what we encounter, whether it is just or unjust. In essence, Jesus says, "Continue steadily on with what I have told you to do, and I will guard your life. If you try to guard it yourself, you remove yourself from My deliverance." Even the most devout among us become atheistic in this regard—we do not believe Him. We put our common sense on the throne and then attach God's name to it. We *do* lean to our own understanding, instead of trusting God with all our hearts (see Proverbs 3:5-6).

HELD BY THE GRIP OF GOD

"I press on, that I may lay hold of that for
which Christ Jesus has also laid hold of me"
(Philippians 3:12).

Never choose to be a worker for God, but once
God has placed His call on you, woe be to you if
you "turn aside to the right hand or to the left"
(Deuteronomy 5:32). We are not here to work for God
because we have chosen to do so, but because God has
"laid hold of" us. And once He has done so, we never
have this thought, "Well, I'm really not suited for this."
What you are to preach is also determined by God, not
by your own natural leanings or desires. Keep your soul
steadfastly related to God, and remember that you are
called not simply to convey your testimony but also to
preach the gospel. Every Christian must testify to the
truth of God, but when it comes to the call to preach,
there must be the agonizing grip of God's hand on you—
your life is in the grip of God for that very purpose. How
many of us are held like that?

Never water down the Word of God, but preach it
in its undiluted sternness. There must be unflinching
faithfulness to the Word of God, but when you come
to personal dealings with others, remember who you
are—you are not some special being created in heaven,
but a sinner saved by grace.

"Brethren, I do not count myself to have appre-
hended; but *one thing I do* . . . I press toward the goal
for the prize of the upward call of God in Christ Jesus"
(Philippians 3:13–14).

THE STRICTEST DISCIPLINE

"If your right hand causes you to sin, cut it off and cast it from you; for it is more profitable for you that one of your members perish, than for your whole body to be cast into hell" (Matthew 5:30).

Jesus did not say that everyone must cut off his right hand, but that "if your right hand causes you to sin" in your walk with Him, then it is better to "cut it off." There are many things that are perfectly legitimate, but if you are going to concentrate on God you cannot do them. Your right hand is one of the best things you have, but Jesus says that if it hinders you in following His precepts, then "cut it off." The principle taught here is the strictest discipline or lesson that ever hit humankind.

When God changes you through regeneration, giving you new life through spiritual rebirth, your life initially has the characteristic of being maimed. There are a hundred and one things that you dare not do—things that would be sin for you, and would be recognized as sin by those who really know you. But the unspiritual people around you will say, "What's so wrong with doing that? How absurd you are!" There has never yet been a saint who has not lived a maimed life initially. Yet it is better to enter into life maimed but lovely in God's sight than to appear lovely to man's eyes but lame to God's. At first, Jesus Christ through His Spirit has to restrain you from doing a great many things that may be perfectly right for everyone else but not right for you. Yet, see that you don't use your restrictions to criticize someone else.

The Christian life is a maimed life initially, but in verse 48 Jesus gave us the picture of a perfectly well-rounded life—"You shall be *perfect*, just as your Father in heaven is perfect."

Do It Now!

"Agree with your adversary quickly . . ."
(Matthew 5:25).

In this verse, Jesus Christ laid down a very important principle by saying, "Do what you know you must do—*now*. Do it quickly. If you don't, an inevitable process will begin to work 'till you have paid the last penny' (5:26) in pain, agony, and distress." God's laws are unchangeable and there is no escape from them. The teachings of Jesus always penetrate right to the heart of our being.

Wanting to make sure that my adversary gives me all my rights is a natural thing. But Jesus says that it is a matter of inescapable and eternal importance to me that I pay my adversary what I owe him. From our Lord's standpoint it doesn't matter whether I am cheated or not, but what does matter is that I don't cheat someone else. Am I insisting on having my own rights, or am I paying what I owe from Jesus Christ's standpoint?

Do it quickly—bring yourself to judgment now. In moral and spiritual matters, you must act immediately. If you don't, the inevitable, relentless process will begin to work. God is determined to have His child as pure, clean, and white as driven snow, and as long as there is disobedience in any point of His teaching, He will allow His Spirit to use whatever process it may take to bring us to obedience. The fact that we insist on proving that we are right is almost always a clear indication that we have some point of disobedience. No wonder the Spirit of God so strongly urges us to stay steadfastly in the light! (see John 3:19–21).

"Agree with your adversary quickly . . . ." Have you suddenly reached a certain place in your relationship with someone, only to find that you have anger in your heart? Confess it quickly—make it right before God. Be reconciled to that person—*do it now!*

THE INEVITABLE PENALTY

"You will by no means get out of there till you have paid the last penny" (Matthew 5:26).

There is no heaven that has a little corner of hell in it. God is determined to make you pure, holy, and right, and He will not allow you to escape from the scrutiny of the Holy Spirit for even one moment. He urged you to come to judgment immediately when He convicted you, but you did not obey. Then the inevitable process began to work, bringing its inevitable penalty. Now you have been "thrown into prison, [and] . . . you will by no means get out of there till you have paid the last penny" (5:25-26). Yet you ask, "Is this a God of mercy and love?" When seen from God's perspective, it is a glorious ministry of love. God is going to bring you out pure, spotless, and undefiled, but He wants you to recognize the nature you were exhibiting—the nature of demanding your right to yourself. The moment you are willing for God to change your nature, His recreating forces will begin to work. And the moment you realize that God's purpose is to get you into the right relationship with Himself and then with others, He will reach to the very limits of the universe to help you take the right road. Decide to do it right now, saying, "Yes, Lord, I *will* write that letter," or, "I *will* be reconciled to that person now."

These sermons of Jesus Christ are meant for your will and your conscience, not for your head. If you dispute these verses from the Sermon on the Mount with your head, you will dull the appeal to your heart.

If you find yourself asking, "I wonder why I'm not growing spiritually with God?"—then ask yourself if you are paying your debts from God's standpoint. Do *now* what you will have to do someday. Every moral question or call comes with an "ought" behind it—the knowledge of knowing what we ought to do.

THE CONDITIONS OF DISCIPLESHIP

> "If anyone comes to Me and does not hate his
> father and mother, wife and children, brothers
> and sisters, yes, and his own life also . . . . And
> whoever does not bear his cross and come after
> Me . . . . So likewise, whoever of you does not
> forsake all that he has cannot be My disciple"
> (Luke 14:26–27, 33).

I f the closest relationships of a disciple's life conflict
with the claims of Jesus Christ, then our Lord requires
instant obedience to Himself. Discipleship means personal, passionate devotion to a Person—our Lord Jesus
Christ. There is a vast difference between devotion to
a person and devotion to principles or to a cause. Our
Lord never proclaimed a cause—He proclaimed personal
devotion to Himself. To be a disciple is to be a devoted
bondservant motivated by love for the Lord Jesus. Many
of us who call ourselves Christians are not truly devoted
to Jesus Christ. No one on earth has this passionate love
for the Lord Jesus unless the Holy Spirit has given it to
him. We may admire, respect, and revere Him, but we
cannot love Him on our own. The only One who truly
loves the Lord Jesus is the Holy Spirit, and it is He who
has "poured out in our hearts" the very "love of God"
(Romans 5:5). Whenever the Holy Spirit sees an opportunity to glorify Jesus through you, He will take your entire
being and set you ablaze with glowing devotion to Jesus
Christ.

The Christian life is a life characterized by true
and spontaneous creativity. Consequently, a disciple is
subject to the same charge that was leveled against Jesus
Christ, namely, the charge of inconsistency. But Jesus
Christ was always consistent in His relationship to God,
and a Christian must be consistent in his relationship
to the life of the Son of God in him, not consistent to
strict, unyielding doctrines. People pour themselves into
their own doctrines, and God has to blast them out of
their preconceived ideas before they can become devoted
to Jesus Christ.

THE CONCENTRATION OF PERSONAL SIN

"Woe is me, for I am undone! Because I am a man of unclean lips . . ." (Isaiah 6:5).

When I come into the very presence of God, I do not realize that I am a sinner in an indefinite sense, but I suddenly realize and the focus of my attention is directed toward the concentration of sin in a particular area of my life. A person will easily say, "Oh yes, I know I am a sinner," but when he comes into the presence of God he cannot get away with such a broad and indefinite statement. Our conviction is focused on our specific sin, and we realize, as Isaiah did, what we really are. This is always the sign that a person is in the presence of God. There is never any vague sense of sin, but a focusing on the concentration of sin in some specific, personal area of life. God begins by convicting us of the very thing to which His Spirit has directed our mind's attention. If we will surrender, submitting to His conviction of that particular sin, He will lead us down to where He can reveal the vast underlying nature of sin. That is the way God always deals with us when we are consciously aware of His presence.

This experience of our attention being directed to our concentration of personal sin is true in everyone's life, from the greatest of saints to the worst of sinners. When a person first begins climbing the ladder of experience, he might say, "I don't know where I've gone wrong," but the Spirit of God will point out some definite and specific thing to him. The effect of Isaiah's vision of the holiness of the Lord was the directing of his attention to the fact that he was "a man of unclean lips." "He touched my mouth with it, and said: 'Behold, this has touched your lips; your iniquity is taken away, and your sin purged' " (6:7). The cleansing fire had to be applied where the sin had been concentrated.

ONE OF GOD'S GREAT "DON'TS"

"Do not fret—it only causes harm" (Psalm 37:8).

Fretting means getting ourselves "out of joint" mentally or spiritually. It is one thing to say, "Do not fret," but something very different to have such a nature that you find yourself unable to fret. It's easy to say, "Rest in the Lord, and wait patiently for Him" (37:7) until our own little world is turned upside down and we are forced to live in confusion and agony like so many other people. Is it possible to "rest in the Lord" then? If this "Do not" doesn't work there, then it will not work anywhere. This "Do not" must work during our days of difficulty and uncertainty, as well as our peaceful days, or it will never work. And if it will not work in your particular case, it will not work for anyone else. Resting in the Lord is not dependent on your external circumstances at all, but on your relationship with God Himself.

Worrying always results in sin. We tend to think that a little anxiety and worry are simply an indication of how wise we really are, yet it is actually a much better indication of just how wicked we are. Fretting rises from our determination to have our own way. Our Lord never worried and was never anxious, because His purpose was never to accomplish His own plans but to fulfill God's plans. Fretting is wickedness for a child of God.

Have you been propping up that foolish soul of yours with the idea that your circumstances are too much for God to handle? Set all your opinions and speculations aside and "abide under the shadow of the Almighty" (Psalm 91:1). Deliberately tell God that you will not fret about whatever concerns you. All our fretting and worrying is caused by planning without God.

DON'T PLAN WITHOUT GOD

"Commit your way to the LORD, trust also in Him, and He shall bring it to pass" (Psalm 37:5).

Don't plan without God. God seems to have a delightful way of upsetting the plans we have made, when we have not taken Him into account. We get ourselves into circumstances that were not chosen by God, and suddenly we realize that we have been making our plans without Him—that we have not even considered Him to be a vital, living factor in the planning of our lives. And yet the only thing that will keep us from even the possibility of worrying is to bring God in as the greatest factor in all of our planning.

In spiritual issues it is customary for us to put God first, but we tend to think that it is inappropriate and unnecessary to put Him first in the practical, everyday issues of our lives. If we have the idea that we have to put on our "spiritual face" before we can come near to God, then we will never come near to Him. We must come as we are.

Don't plan with a concern for evil in mind. Does God really mean for us to plan without taking the evil around us into account? "Love . . . thinks no evil" (1 Corinthians 13:4–5). Love is not ignorant of the existence of evil, but it does not take it into account as a factor in planning. When we were apart from God, we did take evil into account, doing all of our planning with it in mind, and we tried to reason out all of our work from its standpoint.

Don't plan with a rainy day in mind. You cannot hoard things for a rainy day if you are truly trusting Christ. Jesus said, "Let not your heart be troubled . . ." (John 14:1). God will not keep your heart from being troubled. It is a command—"Let not . . . ." To do it, continually pick yourself up, even if you fall a hundred and one times a day, until you get into the habit of putting God first and planning with Him in mind.

VISIONS BECOMING REALITY

"The parched ground shall become a pool . . ."
(Isaiah 35:7).

We always have a vision of something before it actually becomes real to us. When we realize that the vision is real, but is not yet real in us, Satan comes to us with his temptations, and we are inclined to say that there is no point in even trying to continue. Instead of the vision becoming real to us, we have entered into a valley of humiliation.

Life is not as idle ore,
But iron dug from central gloom,
And battered by the shocks of doom
To shape and use.

God gives us a vision, and then He takes us down to the valley to batter us into the shape of that vision. It is in the valley that so many of us give up and faint. Every God-given vision will become real if we will only have patience. Just think of the enormous amount of free time God has! He is never in a hurry. Yet we are always in such a frantic hurry. While still in the light of the glory of the vision, we go right out to do things, but the vision is not yet real in us. God has to take us into the valley and put us through fires and floods to batter us into shape, until we get to the point where He can trust us with the reality of the vision. Ever since God gave us the vision, He has been at work. He is getting us into the shape of the goal He has for us, and yet over and over again we try to escape from the Sculptor's hand in an effort to batter ourselves into the shape of our own goal.

The vision that God gives is not some unattainable castle in the sky, but a vision of what God wants you to be down here. Allow the Potter to put you on His wheel and whirl you around as He desires. Then as surely as God is God, and you are you, you will turn out as an exact likeness of the vision. But don't lose heart in the process. If you have ever had a vision from God, you may try as you will to be satisfied on a lower level, but God will never allow it.

JULY 6

ALL EFFORTS OF WORTH AND EXCELLENCE ARE DIFFICULT

> "Enter by the narrow gate . . . . Because narrow is the gate and difficult is the way which leads to life . . ." (Matthew 7:13-14).

I f we are going to live as disciples of Jesus, we have to remember that all efforts of worth and excellence are difficult. The Christian life is gloriously difficult, but its difficulty does not make us faint and cave in—it stirs us up to overcome. Do we appreciate the miraculous salvation of Jesus Christ enough to be our utmost for His highest—our best for His glory?

God saves people by His sovereign grace through the atonement of Jesus, and "it is God who works in you both to will and to do for His good pleasure" (Philippians 2:13). But we have to "work out" that salvation in our everyday, practical living (Philippians 2:12). If we will only start on the basis of His redemption to do what He commands, then we will find that we can do it. If we fail, it is because we have not yet put into practice what God has placed within us. But a crisis will reveal whether or not we have been putting it into practice. If we will obey the Spirit of God and practice in our physical life what God has placed within us by His Spirit, then when a crisis does come we will find that our own nature, as well as the grace of God, will stand by us.

Thank God that He does give us difficult things to do! His salvation is a joyous thing, but it is also something that requires bravery, courage, and holiness. It tests us for all we are worth. Jesus is "bringing many sons to glory" (Hebrews 2:10), and God will not shield us from the requirements of sonship. God's grace produces men and women with a strong family likeness to Jesus Christ, not pampered, spoiled weaklings. It takes a tremendous amount of discipline to live the worthy and excellent life of a disciple of Jesus in the realities of life. And it is always necessary for us to make an effort to live a life of worth and excellence.

WILL TO BE FAITHFUL

**". . . choose for yourselves this day whom you
will serve . . ." (Joshua 24:15).**

A person's will is embodied in the actions of the
whole person. I cannot *give up* my will—I must
exercise it, putting it into action. I must *will* to
obey, and I must *will* to receive God's Spirit. When God
gives me a vision of truth, there is never a question of
what He will do, but only of what I will do. The Lord has
been placing in front of each of us some big proposals
and plans. The best thing to do is to remember what you
did before when you were touched by God. Recall the
moment when you were saved, or first recognized Jesus,
or realized some truth. It was easy then to yield your allegiance to God. Immediately recall those moments each
time the Spirit of God brings some new proposal before
you.

". . . choose for yourselves this day whom you will
serve. . . ." Your choice must be a deliberate determination—it is not something into which you will automatically drift. And everything else in your life will be held
in temporary suspension until you make a decision. The
proposal is between you and God—do not "confer with
flesh and blood" about it (Galatians 1:16). With every
new proposal, the people around us seem to become
more and more isolated, and that is where the tension
develops. God allows the opinion of His other saints to
matter to you, and yet you become less and less certain
that others really understand the step you are taking. You
have no business trying to find out where God is leading—the only thing God will explain to you is Himself.

Openly declare to Him, "I will be faithful." But
remember that as soon as you choose to be faithful to
Jesus Christ, "You are witnesses against yourselves . . ."
(Joshua 24:22). Don't consult with other Christians, but
simply and freely declare before Him, "I will serve You."
Will to be faithful—and give other people credit for
being faithful too.

WILL YOU EXAMINE YOURSELF?

"Joshua said to the people, 'You cannot serve the LORD . . .' " (Joshua 24:19).

Do you have even the slightest reliance on anything or anyone other than God? Is there a remnant of reliance left on any natural quality within you, or on any particular set of circumstances? Are you relying on yourself in any manner whatsoever regarding this new proposal or plan which God has placed before you? Will you examine yourself by asking these probing questions? It really is true to say, "I cannot live a holy life," but you can decide to let Jesus Christ make you holy. "You cannot serve the LORD . . ."—but you can place yourself in the proper position where God's almighty power will flow through you. Is your relationship with God sufficient for you to expect Him to exhibit His wonderful life in you?

"The people said to Joshua, 'No, but we will serve the LORD!' " (24:21). This is not an impulsive action, but a deliberate commitment. We tend to say, "But God could never have called *me* to this. I'm too unworthy. It can't mean *me*." It does mean you, and the more weak and feeble you are, the better. The person who is still relying and trusting in anything within himself is the last person to even come close to saying, "I will serve the Lord."

We say, "Oh, if only I really could believe!" The question is, "*Will* I believe?" No wonder Jesus Christ placed such emphasis on the sin of unbelief. "He did not do many mighty works there because of their unbelief" (Matthew 13:58). If we really believed that God meant what He said, just imagine what we would be like! Do I really dare to let God be to me all that He says He will be?

The Spiritually Lazy Saint

"Let us consider one another in order to stir up love and good works, not forsaking the assembling of ourselves together . . ." (Hebrews 10:24–25).

We are all capable of being spiritually lazy saints. We want to stay off the rough roads of life, and our primary objective is to secure a peaceful retreat from the world. The ideas put forth in these verses from Hebrews 10 are those of stirring up one another and of keeping ourselves together. Both of these require initiative—our willingness to take the first step toward Christ-realization, not the initiative toward self-realization. To live a distant, withdrawn, and secluded life is diametrically opposed to spirituality as Jesus Christ taught it.

The true test of our spirituality occurs when we come up against injustice, degradation, ingratitude, and turmoil, all of which have the tendency to make us spiritually lazy. While being tested, we want to use prayer and Bible reading for the purpose of finding a quiet retreat. We use God only for the sake of getting peace and joy. We seek only our enjoyment of Jesus Christ, not a true realization of Him. This is the first step in the wrong direction. All these things we are seeking are simply effects, and yet we try to make them causes.

"Yes, I think it is right," Peter said, ". . . to stir you up by reminding you . . ." (2 Peter 1:13). It is a most disturbing thing to be hit squarely in the stomach by someone being used of God to stir us up—someone who is full of spiritual activity. Simple active work and spiritual activity are not the same thing. Active work can actually be the counterfeit of spiritual activity. The real danger in spiritual laziness is that we do not want to be stirred up—all we want to hear about is a spiritual retirement from the world. Yet Jesus Christ never encourages the idea of retirement—He says, "Go and tell My brethren . . ." (Matthew 28:10).

THE SPIRITUALLY
VIGOROUS SAINT

". . . that I may know Him . . ." (Philippians 3:10).

A saint is not to take the initiative toward self-realization, but toward knowing Jesus Christ. A spiritually vigorous saint never believes that his circumstances simply happen at random, nor does he ever think of his life as being divided into the secular and the sacred. He sees every situation in which he finds himself as the means of obtaining a greater knowledge of Jesus Christ, and he has an attitude of unrestrained abandon and total surrender about him. The Holy Spirit is determined that we will have the realization of Jesus Christ in every area of our lives, and He will bring us back to the same point over and over again until we do. Self-realization only leads to the glorification of good works, whereas a saint of God glorifies Jesus Christ through his good works. Whatever we may be doing—even eating, drinking, or washing disciples' feet—we have to take the initiative of realizing and recognizing Jesus Christ in it. Every phase of our life has its counterpart in the life of Jesus. Our Lord realized His relationship to the Father even in the most menial task. "Jesus, knowing . . . that He had come from God and was going to God, . . . took a towel . . . and began to wash the disciples' feet . . ." (John 13:3-5).

The aim of a spiritually vigorous saint is "that I may know Him . . ." Do I know Him where I am today? If not, I am failing Him. I am not here for self-realization, but to know Jesus Christ. In Christian work our initiative and motivation are too often simply the result of realizing that there is work to be done and that we must do it. Yet that is never the attitude of a spiritually vigorous saint. His aim is to achieve the realization of Jesus Christ in every set of circumstances.

THE SPIRITUALLY
SELF-SEEKING CHURCH

". . . till we all come . . . to the measure of
the stature of the fullness of Christ . . ."
(Ephesians 4:13).

Reconciliation means the restoring of the relationship between the entire human race and God, putting it back to what God designed it to be. This is what Jesus Christ did in redemption. The church ceases to be spiritual when it becomes self-seeking, only interested in the development of its own organization. The reconciliation of the human race according to His plan means realizing Him not only in our lives individually, but also in our lives collectively. Jesus Christ sent apostles and teachers for this very purpose—that the corporate Person of Christ and His church, made up of many members, might be brought into being and made known. We are not here to develop a spiritual life of our own, or to enjoy a quiet spiritual retreat. We are here to have the full realization of Jesus Christ, for the purpose of building His body.

Am I building up the body of Christ, or am I only concerned about my own personal development? The essential thing is my personal relationship with Jesus Christ—". . . that *I* may know *Him* . . ." (Philippians 3:10). To fulfill God's perfect design for me requires my total surrender—complete abandonment of myself to Him. Whenever I only want things for myself, the relationship is distorted. And I will suffer great humiliation once I come to acknowledge and understand that I have not really been concerned about realizing Jesus Christ Himself, but only concerned with knowing what He has done for me.

> My goal is God Himself, not joy nor peace,
> Nor even blessing, but Himself, my God.

Am I measuring my life by this standard or by something less?

THE PRICE OF THE VISION

"In the year that King Uzziah died, I saw the Lord . . ." (Isaiah 6:1).

Our soul's personal history with God is often an account of the death of our heroes. Over and over again God has to remove our friends to put Himself in their place, and that is when we falter, fail, and become discouraged. Let me think about this personally—when the person died who represented for me all that God was, did I give up on everything in life? Did I become ill or disheartened? Or did I do as Isaiah did and see the Lord?

My vision of God is dependent upon the condition of my character. My character determines whether or not truth can even be revealed to me. Before I can say, "I saw the Lord," there must be something in my character that conforms to the likeness of God. Until I am born again and really begin to see the kingdom of God, I only see from the perspective of my own biases. What I need is God's surgical procedure—His use of external circumstances to bring about internal purification.

Your priorities must be God first, God second, and God third, until your life is continually face to face with God and no one else is taken into account whatsoever. Your prayer will then be, "In all the world there is no one but You, dear God; there is no one but You."

Keep paying the price. Let God see that you are willing to live up to the vision.

SUFFERING AFFLICTIONS AND GOING THE SECOND MILE

"I tell you not to resist an evil person. But whoever slaps you on your right cheek, turn the other to him also" (Matthew 5:39).

This verse reveals the humiliation of being a Christian. In the natural realm, if a person does not hit back, it is because he is a coward. But in the spiritual realm, it is the very evidence of the Son of God in him if he does not hit back. When you are insulted, you must not only not resent it, but you must make it an opportunity to exhibit the Son of God in your life. And you cannot imitate the nature of Jesus—it is either in you or it is not. A personal insult becomes an opportunity for a saint to reveal the incredible sweetness of the Lord Jesus.

The teaching of the Sermon on the Mount is not, "Do your duty," but is, in effect, "Do what is not your duty." It is not your duty to go the second mile, or to turn the other cheek, but Jesus said that if we are His disciples, we will always do these things. We will not say, "Oh well, I just can't do any more, and I've been so misrepresented and misunderstood." Every time I insist on having my own rights, I hurt the Son of God, while in fact I can prevent Jesus from being hurt if I will take the blow myself. That is the real meaning of filling "up in my flesh what is lacking in the afflictions of Christ . . ." (Colossians 1:24). A disciple realizes that it is his Lord's honor that is at stake in his life, not his own honor.

Never look for righteousness in the other person, but never cease to be righteous yourself. We are always looking for justice, yet the essence of the teaching of the Sermon on the Mount is—Never look for justice, but never cease to give it.

MY LIFE'S SPIRITUAL HONOR AND DUTY

"I am a debtor both to Greeks and to barbarians . . ." (Romans 1:14).

Paul was overwhelmed with the sense of his indebtedness to Jesus Christ, and he spent his life to express it. The greatest inspiration in Paul's life was his view of Jesus Christ as his spiritual creditor. Do I feel that same sense of indebtedness to Christ regarding every unsaved soul? As a saint, my life's spiritual honor and duty is to fulfill my debt to Christ in relation to these lost souls. Every tiny bit of my life that has value I owe to the redemption of Jesus Christ. Am I doing anything to enable Him to bring His redemption into evident reality in the lives of others? I will only be able to do this as the Spirit of God works into me this sense of indebtedness.

I am not a superior person among other people—I am a bondservant of the Lord Jesus. Paul said, ". . . you are not your own . . . you were bought at a price . . ." (1 Corinthians 6:19-20). Paul sold himself to Jesus Christ and he said, in effect, "I am a debtor to everyone on the face of the earth because of the gospel of Jesus; I am free only that I may be an absolute bondservant of His." That is the characteristic of a Christian's life once this level of spiritual honor and duty becomes real. Quit praying about yourself and spend your life for the sake of others as the bondservant of Jesus. That is the true meaning of being broken bread and poured-out wine in real life.

THE CONCEPT OF
DIVINE CONTROL

"... how much more will your Father who is in heaven give good things to those who ask Him!" (Matthew 7:11).

Jesus is laying down the rules of conduct in this passage for those people who have His Spirit. He urges us to keep our minds filled with the concept of God's control over everything, which means that a disciple must maintain an attitude of perfect trust and an eagerness to ask and to seek.

Fill your mind with the thought that God is there. And once your mind is truly filled with that thought, when you experience difficulties it will be as easy as breathing for you to remember, "My heavenly Father knows all about this!" This will be no effort at all, but will be a natural thing for you when difficulties and uncertainties arise. Before you formed this concept of divine control so powerfully in your mind, you used to go from person to person seeking help, but now you go to God about it. Jesus is laying down the rules of conduct for those people who have His Spirit, and it works on the following principle: God is my Father, He loves me, and I will never think of anything that He will forget, so why should I worry?

Jesus said there are times when God cannot lift the darkness from you, but you should trust Him. At times God will appear like an unkind friend, but He is not; He will appear like an unnatural father, but He is not; He will appear like an unjust judge, but He is not. Keep the thought that the mind of God is behind all things strong and growing. Not even the smallest detail of life happens unless God's will is behind it. Therefore, you can rest in perfect confidence in Him. Prayer is not only asking, but is an attitude of the mind which produces the atmosphere in which asking is perfectly natural. "Ask, and it will be given to you ..." (7:7).

THE MIRACLE OF BELIEF

"My speech and my preaching were not with persuasive words of human wisdom . . ." (1 Corinthians 2:4).

Paul was a scholar and an orator of the highest degree; he was not speaking here out of a deep sense of humility, but was saying that when he preached the gospel, he would veil the power of God if he impressed people with the excellency of his speech. Belief in Jesus is a miracle produced only by the effectiveness of redemption, not by impressive speech, nor by wooing and persuading, but only by the sheer unaided power of God. The creative power of redemption comes through the preaching of the gospel, but never because of the personality of the preacher.

Real and effective fasting by a preacher is not fasting from food, but fasting from eloquence, from impressive diction, and from everything else that might hinder the gospel of God being presented. The preacher is there as the representative of God—". . . as though God were pleading through us . . ." (2 Corinthians 5:20). He is there to present the gospel of God. If it is only because of my preaching that people desire to be better, they will never get close to Jesus Christ. Anything that flatters me in my preaching of the gospel will result in making me a traitor to Jesus, and I prevent the creative power of His redemption from doing its work.

"And I, if I am lifted up . . . , will draw all peoples to Myself" (John 12:32).

THE MYSTERY OF BELIEVING

"He said, 'Who are You, Lord?' " (Acts 9:5).

Through the miracle of redemption, Saul of Tarsus was instantly changed from a strong-willed and forceful Pharisee into a humble and devoted bond-servant of the Lord Jesus.

There is nothing miraculous or mysterious about the things we can explain. We control what we are able to explain, consequently it is only natural to seek an explanation for everything. It is not natural to obey, yet it is not necessarily sinful to disobey. There can be no real disobedience, nor any moral virtue in obedience, unless a person recognizes the higher authority of the one giving the orders. If this recognition does not exist, even the one giving the orders may view the other person's disobedience as freedom. If one rules another by saying, "You must do this," and, "You will do that," he breaks the human spirit, making it unfit for God. A person is simply a slave for obeying, unless behind his obedience is the recognition of a holy God.

Many people begin coming to God once they stop being religious, because there is only one master of the human heart—Jesus Christ, not religion. But "Woe is me" if after seeing *Him* I still *will not* obey (Isaiah 6:5, also see verse 1). Jesus will never insist that I obey, but if I don't, I have already begun to sign the death certificate of the Son of God in my soul. When I stand face to face with Jesus Christ and say, "I will not obey," He will never insist. But when I do this, I am backing away from the recreating power of His redemption. It makes no difference to God's grace what an abomination I am, if I will only come to the light. But "Woe is me" if I refuse the light (see John 3:19-21).

THE SUBMISSION OF THE BELIEVER

"You call Me Teacher and Lord, and you say well, for so I am" (John 13:13).

Our Lord never insists on having authority over us. He never says, "You *will* submit to me." No, He leaves us perfectly free to choose—so free, in fact, that we can spit in His face or we can put Him to death, as others have done; and yet He will never say a word. But once His life has been created in me through His redemption, I instantly recognize His right to absolute authority over me. It is a complete and effective domination, in which I acknowledge that "You are *worthy*, O Lord . . ." (Revelation 4:11). It is simply the unworthiness within me that refuses to bow down or to submit to one who is worthy. When I meet someone who is more holy than myself, and I don't recognize his worthiness, nor obey his instructions for me, it is a sign of my own unworthiness being revealed. God teaches us by using these people who are a little better than we are; not better intellectually, but more holy. And He continues to do so until we willingly submit. Then the whole attitude of our life is one of obedience to Him.

If our Lord insisted on our obedience, He would simply become a taskmaster and cease to have any real authority. He never insists on obedience, but when we truly see Him we will instantly obey Him. Then He is easily Lord of our life, and we live in adoration of Him from morning till night. The level of my growth in grace is revealed by the way I look at obedience. We should have a much higher view of the word *obedience*, rescuing it from the mire of the world. Obedience is only possible between people who are equals in their relationship to each other; like the relationship between father and son, not that between master and servant. Jesus showed this relationship by saying, "I and My Father are one" (John 10:30). ". . . though He was a Son, yet He learned obedience by the things which He suffered" (Hebrews 5:8). The Son was obedient as our Redeemer, *because He was the Son*, not in order to become God's Son.

DEPENDENT ON GOD'S PRESENCE

"Those who wait on the LORD . . . shall walk and not faint" (Isaiah 40:31).

There is no thrill for us in walking, yet it is the test for all of our steady and enduring qualities. To "walk and not faint" is the highest stretch possible as a measure of strength. The word *walk* is used in the Bible to express the character of a person— ". . . John . . . looking at Jesus *as He walked* . . . said, 'Behold the Lamb of God!' " (John 1:35–36). There is nothing abstract or obscure in the Bible; everything is vivid and real. God does not say, "Be spiritual," but He says, *"Walk before Me . . ."* (Genesis 17:1).

When we are in an unhealthy condition either physically or emotionally, we always look for thrills in life. In our physical life this leads to our efforts to counterfeit the work of the Holy Spirit; in our emotional life it leads to obsessions and to the destruction of our morality; and in our spiritual life, if we insist on pursuing only thrills, on mounting up "with wings like eagles" (40:31), it will result in the destruction of our spirituality.

Having the reality of God's presence is not dependent on our being in a particular circumstance or place, but is only dependent on our determination to keep the Lord before us continually. Our problems arise when we refuse to place our trust in the reality of His presence. The experience the psalmist speaks of—"We will not fear, even though . . ." (Psalm 46:2)—will be ours once we are grounded on the truth of the reality of God's presence, not just a simple awareness of it, but an understanding of the reality of it. Then we will exclaim, "He has been here all the time!" At critical moments in our lives it is necessary to ask God for guidance, but it should be unnecessary to be constantly saying, "Oh, Lord, direct me in this, and in that." Of course He will, and in fact, He is doing it already! If our everyday decisions are not according to His will, He will press through them, bringing restraint to our spirit. Then we must be quiet and wait for the direction of His presence.

The Doorway to the Kingdom

"Blessed are the poor in spirit . . ." (Matthew 5:3).

Beware of thinking of our Lord as only a teacher. If Jesus Christ is only a teacher, then all He can do is frustrate me by setting a standard before me I cannot attain. What is the point of presenting me with such a lofty ideal if I cannot possibly come close to reaching it? I would be happier if I never knew it. What good is there in telling me to be what I can never be—to be "pure in heart" (5:8), to do more than my duty, or to be completely devoted to God? I must know Jesus Christ as my Savior before His teaching has any meaning for me other than that of a lofty ideal which only leads to despair. But when I am born again by the Spirit of God, I know that Jesus Christ did not come only to *teach*—He came to *make me what He teaches I should be*. The redemption means that Jesus Christ can place within anyone the same nature that ruled His own life, and all the standards God gives us are based on that nature.

The teaching of the Sermon on the Mount produces a sense of despair in the natural man—exactly what Jesus means for it to do. As long as we have some self-righteous idea that we can carry out our Lord's teaching, God will allow us to continue until we expose our own ignorance by stumbling over some obstacle in our way. Only then are we willing to come to Him as paupers and receive from Him. "Blessed are the poor in spirit . . . ." This is the first principle in the kingdom of God. The underlying foundation of Jesus Christ's kingdom is poverty, not possessions; not making decisions for Jesus, but having such a sense of absolute futility that we finally admit, "Lord, I cannot even begin to do it." Then Jesus says, "Blessed are you . . ." (5:11). This is the doorway to the kingdom, and yet it takes us so long to believe that we are actually poor! The knowledge of our own poverty is what brings us to the proper place where Jesus Christ accomplishes His work.

SANCTIFICATION

"This is the will of God, your sanctification . . ." (1 Thessalonians 4:3).

The Death Side. In sanctification God has to deal with us on the death side as well as on the life side. Sanctification requires our coming to the place of death, but many of us spend so much time there that we become morbid. There is always a tremendous battle before sanctification is realized—something within us pushing with resentment against the demands of Christ. When the Holy Spirit begins to show us what sanctification means, the struggle starts immediately. Jesus said, "If anyone comes to Me and does not hate . . . his own life . . . he cannot be My disciple" (Luke 14:26).

In the process of sanctification, the Spirit of God will strip me down until there is nothing left but myself, and that is the place of death. Am I willing to be myself and nothing more? Am I willing to have no friends, no father, no brother, and no self-interest—simply to be ready for death? That is the condition required for sanctification. No wonder Jesus said, "I did not come to bring peace but a sword" (Matthew 10:34). This is where the battle comes, and where so many of us falter. We refuse to be identified with the death of Jesus Christ on this point. We say, "But this is so strict. Surely He does not require that of me." Our Lord *is* strict, and He *does* require that of us.

Am I willing to reduce myself down to simply "me"? Am I determined enough to strip myself of all that my friends think of me, and all that I think of myself? Am I willing and determined to hand over my simple naked self to God? Once I am, He will immediately sanctify me completely, and my life will be free from being determined and persistent toward anything except God (see 1 Thessalonians 5:23-24).

When I pray, "Lord, show me what sanctification means for me," He will show me. It means being made one with Jesus. Sanctification is not something Jesus puts in me—it is *Himself* in me (see 1 Corinthians 1:30).

SANCTIFICATION

**"But of Him you are in Christ Jesus, who became for us . . . sanctification . . ."
(1 Corinthians 1:30).**

The Life Side. The mystery of sanctification is that the perfect qualities of Jesus Christ are imparted as a gift to me, not gradually, but instantly once I enter by faith into the realization that He "became for [me] . . . sanctification . . . ." Sanctification means nothing less than the holiness of Jesus becoming mine and being exhibited in my life.

The most wonderful secret of living a holy life does not lie in imitating Jesus, but in letting the perfect qualities of Jesus exhibit themselves in my human flesh. Sanctification is "Christ in you . . ." (Colossians 1:27). It is *His* wonderful life that is imparted to me in sanctification—imparted by faith as a sovereign gift of God's grace. Am I willing for God to make sanctification as real in me as it is in His Word?

Sanctification means the impartation of the holy qualities of Jesus Christ to me. It is the gift of His patience, love, holiness, faith, purity, and godliness that is exhibited in and through every sanctified soul. Sanctification is not drawing from Jesus the power to be holy—it is drawing from Jesus the very holiness that was exhibited in Him, and that He now exhibits in me. Sanctification is an impartation, not an imitation. Imitation is something altogether different. The perfection of everything is in Jesus Christ, and the mystery of sanctification is that all the perfect qualities of Jesus are at my disposal. Consequently, I slowly but surely begin to live a life of inexpressible order, soundness, and holiness—". . . kept by the power of God . . ." (1 Peter 1:5).

His Nature and Our Motives

". . . unless your righteousness exceeds the righteousness of the scribes and Pharisees, you will by no means enter the kingdom of heaven" (Matthew 5:20).

The characteristic of a disciple is not that he does good things, but that he is good in his motives, having been made good by the supernatural grace of God. The only thing that exceeds right-*doing* is right-*being*. Jesus Christ came to place within anyone who would let Him a new heredity that would have a righteousness exceeding that of the scribes and Pharisees. Jesus is saying, "If you are My disciple, you must be right not only in your actions, but also in your motives, your aspirations, and in the deep recesses of the thoughts of your mind." Your motives must be so pure that God Almighty can see nothing to rebuke. Who can stand in the eternal light of God and have nothing for Him to rebuke? Only the Son of God, and Jesus Christ claims that through His redemption He can place within anyone His own nature and make that person as pure and as simple as a child. The purity that God demands is impossible unless I can be remade within, and that is exactly what Jesus has undertaken to do through His redemption.

No one can make himself pure by obeying laws. Jesus Christ does not give us rules and regulations—He gives us His teachings which are truths that can only be interpreted by His nature which He places within us. The great wonder of Jesus Christ's salvation is that He changes our heredity. He does not change human nature—He changes its source, and thereby its motives as well.

AM I BLESSED LIKE THIS?

"Blessed are . . ." (Matthew 5:3–11).

When we first read the statements of Jesus, they seem wonderfully simple and unstartling, and they sink unnoticed into our subconscious minds. For instance, the Beatitudes initially seem to be merely soothing and beautiful precepts for overly spiritual and seemingly useless people, but of very little practical use in the rigid, fast-paced workdays of the world in which *we* live. We soon find, however, that the Beatitudes contain the "dynamite" of the Holy Spirit. And they "explode" when the circumstances of our lives cause them to do so. When the Holy Spirit brings to our remembrance one of the Beatitudes, we say, "What a startling statement that is!" Then we must decide whether or not we will accept the tremendous spiritual upheaval that will be produced in our circumstances if we obey His words. That is the way the Spirit of God works. We do not need to be born again to apply the Sermon on the Mount literally. The literal interpretation of the Sermon on the Mount is as easy as child's play. But the interpretation by the Spirit of God as He applies our Lord's statements to our circumstances is the strict and difficult work of a saint.

The teachings of Jesus are all out of proportion when compared to our natural way of looking at things, and they come to us initially with astonishing discomfort. We gradually have to conform our walk and conversation to the precepts of Jesus Christ as the Holy Spirit applies them to our circumstances. The Sermon on the Mount is not a set of rules and regulations—it is a picture of the life we will live when the Holy Spirit is having His unhindered way with us.

THE WAY TO PURITY

> "Those things which proceed out of the mouth come from the heart . . . . For out of the heart proceed evil thoughts, murders, adulteries, fornications, thefts, false witness, blasphemies. These are the things which defile a man . . ." (Matthew 15:18-20).

I nitially we trust in our ignorance, calling it innocence, and next we trust our innocence, calling it purity. Then when we hear these strong statements from our Lord, we shrink back, saying, "But I never felt any of those awful things in my heart." We resent what He reveals. Either Jesus Christ is the supreme authority on the human heart, or He is not worth paying any attention to. Am I prepared to trust the penetration of His Word into my heart, or would I prefer to trust my own "innocent ignorance"? If I will take an honest look at myself, becoming fully aware of my so-called innocence and putting it to the test, I am very likely to have a rude awakening that what Jesus Christ said is true, and I will be appalled at the possibilities of the evil and the wrong within me. But as long as I remain under the false security of my own "innocence," I am living in a fool's paradise. If I have never been an openly rude and abusive person, the only reason is my own cowardice coupled with the sense of protection I receive from living a civilized life. But when I am open and completely exposed before God, I find that Jesus Christ is right in His diagnosis of me.

The only thing that truly provides protection is the redemption of Jesus Christ. If I will simply hand myself over to Him, I will never have to experience the terrible possibilities that lie within my heart. Purity is something far too deep for me to arrive at naturally. But when the Holy Spirit comes into me, He brings into the center of my personal life the very Spirit that was exhibited in the life of Jesus Christ, namely, the *Holy* Spirit, which is absolute unblemished purity.

THE WAY TO KNOWLEDGE

"If anyone wills to do His will, he shall know concerning the doctrine . . ." (John 7:17).

The golden rule to follow to obtain spiritual understanding is not one of intellectual pursuit, but one of obedience. If a person wants scientific knowledge, then intellectual curiosity must be his guide. But if he desires knowledge and insight into the teachings of Jesus Christ, he can only obtain it through obedience. If spiritual things seem dark and hidden to me, then I can be sure that there is a point of disobedience somewhere in my life. Intellectual darkness is the result of ignorance, but spiritual darkness is the result of something that I do not intend to obey.

No one ever receives a word from God without instantly being put to the test regarding it. We disobey and then wonder why we are not growing spiritually. Jesus said, "If you bring your gift to the altar, and there remember that your brother has something against you, leave your gift there before the altar, and go your way. First be reconciled to your brother, and then come and offer your gift" (Matthew 5:23-24). He is saying, in essence, "Don't say another word to me; first be obedient by making things right." The teachings of Jesus hit us where we live. We cannot stand as impostors before Him for even one second. He instructs us down to the very last detail. The Spirit of God uncovers our spirit of self-vindication and makes us sensitive to things that we have never even thought of before.

When Jesus drives something home to you through His Word, don't try to evade it. If you do, you will become a religious impostor. Examine the things you tend simply to shrug your shoulders about, and where you have refused to be obedient, and you will know why you are not growing spiritually. As Jesus said, *"First . . . go . . . ."* Even at the risk of being thought of as fanatical, you must obey what God tells you.

GOD'S PURPOSE OR MINE?

"He made His disciples get into the boat and go before Him to the other side . . ." (Mark 6:45).

We tend to think that if Jesus Christ compels us to do something and we are obedient to Him, He will lead us to great success. We should never have the thought that our dreams of success are God's purpose for us. In fact, His purpose may be exactly the opposite. We have the idea that God is leading us toward a particular end or a desired goal, but He is not. The question of whether or not we arrive at a particular goal is of little importance, and reaching it becomes merely an episode along the way. What we see as only the process of reaching a particular end, God sees as the goal itself.

What is my vision of God's purpose for me? Whatever it may be, His purpose is for me to depend on Him and on His power *now*. If I can stay calm, faithful, and unconfused while in the middle of the turmoil of life, the goal of the purpose of God is being accomplished in me. God is not working toward a particular finish—His purpose is the process itself. What He desires for me is that I see "Him walking on the sea" with no shore, no success, nor goal in sight, but simply having the absolute certainty that everything is all right because I see "Him walking on the sea" (6:49). It is the process, not the outcome, that is glorifying to God.

God's training is for now, not later. His purpose is for this very minute, not for sometime in the future. We have nothing to do with what will follow our obedience, and we are wrong to concern ourselves with it. What people call preparation, God sees as the goal itself.

God's purpose is to enable me to see that He can walk on the storms of my life right now. If we have a further goal in mind, we are not paying enough attention to the present time. However, if we realize that moment-by-moment obedience is the goal, then each moment as it comes is precious.

DO YOU SEE JESUS IN YOUR CLOUDS?

"Behold, He is coming with clouds . . ."
(Revelation 1:7).

I n the Bible clouds are always associated with God. Clouds are the sorrows, sufferings, or providential circumstances, within or without our personal lives, which actually seem to contradict the sovereignty of God. Yet it is through these very clouds that the Spirit of God is teaching us how to walk by faith. If there were never any clouds in our lives, we would have no faith. "The clouds are the dust of His feet" (Nahum 1:3). They are a sign that God is there. What a revelation it is to know that sorrow, bereavement, and suffering are actually the clouds that come along with God! God cannot come near us without clouds—He does not come in clear-shining brightness.

It is not true to say that God wants to teach us something in our trials. Through every cloud He brings our way, He wants us to *unlearn* something. His purpose in using the cloud is to simplify our beliefs until our relationship with Him is exactly like that of a child—a relationship simply between God and our own souls, and where other people are but shadows. Until other people become shadows to us, clouds and darkness will be ours every once in a while. Is our relationship with God becoming more simple than it has ever been?

There is a connection between the strange providential circumstances allowed by God and what we know of Him, and we have to learn to interpret the mysteries of life in the light of our knowledge of God. Until we can come face to face with the deepest, darkest fact of life without damaging our view of God's character, we do not yet know Him.

". . . they were fearful as they entered the cloud" (Luke 9:34). Is there anyone except Jesus in your cloud? If so, it will only get darker until you get to the place where there is "no one anymore, but only Jesus . . ." (Mark 9:8; also see verses 2–7).

THE TEACHING OF DISILLUSIONMENT

"Jesus did not commit Himself to them . . . , for He knew what was in man" (John 2:24–25).

Disillusionment means having no more misconceptions, false impressions, and false judgments in life; it means being free from these deceptions. However, though no longer deceived, our experience of disillusionment may actually leave us cynical and overly critical in our judgment of others. But the disillusionment that comes from God brings us to the point where we see people as they really are, yet without any cynicism or any stinging and bitter criticism. Many of the things in life that inflict the greatest injury, grief, or pain, stem from the fact that we suffer from illusions. We are not true to one another as *facts*, seeing each other as we really are; we are only true to our misconceived *ideas* of one another. According to our thinking, everything is either delightful and good, or it is evil, malicious, and cowardly.

Refusing to be disillusioned is the cause of much of the suffering of human life. And this is how that suffering happens—if we love someone, but do not love God, we demand total perfection and righteousness from that person, and when we do not get it we become cruel and vindictive; yet we are demanding of a human being something which he or she cannot possibly give. There is only one Being who can completely satisfy to the absolute depth of the hurting human heart, and that is the Lord Jesus Christ. Our Lord is so obviously uncompromising with regard to every human relationship because He knows that every relationship that is not based on faithfulness to Himself will end in disaster. Our Lord trusted no one, and never placed His faith in people, yet He was never suspicious or bitter. Our Lord's confidence in God, and in what God's grace could do for anyone, was so perfect that He never despaired, never giving up hope for any person. If our trust is placed in human beings, we will end up despairing of everyone.

BECOMING ENTIRELY HIS

"Let patience have its perfect work, that you may be perfect and complete, lacking nothing" (James 1:4).

Many of us appear to be all right in general, but there are still some areas in which we are careless and lazy; it is not a matter of sin, but the remnants of our carnal life that tend to make us careless. Carelessness is an insult to the Holy Spirit. We should have no carelessness about us either in the way we worship God, or even in the way we eat and drink.

Not only must our relationship to God be right, but the outward expression of that relationship must also be right. Ultimately, God will allow nothing to escape; every detail of our lives is under His scrutiny. God will bring us back in countless ways to the same point over and over again. And He never tires of bringing us back to that one point until we learn the lesson, because His purpose is to produce the finished product. It may be a problem arising from our impulsive nature, but again and again, with the most persistent patience, God has brought us back to that one particular point. Or the problem may be our idle and wandering thinking, or our independent nature and self-interest. Through this process, God is trying to impress upon us the one thing that is not entirely right in our lives.

We have been having a wonderful time in our studies over the revealed truth of God's redemption, and our hearts are perfect toward Him. And His wonderful work in us makes us know that overall we are right with Him. "Let patience have its perfect work . . . ." The Holy Spirit speaking through James said, "Now let your patience become a finished product." Beware of becoming careless over the small details of life and saying, "Oh, that will have to do for now." Whatever it may be, God will point it out with persistence until we become entirely His.

LEARNING ABOUT HIS WAYS

"When Jesus finished commanding His twelve disciples . . . He departed from there to teach and to preach in their cities" (Matthew 11:1).

He comes where He commands us to leave. If you stayed home when God told you to go because you were so concerned about your own people there, then you actually robbed them of the teaching of Jesus Christ Himself. When you obeyed and left all the consequences to God, the Lord went into your city to teach, but as long as you were disobedient, you blocked His way. Watch where you begin to debate with Him and put what you call your duty into competition with His commands. If you say, "I know that He told me to go, but my duty is here," it simply means that you do not believe that Jesus means what He says.

He teaches where He instructs us not to teach.

"Master . . . let us make three tabernacles . . ." (Luke 9:33).

Are we playing the part of an amateur providence, trying to play God's role in the lives of others? Are we so noisy in our instruction of other people that God cannot get near them? We must learn to keep our mouths shut and our spirits alert. God wants to instruct us regarding His Son, and He wants to turn our times of prayer into mounts of transfiguration. When we become certain that God is going to work in a particular way, He will never work in that way again.

He works where He sends us to wait.

". . . tarry . . . until . . ." (Luke 24:49).

"Wait on the LORD" and He will work (Psalm 37:34). But don't wait sulking spiritually and feeling sorry for yourself, just because you can't see one inch in front of you! Are we detached enough from our own spiritual fits of emotion to "wait patiently for Him"? (37:7). Waiting is not sitting with folded hands doing nothing, but it is learning to do what we are told.

These are some of the facets of His ways that we rarely recognize.

THE TEACHING OF ADVERSITY

"In the world you will have tribulation; but be of good cheer, I have overcome the world" (John 16:33).

The typical view of the Christian life is that it means being delivered from all adversity. But it actually means being delivered *in* adversity, which is something very different. "He who dwells in the secret place of the Most High shall abide under the shadow of the Almighty. No evil shall befall you, nor shall any plague come near your dwelling . . ." (Psalm 91:1, 10)—the place where you are at one with God.

If you are a child of God, you will certainly encounter adversities, but Jesus says you should not be surprised when they come. "In the world you will have tribulation; but be of good cheer, I have overcome the world." He is saying, "There is nothing for you to fear." The same people who refused to talk about their adversities before they were saved often complain and worry after being born again because they have the wrong idea of what it means to live the life of a saint.

God does not give us overcoming life—He gives us life as we overcome. The strain of life is what builds our strength. If there is no strain, there will be no strength. Are you asking God to give you life, liberty, and joy? He cannot, unless you are willing to accept the strain. And once you face the strain, you will immediately get the strength. Overcome your own timidity and take the first step. Then God will give you nourishment—"To him who overcomes I will give to eat from the tree of life . . ." (Revelation 2:7). If you completely give of yourself physically, you become exhausted. But when you give of yourself spiritually, you get more strength. God never gives us strength for tomorrow, or for the next hour, but only for the strain of the moment. Our temptation is to face adversities from the standpoint of our own common sense. But a saint can "be of good cheer" even when seemingly defeated by adversities, because victory is absurdly impossible to everyone, except God.

THE COMPELLING
PURPOSE OF GOD

"He . . . said to them, 'Behold, we are going up to Jerusalem . . .'" (Luke 18:31).

Jerusalem, in the life of our Lord, represents the place where He reached the culmination of His Father's will. Jesus said, "I do not seek My own will but the will of the Father who sent Me" (John 5:30). Seeking to do "the will of the Father" was the one dominating concern throughout our Lord's life. And whatever He encountered along the way, whether joy or sorrow, success or failure, He was never deterred from that purpose. ". . . He steadfastly set His face to go to Jerusalem . . ." (Luke 9:51).

The greatest thing for us to remember is that we go up to Jerusalem to fulfill God's purpose, not our own. In the natural life our ambitions are our own, but in the Christian life we have no goals of our own. We talk so much today about our decisions for Christ, our determination to be Christians, and our decisions for this and that, but in the New Testament the only aspect that is brought out is the compelling purpose of God. "You did not choose Me, but I chose you . . ." (John 15:16).

We are not taken into a conscious agreement with God's purpose—we are taken into God's purpose with no awareness of it at all. We have no idea what God's goal may be; as we continue, His purpose becomes even more and more vague. God's aim appears to have missed the mark, because we are too nearsighted to see the target at which He is aiming. At the beginning of the Christian life, we have our own ideas as to what God's purpose is. We say, "God means for me to go over there," and, "God has called me to do this special work." We do what we think is right, and yet the compelling purpose of God remains upon us. The work we do is of no account when compared with the compelling purpose of God. It is simply the scaffolding surrounding His work and His plan. "He took the twelve aside . . ." (Luke 18:31). God takes us aside all the time. We have not yet understood all there is to know of the compelling purpose of God.

THE BRAVE FRIENDSHIP OF GOD

"He took the twelve aside . . ." (Luke 18:31).

Oh, the bravery of God in trusting us! Do you say, "But He has been unwise to choose me, because there is nothing good in me and I have no value"? That is exactly why He chose you. As long as you think that you are of value to Him He cannot choose you, because you have purposes of your own to serve. But if you will allow Him to take you to the end of your own self-sufficiency, then He can choose you to go with Him "to Jerusalem" (18:31). And that will mean the fulfillment of purposes which He does not discuss with you.

We tend to say that because a person has natural ability, he will make a good Christian. It is not a matter of our equipment, but a matter of our poverty; not of what we bring with us, but of what God puts into us; not a matter of natural virtues, of strength of character, of knowledge, or of experience—all of that is of no avail in this concern. The only thing of value is being taken into the compelling purpose of God and being made His friends (see 1 Corinthians 1:26-31). God's friendship is with people who know their poverty. He can accomplish nothing with the person who thinks that he is of use to God. As Christians we are not here for our own purpose at all—we are here for the purpose of God, and the two are not the same. We do not know what God's compelling purpose is, but whatever happens, we must maintain our relationship with Him. We must never allow anything to damage our relationship with God, but if something does damage it, we must take the time to make it right again. The most important aspect of Christianity is not the work we do, but the relationship we maintain and the surrounding influence and qualities produced by that relationship. That is all God asks us to give our attention to, and it is the one thing that is continually under attack.

THE BEWILDERING CALL OF GOD

" '. . . and all things that are written by the prophets concerning the Son of Man will be accomplished.' . . . But they understood none of these things . . ." (Luke 18:31, 34).

God called Jesus Christ to what seemed absolute disaster. And Jesus Christ called His disciples to see Him put to death, leading every one of them to the place where their hearts were broken. His life was an absolute failure from every standpoint except God's. But what seemed to be failure from man's standpoint was a triumph from God's standpoint, because God's purpose is never the same as man's purpose.

This bewildering call of God comes into our lives as well. The call of God can never be understood absolutely or explained externally; it is a call that can only be perceived and understood internally by our true inner nature. The call of God is like the call of the sea—no one hears it except the person who has the nature of the sea in him. What God calls us to cannot be definitely stated, because His call is simply to be His friend to accomplish His own purposes. Our real test is in truly believing that God knows what He desires. The things that happen do not happen by chance—they happen entirely by the decree of God. God is sovereignly working out His own purposes.

If we are in fellowship and oneness with God and recognize that He is taking us into His purposes, then we will no longer strive to find out what His purposes are. As we grow in the Christian life, it becomes simpler to us, because we are less inclined to say, "I wonder why God allowed this or that?" And we begin to see that the compelling purpose of God lies behind everything in life, and that God is divinely shaping us into oneness with that purpose. A Christian is someone who trusts in the knowledge and the wisdom of God, not in his own abilities. If we have a purpose of our own, it destroys the simplicity and the calm, relaxed pace which should be characteristic of the children of God.

THE CROSS IN PRAYER

**"In that day you will ask in My name . . ."
(John 16:26).**

W e too often think of the Cross of Christ as
something we have to get through, yet we get
through for the purpose of getting *into* it. The
Cross represents only one thing for us—complete, entire,
absolute identification with the Lord Jesus Christ—and
there is nothing in which this identification is more real
to us than in prayer.

"Your Father knows the things you have need of
before you ask Him" (Matthew 6:8). Then why should
we ask? The point of prayer is not to get answers from
God, but to have perfect and complete oneness with
Him. If we pray only because we want answers, we will
become irritated and angry with God. We receive an
answer every time we pray, but it does not always come
in the way we expect, and our spiritual irritation shows
our refusal to identify ourselves truly with our Lord
in prayer. We are not here to prove that God answers
prayer, but to be living trophies of God's grace.

". . . I do not say to you that I shall pray the Father
for you; for the Father Himself loves you . . ." (John
16:26-27). Have you reached such a level of intimacy
with God that the only thing that can account for your
prayer life is that it has become one with the prayer life
of Jesus Christ? Has our Lord exchanged your life with
His vital life? If so, then "in that day" you will be so
closely identified with Jesus that there will be no distinction.

When prayer seems to be unanswered, beware of
trying to place the blame on someone else. That is always
a trap of Satan. When you seem to have no answer, there
is always a reason—God uses these times to give you deep
personal instruction, and it is not for anyone else but
you.

PRAYER IN THE FATHER'S HOUSE

". . . they found Him in the temple . . . . And He said to them, '. . . Did you not know that I must be about My Father's business?' " (Luke 2:46, 49).

Our Lord's childhood was not immaturity waiting to grow into manhood—His childhood is an eternal fact. Am I a holy, innocent child of God as a result of my identification with my Lord and Savior? Do I look at my life as being in my Father's house? Is the Son of God living in His Father's house within me?

The only abiding reality is God Himself, and His order comes to me moment by moment. Am I continually in touch with the reality of God, or do I pray only when things have gone wrong—when there is some disturbance in my life? I must learn to identify myself closely with my Lord in ways of holy fellowship and oneness that some of us have not yet even begun to learn. ". . . I must be about My Father's business"—and I must learn to live every moment of my life in my Father's house.

Think about your own circumstances. Are you so closely identified with the Lord's life that you are simply a child of God, continually talking to Him and realizing that everything comes from His hands? Is the eternal Child in you living in His Father's house? Is the grace of His ministering life being worked out through you in your home, your business, and in your circle of friends? Have you been wondering why you are going through certain circumstances? In fact, it is not that *you* have to go through them. It is because of your relationship with the Son of God who comes, through the providential will of His Father, into your life. You must allow *Him* to have His way with you, staying in perfect oneness with Him.

The life of your Lord is to become your vital, simple life, and the way He worked and lived among people while here on earth must be the way He works and lives in you.

AUGUST 7

PRAYER IN THE FATHER'S HONOR

". . . that Holy One who is to be born will be called the Son of God" (Luke 1:35).

If the Son of God has been born into my human flesh, then am I allowing His holy innocence, simplicity, and oneness with the Father the opportunity to exhibit itself in me? What was true of the Virgin Mary in the history of the Son of God's birth on earth is true of every saint. God's Son is born into me through the direct act of God; then I as His child must exercise the right of a child—the right of always being face to face with my Father through prayer. Do I find myself continually saying in amazement to the commonsense part of my life, "Why did you want me to turn here or to go over there? 'Did you not know that I must be about My Father's business?' " (Luke 2:49). Whatever our circumstances may be, that holy, innocent, and eternal Child must be in contact with His Father.

Am I simple enough to identify myself with my Lord in this way? Is He having His wonderful way with me? Is God's will being fulfilled in that His Son has been formed in me (see Galatians 4:19), or have I carefully pushed Him to one side? Oh, the noisy outcry of today! Why does everyone seem to be crying out so loudly? People today are crying out for the Son of God to be put to death. There is no room here for God's Son right now—no room for quiet, holy fellowship and oneness with the Father.

Is the Son of God praying in me, bringing honor to the Father, or am I dictating my demands to Him? Is He ministering in me as He did in the time of His manhood here on earth? Is God's Son in me going through His passion, suffering so that His own purposes might be fulfilled? The more a person knows of the inner life of God's most mature saints, the more he sees what God's purpose really is: to ". . . fill up in my flesh what is lacking in the afflictions of Christ . . ." (Colossians 1:24). And when we think of what it takes to "fill up," there is always something yet to be done.

Prayer in the Father's Hearing

"Jesus lifted up His eyes and said, 'Father, I thank You that You have heard Me' " (John 11:41).

When the Son of God prays, He is mindful and consciously aware of only His Father. God always hears the prayers of His Son, and if the Son of God has been formed in me (see Galatians 4:19) the Father will always hear my prayers. But I must see to it that the Son of God is exhibited in my human flesh. ". . . your body is the temple of the Holy Spirit . . . " (1 Corinthians 6:19), that is, your body is the Bethlehem of God's Son. Is the Son of God being given His opportunity to work in me? Is the direct simplicity of His life being worked out in me exactly as it was worked out in His life while here on earth? When I come into contact with the everyday occurrences of life as an ordinary human being, is the prayer of God's eternal Son to His Father being prayed in me? Jesus says, "In that day you will ask in My name . . ." (John 16:26). What day does He mean? He is referring to the day when the Holy Spirit has come to me and made me one with my Lord.

Is the Lord Jesus Christ being abundantly satisfied by your life, or are you exhibiting a walk of spiritual pride before Him? Never let your common sense become so prominent and forceful that it pushes the Son of God to one side. Common sense is a gift that God gave to our human nature—but common sense is not the gift of His Son. Supernatural sense is the gift of His Son, and we should never put our common sense on the throne. The Son always recognizes and identifies with the Father, but common sense has never yet done so and never will. Our ordinary abilities will never worship God unless they are transformed by the indwelling Son of God. We must make sure that our human flesh is kept in perfect submission to Him, allowing Him to work through it moment by moment. Are we living at such a level of human dependence upon Jesus Christ that His life is being exhibited moment by moment in us?

THE HOLY SUFFERING
OF THE SAINT

> "Let those who suffer according to the will of God commit their souls to Him in doing good . . ." (1 Peter 4:19).

Choosing to suffer means that there must be something wrong with you, but choosing God's will—even if it means you will suffer—is something very different. No normal, healthy saint ever chooses suffering; he simply chooses God's will, just as Jesus did, whether it means suffering or not. And no saint should ever dare to interfere with the lesson of suffering being taught in another saint's life.

The saint who satisfies the heart of Jesus will make other saints strong and mature for God. But the people used to strengthen us are never those who sympathize with us; in fact, we are hindered by those who give us their sympathy, because sympathy only serves to weaken us. No one better understands a saint than the saint who is as close and as intimate with Jesus as possible. If we accept the sympathy of another saint, our spontaneous feeling is, "God is dealing too harshly with me and making my life too difficult." That is why Jesus said that self-pity was of the devil (see Matthew 16:21-23). We must be merciful to God's reputation. It is easy for us to tarnish God's character because He never argues back; He never tries to defend or vindicate Himself. Beware of thinking that Jesus needed sympathy during His life on earth. He refused the sympathy of people because in His great wisdom He knew that no one on earth understood His purpose (see 16:23). He accepted only the sympathy of His Father and the angels (see Luke 15:10).

Look at God's incredible waste of His saints, according to the world's judgment. God seems to plant His saints in the most useless places. And then we say, "God intends for me to be here because I am so useful to Him." Yet Jesus never measured His life by how or where He was of the greatest use. God places His saints where they will bring the most glory to Him, and we are totally incapable of judging where that may be.

THIS EXPERIENCE MUST COME

"Elijah went up by a whirlwind into heaven. And Elisha . . . saw him no more" (2 Kings 2:11–12).

It is not wrong for you to depend on your "Elijah" for as long as God gives him to you. But remember that the time will come when he must leave and will no longer be your guide and your leader, because God does not intend for him to stay. Even the thought of that causes you to say, "I cannot continue without my 'Elijah.'" Yet God says you must continue.

Alone at Your "Jordan" (2:14). The Jordan River represents the type of separation where you have no fellowship with anyone else, and where no one else can take your responsibility from you. You now have to put to the test what you learned when you were with your "Elijah." You have been to the Jordan over and over again with Elijah, but now you are facing it alone. There is no use in saying that you cannot go—the experience is here, and you must go. If you truly want to know whether or not God is the God your faith believes Him to be, then go through your "Jordan" alone.

Alone at Your "Jericho" (2:15). Jericho represents the place where you have seen your "Elijah" do great things. Yet when you come alone to your "Jericho," you have a strong reluctance to take the initiative and trust in God, wanting, instead, for someone else to take it for you. But if you remain true to what you learned while with your "Elijah," you will receive a sign, as Elisha did, that God is with you.

Alone at Your "Bethel" (2:23). At your "Bethel" you will find yourself at your wits' end but at the beginning of God's wisdom. When you come to your wits' end and feel inclined to panic—don't! Stand true to God and He will bring out His truth in a way that will make your life an expression of worship. Put into practice what you learned while with your "Elijah"—use his mantle and pray (see 2:13–14). Make a determination to trust in God, and do not even look for Elijah anymore.

THE THEOLOGY OF
RESTING IN GOD

**"Why are you fearful, O you of little faith?"
(Matthew 8:26).**

When we are afraid, the least we can do is pray to God. But our Lord has a right to expect that those who name His name have an underlying confidence in Him. God expects His children to be so confident in Him that in any crisis they are the ones who are reliable. Yet our trust is only in God up to a certain point, then we turn back to the elementary panic-stricken prayers of those people who do not even know God. We come to our wits' end, showing that we don't have even the slightest amount of confidence in Him or in His sovereign control of the world. To us He seems to be asleep, and we can see nothing but giant, breaking waves on the sea ahead of us.

". . . O you of little faith!" What a stinging pain must have shot through the disciples as they surely thought to themselves, "We missed the mark again!" And what a sharp pain will go through us when we suddenly realize that we could have produced complete and utter joy in the heart of Jesus by remaining absolutely confident in Him, in spite of what we were facing.

There are times when there is no storm or crisis in our lives, and we do all that is humanly possible. But it is when a crisis arises that we instantly reveal upon whom we rely. If we have been learning to worship God and to place our trust in Him, the crisis will reveal that we can go to the point of breaking, yet without breaking our confidence in Him.

We have been talking quite a lot about sanctification, but what will be the result in our lives? It will be expressed in our lives as a peaceful resting in God, which means a total oneness with Him. And this oneness will make us not only blameless in His sight, but also a profound joy to Him.

"DO NOT QUENCH THE SPIRIT"

"Do not quench the Spirit" (1 Thessalonians 5:19).

The voice of the Spirit of God is as gentle as a summer breeze—so gentle that unless you are living in complete fellowship and oneness with God, you will never hear it. The sense of warning and restraint that the Spirit gives comes to us in the most amazingly gentle ways. And if you are not sensitive enough to detect His voice, you will quench it, and your spiritual life will be impaired. This sense of restraint will always come as a "still small voice" (1 Kings 19:12), so faint that no one except a saint of God will notice it.

Beware if in sharing your personal testimony you continually have to look back, saying, "Once, a number of years ago, I was saved." If you have put your "hand to the plow" and are walking in the light, there is no "looking back"—the past is instilled into the present wonder of fellowship and oneness with God (Luke 9:62; also see 1 John 1:6-7). If you get out of the light, you become a sentimental Christian, and live only on your memories, and your testimony will have a hard metallic ring to it. Beware of trying to cover up your present refusal to "walk in the light" by recalling your past experiences when you did "walk in the light" (1 John 1:7). Whenever the Spirit gives you that sense of restraint, call a halt and make things right, or else you will go on quenching and grieving Him without even knowing it.

Suppose God brings you to a crisis and you almost endure it, but not completely. He will engineer the crisis again, but this time some of the intensity will be lost. You will have less discernment and more humiliation at having disobeyed. If you continue to grieve His Spirit, there will come a time when that crisis cannot be repeated, because you have totally quenched Him. But if you will go on through the crisis, your life will become a hymn of praise to God. Never become attached to anything that continues to hurt God. For you to be free of it, God must be allowed to hurt whatever it may be.

THE DISCIPLINE OF THE LORD

"My son, do not despise the chastening of the LORD, nor be discouraged when you are rebuked by Him" (Hebrews 12:5).

It is very easy to grieve the Spirit of God; we do it by despising the discipline of the Lord, or by becoming discouraged when He rebukes us. If our experience of being set apart from sin and being made holy through the process of sanctification is still very shallow, we tend to mistake the reality of God for something else. And when the Spirit of God gives us a sense of warning or restraint, we are apt to say mistakenly, "Oh, that must be from the devil."

"Do not quench the Spirit" (1 Thessalonians 5:19), and do not despise Him when He says to you, in effect, "Don't be blind on this point anymore—you are not as far along spiritually as you thought you were. Until now I have not been able to reveal this to you, but I'm revealing it to you right now." When the Lord disciplines you like that, let Him have His way with you. Allow Him to put you into a right-standing relationship before God.

". . . nor be discouraged when you are rebuked by Him." We begin to pout, become irritated with God, and then say, "Oh well, I can't help it. I prayed and things didn't turn out right anyway. So I'm simply going to give up on everything." Just think what would happen if we acted like this in any other area of our lives!

Am I fully prepared to allow God to grip me by His power and do a work in me that is truly worthy of Himself? Sanctification is not my idea of what I want God to do for me—sanctification is God's idea of what He wants to do for me. But He has to get me into the state of mind and spirit where I will allow Him to sanctify me completely, whatever the cost (see 1 Thessalonians 5:23-24).

THE EVIDENCE OF THE NEW BIRTH

"You must be born again" (John 3:7).

The answer to Nicodemus' question, "How can a man be born when he is old?" is: Only when he is willing to die to everything in his life, including his rights, his virtues, and his religion, and becomes willing to receive into himself a new life that he has never before experienced (3:4). This new life exhibits itself in our conscious repentance and through our unconscious holiness.

"But as many as received Him . . ." (John 1:12). Is my knowledge of Jesus the result of my own internal spiritual perception, or is it only what I have learned through listening to others? Is there something in my life that unites me with the Lord Jesus as my personal Savior? My spiritual history must have as its underlying foundation a personal knowledge of Jesus Christ. To be born again means that I see Jesus.

". . . unless one is born again, he cannot see the kingdom of God" (John 3:3). Am I seeking only for the evidence of God's kingdom, or am I actually recognizing His absolute sovereign control? The new birth gives me a new power of vision by which I begin to discern God's control. His sovereignty was there all the time, but with God being true to His nature, I could not see it until I received His very nature myself.

"Whoever has been born of God does not sin . . ." (1 John 3:9). Am I seeking to stop sinning or have I actually stopped? To be born of God means that I have His supernatural power to stop sinning. The Bible never asks, "Should a Christian sin?" The Bible emphatically states that *a Christian must not sin.* The work of the new birth is being effective in us when we do not commit sin. It is not merely that we have the power not to sin, but that we have actually stopped sinning. Yet 1 John 3:9 does not mean that we *cannot* sin—it simply means that if we will obey the life of God in us, that we *do not have to sin.*

DOES HE KNOW ME . . . ?

"He calls his own ... by name ..." (John 10:3).

W hen I have sadly misunderstood Him? (see John 20:11-18). It is possible to know all about doctrine and still not know Jesus. A person's soul is in grave danger when the knowledge of doctrine surpasses Jesus, avoiding intimate touch with Him. Why was Mary weeping? Doctrine meant no more to her than the grass under her feet. In fact, any Pharisee could have made a fool of Mary doctrinally, but one thing they could never ridicule was the fact that Jesus had cast seven demons out of her (see Luke 8:2); yet His blessings were nothing to her in comparison with knowing Jesus Himself. ". . . she turned around and saw Jesus standing there, and did not know that it was Jesus. . . . Jesus said to her, 'Mary!' " (John 20:14, 16). Once He called Mary by her name, she immediately knew that she had a personal history with the One who spoke. "She turned and said to Him, 'Rabboni!' " (20:16).

When I have stubbornly doubted? (see John 20:24-29). Have I been doubting something about Jesus—maybe an experience to which others testify, but which I have not yet experienced? The other disciples said to Thomas, "We have seen the Lord" (20:25). But Thomas doubted, saying, "Unless I see . . . I will not believe" (20:25). Thomas needed the personal touch of Jesus. When His touches will come we never know, but when they do come they are indescribably precious. "Thomas . . . said to Him, 'My Lord and my God!' " (20:28).

When I have selfishly denied Him? (see John 21:15-17). Peter denied Jesus Christ with oaths and curses (see Matthew 26:69-75), and yet after His resurrection Jesus appeared to Peter alone. Jesus restored Peter in private, and then He restored him publicly before the others. And Peter said to Him, "Lord . . . You know that I love You" (John 21:17).

Do I have a personal history with Jesus Christ? The one true sign of discipleship is intimate oneness with Him—a knowledge of Jesus that nothing can shake.

ARE YOU DISCOURAGED OR DEVOTED?

"... Jesus ... said to him, 'You still lack one thing. Sell all that you have ... and come, follow Me.' But when he heard this, he became very sorrowful, for he was very rich" (Luke 18:22–23).

Have you ever heard the Master say something very difficult to you? If you haven't, I question whether you have ever heard Him say anything at all. Jesus says a tremendous amount to us that we listen to, but do not actually hear. And once we do hear Him, His words are harsh and unyielding.

Jesus did not show the least concern that this rich young ruler should do what He told him, nor did Jesus make any attempt to keep this man with Him. He simply said to him, "Sell all that you have ... and come, follow Me." Our Lord never pleaded with him; He never tried to lure him—He simply spoke the strictest words that human ears have ever heard, and then left him alone.

Have I ever heard Jesus say something difficult and unyielding to me? Has He said something personally to me to which I have deliberately listened—not something I can explain for the sake of others, but something I have heard Him say directly to me? This man understood what Jesus said. He heard it clearly, realizing the full impact of its meaning, and it broke his heart. He did not go away as a defiant person, but as one who was sorrowful and discouraged. He had come to Jesus on fire with zeal and determination, but the words of Jesus simply froze him. Instead of producing enthusiastic devotion to Jesus, they produced heartbreaking discouragement. And Jesus did not go after him, but let him go. Our Lord knows perfectly well that once His word is truly heard, it will bear fruit sooner or later. What is so terrible is that some of us prevent His words from bearing fruit in our present life. I wonder what we will say when we finally make up our minds to be devoted to Him on that particular point? One thing is certain—He will never throw our past failures back in our faces.

HAVE YOU EVER BEEN SPEECHLESS WITH SORROW?

"When he heard this, he became very sorrowful, for he was very rich" (Luke 18:23).

The rich young ruler went away from Jesus speechless with sorrow, having nothing to say in response to Jesus' words. He had no doubt about what Jesus had said or what it meant, and it produced in him a sorrow with no words with which to respond. Have you ever been there? Has God's Word ever come to you, pointing out an area of your life, requiring you to yield it to Him? Maybe He has pointed out certain personal qualities, desires, and interests, or possibly relationships of your heart and mind. If so, then you have often been speechless with sorrow. The Lord will not go after you, and He will not plead with you. But every time He meets you at the place where He has pointed, He will simply repeat His words, saying, "If you really mean what you say, these are the conditions."

"Sell all that you have . . ." (18:22). In other words, rid yourself before God of everything that might be considered a possession until you are a mere conscious human being standing before Him, and then give God that. That is where the battle is truly fought—in the realm of your will before God. Are you more devoted to your idea of what Jesus wants than to Jesus Himself? If so, you are likely to hear one of His harsh and unyielding statements that will produce sorrow in you. What Jesus says *is* difficult—it is only easy when it is heard by those who have His nature in them. Beware of allowing anything to soften the hard words of Jesus Christ.

I can be so rich in my own poverty, or in the awareness of the fact that I am nobody, that I will never be a disciple of Jesus. Or I can be so rich in the awareness that I am somebody that I will never be a disciple. Am I willing to be destitute and poor even in my sense of awareness of my destitution and poverty? If not, that is why I become discouraged. Discouragement is disillusioned self-love, and self-love may be love for my devotion to Jesus—not love for Jesus Himself.

SELF-AWARENESS

"Come to Me . . ." (Matthew 11:28).

God intends for us to live a well-rounded life in Christ Jesus, but there are times when that life is attacked from the outside. Then we tend to fall back into self-examination, a habit that we thought was gone. Self-awareness is the first thing that will upset the completeness of our life in God, and self-awareness continually produces a sense of struggling and turmoil in our lives. Self-awareness is not sin, and it can be produced by nervous emotions or by suddenly being dropped into a totally new set of circumstances. Yet it is never God's will that we should be anything less than absolutely complete in Him. Anything that disturbs our rest in Him must be rectified at once, and it is not rectified by being ignored but only by coming to Jesus Christ. If we will come to Him, asking Him to produce Christ-awareness in us, He will always do it, until we fully learn to abide in Him.

Never allow anything that divides or destroys the oneness of your life with Christ to remain in your life without facing it. Beware of allowing the influence of your friends or your circumstances to divide your life. This only serves to sap your strength and slow your spiritual growth. Beware of anything that can split your oneness with Him, causing you to see yourself as separate from Him. Nothing is as important as staying right spiritually. And the only solution is a very simple one—"Come to Me . . . ." The intellectual, moral, and spiritual depth of our reality as a person is tested and measured by these words. Yet in every detail of our lives where we are found not to be real, we would rather dispute the findings than come to Jesus.

CHRIST-AWARENESS

". . . and I will give you rest" (Matthew 11:28).

Whenever anything begins to disintegrate your life with Jesus Christ, turn to Him at once, asking Him to re-establish your rest. Never allow anything to remain in your life that is causing the unrest. Think of every detail of your life that is causing the disintegration as something to fight against, not as something you should allow to remain. Ask the Lord to put awareness of Himself in you, and your self-awareness will disappear. Then He will be your all in all. Beware of allowing your self-awareness to continue, because slowly but surely it will awaken self-pity, and self-pity is satanic. Don't allow yourself to say, "Well, they have just misunderstood me, and this is something over which they should be apologizing to me; I'm sure I must have this cleared up with them already." Learn to leave others alone regarding this. Simply ask the Lord to give you Christ-awareness, and He will steady you until your completeness in Him is absolute.

A complete life is the life of a child. When I am fully conscious of my awareness of Christ, there is something wrong. It is the sick person who really knows what health is. A child of God is not aware of the will of God because he *is* the will of God. When we have deviated even slightly from the will of God, we begin to ask, "Lord, what is your will?" A child of God never prays to be made aware of the fact that God answers prayer, because he is so restfully certain that God always answers prayer.

If we try to overcome our self-awareness through any of our own commonsense methods, we will only serve to strengthen our self-awareness tremendously. Jesus says, "Come to Me . . . and I will give you rest," that is, Christ-awareness will take the place of self-awareness. Wherever Jesus comes He establishes rest—the rest of the completion of activity in our lives that is never aware of itself.

THE MINISTRY OF THE UNNOTICED

"Blessed are the poor in spirit . . ." (Matthew 5:3).

The New Testament notices things that do not seem worthy of notice by our standards. "Blessed are the poor in spirit . . . ." This literally means, "Blessed are the paupers." Paupers are remarkably commonplace! The preaching of today tends to point out a person's strength of will or the beauty of his character—things that are easily noticed. The statement we so often hear, "Make a decision for Jesus Christ," places the emphasis on something our Lord never trusted. He never asks us to decide for Him, but to yield to Him—something very different. At the foundation of Jesus Christ's kingdom is the genuine loveliness of those who are commonplace. I am truly blessed in my poverty. If I have no strength of will and a nature without worth or excellence, then Jesus says to me, "Blessed are you, because it is through your poverty that you can enter My kingdom." I cannot enter His kingdom by virtue of my goodness—I can only enter it as an absolute pauper.

The true character of the loveliness that speaks for God is always unnoticed by the one possessing that quality. Conscious influence is prideful and unchristian. If I wonder if I am being of any use to God, I instantly lose the beauty and the freshness of the touch of the Lord. "He who believes in Me . . . out of his heart will flow rivers of living water" (John 7:38). And if I examine the outflow, I lose the touch of the Lord.

Who are the people who have influenced us most? Certainly not the ones who thought they did, but those who did not have even the slightest idea that they were influencing us. In the Christian life, godly influence is never conscious of itself. If we are conscious of our influence, it ceases to have the genuine loveliness which is characteristic of the touch of Jesus. We always know when Jesus is at work because He produces in the commonplace something that is inspiring.

"I Indeed . . . But He"

"I indeed baptize you with water . . . but He . . . will baptize you with the Holy Spirit and fire" (Matthew 3:11).

Have I ever come to the point in my life where I can say, "I indeed . . . but He . . ."? Until that moment comes, I will never know what the baptism of the Holy Spirit means. *I indeed* am at the end, and I cannot do anything more—*but He* begins right there—He does the things that no one else can ever do. Am I prepared for His coming? Jesus cannot come and do His work in me as long as there is anything blocking the way, whether it is something good or bad. When He comes to me, am I prepared for Him to drag every wrong thing I have ever done into the light? That is exactly where He comes. Wherever I know I am unclean is where He will put His feet and stand, and wherever I think I am clean is where He will remove His feet and walk away.

Repentance does not cause a sense of sin—it causes a sense of inexpressible unworthiness. When I repent, I realize that I am absolutely helpless, and I know that through and through I am not worthy even to carry His sandals. Have I repented like that, or do I have a lingering thought of possibly trying to defend my actions? The reason God cannot come into my life is that I am not at the point of complete repentance.

"He will baptize you with the Holy Spirit and fire." John is not speaking here of the baptism of the Holy Spirit as an experience, but as a work performed by Jesus Christ. "*He* will baptize you . . . ." The only experience that those who are baptized with the Holy Spirit are ever conscious of is the experience of sensing their absolute unworthiness.

"*I indeed*" was this in the past, "*but He*" came and something miraculous happened. Get to the end of yourself where you can do nothing, but where He does everything.

PRAYER—BATTLE IN "THE SECRET PLACE"

> "When you pray, go into your room, and when you have shut your door, pray to your Father who is in the secret place; and your Father who sees in secret will reward you openly" (Matthew 6:6).

Jesus did not say, "Dream about your Father who is in the secret place," but He said, ". . . *pray* to your Father who is in the secret place. . . ." Prayer is an effort of the will. After we have entered our secret place and shut the door, the most difficult thing to do is to pray. We cannot seem to get our minds into good working order, and the first thing we have to fight is wandering thoughts. The great battle in private prayer is overcoming this problem of our idle and wandering thinking. We have to learn to discipline our minds and concentrate on willful, deliberate prayer.

We must have a specially selected place for prayer, but once we get there this plague of wandering thoughts begins, as we begin to think to ourselves, "This needs to be done, and I have to do that today." Jesus says to "shut your door." Having a secret stillness before God means deliberately shutting the door on our emotions and remembering Him. God is in secret, and He sees us from "the secret place"—He does not see us as other people do, or as we see ourselves. When we truly live in "the secret place," it becomes impossible for us to doubt God. We become more sure of Him than of anyone or anything else. Enter into "the secret place," and you will find that God was right in the middle of your everyday circumstances all the time. Get into the habit of dealing with God about everything. Unless you learn to open the door of your life completely and let God in from your first waking moment of each new day, you will be working on the wrong level throughout the day. But if you will swing the door of your life fully open and "pray to your Father who is in the secret place," every public thing in your life will be marked with the lasting imprint of the presence of God.

AUGUST 23

THE SPIRITUAL SEARCH

**"What man is there among you who, if his son asks for bread, will give him a stone?"
(Matthew 7:9).**

The illustration of prayer that our Lord used here is one of a good child who is asking for something good. We talk about prayer as if God hears us regardless of what our relationship is to Him (see Matthew 5:45). Never say that it is not God's will to give you what you ask. Don't faint and give up, but find out the reason you have not received; increase the intensity of your search and examine the evidence. Is your relationship right with your spouse, your children, and your fellow students? Are you a "good child" in those relationships? Do you have to say to the Lord, "I have been irritable and cross, but I still want spiritual blessings"? You cannot receive and will have to do without them until you have the attitude of a "good child."

We mistake defiance for devotion, arguing with God instead of surrendering. We refuse to look at the evidence that clearly indicates where we are wrong. Have I been asking God to give me money for something I want, while refusing to pay someone what I owe him? Have I been asking God for liberty while I am withholding it from someone who belongs to me? Have I refused to forgive someone, and have I been unkind to that person? Have I been living as God's child among my relatives and friends? (see Matthew 7:12).

I am a child of God only by being born again, and as His child I am good only as I "walk in the light" (1 John 1:7). For most of us, prayer simply becomes some trivial religious expression, a matter of mystical and emotional fellowship with God. We are all good at producing spiritual fog that blinds our sight. But if we will search out and examine the evidence, we will see very clearly what is wrong—a friendship, an unpaid debt, or an improper attitude. There is no use praying unless we are living as children of God. Then Jesus says, regarding His children, "Everyone who asks receives . . ." (Matthew 7:8).

SACRIFICE AND FRIENDSHIP

"I have called you friends . . ." (John 15:15).

We will never know the joy of self-sacrifice until we surrender in every detail of our lives. Yet self-surrender is the most difficult thing for us to do. We make it conditional by saying, "I'll surrender if . . . !" Or we approach it by saying, "I suppose I have to devote my life to God." We will never find the joy of self-sacrifice in either of these ways.

But as soon as we do totally surrender, abandoning ourselves to Jesus, the Holy Spirit gives us a taste of His joy. The ultimate goal of self-sacrifice is to lay down our lives for our Friend (see 15:13-14). When the Holy Spirit comes into our lives, our greatest desire is to lay down our lives for Jesus. Yet the thought of self-sacrifice never even crosses our minds, because sacrifice is the Holy Spirit's ultimate expression of love.

Our Lord is our example of a life of self-sacrifice, and He perfectly exemplified Psalm 40:8, "I delight to do Your will, O my God . . . ." He endured tremendous personal sacrifice, yet with overflowing joy. Have I ever yielded myself in absolute submission to Jesus Christ? If He is not the One to whom I am looking for direction and guidance, then there is no benefit in my sacrifice. But when my sacrifice is made with my eyes focused on Him, slowly but surely His molding influence becomes evident in my life (see Hebrews 12:1-2).

Beware of letting your natural desires hinder your walk in love before God. One of the cruelest ways to kill natural love is through the rejection that results from having built the love on natural desires. But the one true desire of a saint is the Lord Jesus. Love for God is not something sentimental or emotional—for a saint to love as God loves is the most practical thing imaginable.

"I have called you friends. . . ." Our friendship with Jesus is based on the new life He created in us, which has no resemblance or attraction to our old life but only to the life of God. It is a life that is completely humble, pure, and devoted to God.

ARE YOU EVER TROUBLED?

"Peace I leave with you, My peace I give to you . . ." (John 14:27).

There are times in our lives when our peace is based simply on our own ignorance. But when we are awakened to the realities of life, true inner peace is impossible unless it is received from Jesus. When our Lord speaks peace, He creates peace, because the words that He speaks are always "spirit, and they are life" (John 6:63). Have I ever received what Jesus speaks? ". . . My *peace I give to you* . . ."—a peace that comes from looking into His face and fully understanding and receiving His quiet contentment.

Are you severely troubled right now? Are you afraid and confused by the waves and the turbulence God sovereignly allows to enter your life? Have you left no stone of your faith unturned, yet still not found any well of peace, joy, or comfort? Does your life seem completely barren to you? Then look up and receive the quiet contentment of the Lord Jesus. Reflecting His peace is proof that you are right with God, because you are exhibiting the freedom to turn your mind to Him. If you are not right with God, you can never turn your mind anywhere but on yourself. Allowing anything to hide the face of Jesus Christ from you either causes you to become troubled or gives you a false sense of security.

With regard to the problem that is pressing in on you right now, are you "looking unto Jesus" (Hebrews 12:2) and receiving peace from Him? If so, He will be a gracious blessing of peace exhibited in and through you. But if you only try to worry your way out of the problem, you destroy His effectiveness in you, and you deserve whatever you get. We become troubled because we have not been taking Him into account. When a person confers with Jesus Christ, the confusion stops, because there is no confusion in Him. Lay everything out before Him, and when you are faced with difficulty, bereavement, and sorrow, listen to Him say, "Let not your heart be troubled . . ." (John 14:27).

LIVING YOUR THEOLOGY

"Walk while you have the light, lest darkness overtake you . . ." (John 12:35).

B eware of not acting upon what you see in your moments on the mountaintop with God. If you do not obey the light, it will turn into darkness. "If therefore the light that is in you is darkness, how great is that darkness!" (Matthew 6:23). The moment you forsake the matter of sanctification or neglect anything else on which God has given you His light, your spiritual life begins to disintegrate within you. Continually bring the truth out into your real life, working it out into every area, or else even the light that you possess will itself prove to be a curse.

The most difficult person to deal with is the one who has the prideful self-satisfaction of a past experience, but is not working that experience out in his everyday life. If you *say* you are sanctified, *show it.* The experience must be so genuine that it shows in your life. Beware of any belief that makes you self-indulgent or self-gratifying; that belief came from the pit of hell itself, regardless of how beautiful it may sound.

Your theology must work itself out, exhibiting itself in your most common everyday relationships. Our Lord said, ". . . unless your righteousness *exceeds* the righteousness of the scribes and Pharisees, you will by no means enter the kingdom of heaven" (Matthew 5:20). In other words, you must be more moral than the most moral person you know. You may know all about the doctrine of sanctification, but are you working it out in the everyday issues of your life? Every detail of your life, whether physical, moral, or spiritual, is to be judged and measured by the standard of the atonement by the Cross of Christ.

THE PURPOSE OF PRAYER

> ". . . one of His disciples said to Him, 'Lord,
> teach us to pray . . .' " (Luke 11:1).

Prayer is not a normal part of the life of the natural
man. We hear it said that a person's life will suffer if he doesn't pray, but I question that. What
will suffer is the life of the Son of God in him, which
is nourished not by food, but by prayer. When a person
is born again from above, the life of the Son of God is
born in him, and he can either starve or nourish that life.
Prayer is the way that the life of God in us is nourished.
Our common ideas regarding prayer are not found in the
New Testament. We look upon prayer simply as a means
of getting things for ourselves, but the biblical purpose of
prayer is that we may get to know God Himself.

"Ask, and you will receive . . ." (John 16:24). We
complain before God, and sometimes we are apologetic
or indifferent to Him, but we actually *ask* Him for very
few things. Yet a child exhibits a magnificent boldness to
ask! Our Lord said, ". . . unless you . . . become as little
children . . ." (Matthew 18:3). Ask and God will do. Give
Jesus Christ the opportunity and the room to work. The
problem is that no one will ever do this until he is at his
wits' end. When a person is at his wits' end, it no longer
seems to be a cowardly thing to pray; in fact, it is the only
way he can get in touch with the truth and the reality of
God Himself. Be yourself before God and present Him
with your problems—the very things that have brought
you to your wits' end. But as long as you think you are
self-sufficient, you do not need to ask God for anything.

To say that "prayer changes things" is not as close to
the truth as saying, "Prayer changes *me* and then I change
things." God has established things so that prayer, on the
basis of redemption, changes the way a person looks at
things. Prayer is not a matter of changing things externally, but one of working miracles in a person's inner
nature.

THE UNSURPASSED INTIMACY
OF TESTED FAITH

**"Jesus said to her, 'Did I not say to you that if you would believe you would see the glory of God?' "
(John 11:40).**

E very time you venture out in your life of faith, you will find something in your circumstances that, from a commonsense standpoint, will flatly contradict your faith. But common sense is not faith, and faith is not common sense. In fact, they are as different as the natural life and the spiritual. Can you trust Jesus Christ where your common sense cannot trust Him? Can you venture out with courage on the words of Jesus Christ, while the realities of your commonsense life continue to shout, "It's all a lie"? When you are on the mountaintop, it's easy to say, "Oh yes, I believe God can do it," but you have to come down from the mountain to the demon-possessed valley and face the realities that scoff at your Mount-of-Transfiguration belief (see Luke 9:28–42). Every time my theology becomes clear to my own mind, I encounter something that contradicts it. As soon as I say, "I believe 'God shall supply all [my] need,' " the testing of my faith begins (Philippians 4:19). When my strength runs dry and my vision is blinded, will I endure this trial of my faith victoriously or will I turn back in defeat?

Faith must be tested, because it can only become your intimate possession through conflict. What is challenging your faith right now? The test will either prove your faith right, or it will kill it. Jesus said, "Blessed is he who is not offended because of Me" (Matthew 11:6). The ultimate thing is confidence in Jesus. "We have become partakers of Christ if we hold the beginning of our confidence steadfast to the end . . ." (Hebrews 3:14). Believe steadfastly on Him and everything that challenges you will strengthen your faith. There is continual testing in the life of faith up to the point of our physical death, which is the last great test. Faith is absolute trust in God—trust that could never imagine that He would forsake us (see Hebrews 13:5–6).

AUGUST 29

USEFULNESS OR RELATIONSHIP?

"Do not rejoice in this, that the spirits are subject to you, but rather rejoice because your names are written in heaven" (Luke 10:20).

Jesus Christ is saying here, "Don't rejoice in your successful service for Me, but rejoice because of your right relationship with Me." The trap you may fall into in Christian work is to rejoice in successful service—rejoicing in the fact that God has used you. Yet you will never be able to measure fully what God will do through you if you do not have a right-standing relationship with Jesus Christ. If you keep your relationship right with Him, then regardless of your circumstances or whoever you encounter each day, He will continue to pour "rivers of living water" through you (John 7:38). And it is actually by His mercy that He does not let you know it. Once you have the right relationship with God through salvation and sanctification, remember that whatever your circumstances may be, you have been placed in them by God. And God uses the reaction of your life to your circumstances to fulfill His purpose, as long as you continue to "walk in the light as He is in the light" (1 John 1:7).

Our tendency today is to put the emphasis on service. Beware of the people who make their request for help on the basis of someone's usefulness. If you make usefulness the test, then Jesus Christ was the greatest failure who ever lived. For the saint, direction and guidance come from God Himself, not some measure of that saint's usefulness. It is the work that God does through us that counts, not what we do for Him. All that our Lord gives His attention to in a person's life is that person's relationship with God—something of great value to His Father. Jesus is "bringing many *sons* to glory . . ." (Hebrews 2:10).

"MY JOY . . . YOUR JOY"

"These things I have spoken to you, that My joy may remain in you, and that your joy may be full" (John 15:11).

What was the joy that Jesus had? Joy should not be confused with happiness. In fact, it is an insult to Jesus Christ to use the word *happiness* in connection with Him. The joy of Jesus was His absolute self-surrender and self-sacrifice to His Father—the joy of doing that which the Father sent Him to do—". . . who for the joy that was set before Him endured the cross . . ." (Hebrews 12:2). "I delight to do Your will, O my God . . ." (Psalm 40:8). Jesus prayed that our joy might continue fulfilling itself until it becomes the same joy as His. Have I allowed Jesus Christ to introduce His joy to me?

Living a full and overflowing life does not rest in bodily health, in circumstances, nor even in seeing God's work succeed, but in the perfect understanding of God, and in the same fellowship and oneness with Him that Jesus Himself enjoyed. But the first thing that will hinder this joy is the subtle irritability caused by giving too much thought to our circumstances. Jesus said, ". . . the cares of this world, . . . choke the word, and it becomes unfruitful" (Mark 4:19). And before we even realize what has happened, we are caught up in our cares. All that God has done for us is merely the threshold—He wants us to come to the place where we will be His witnesses and proclaim who Jesus is.

Have the right relationship with God, finding your joy there, and out of you "will flow rivers of living water" (John 7:38). Be a fountain through which Jesus can pour His "living water." Stop being hypocritical and proud, aware only of yourself, and live "your life . . . hidden with Christ in God" (Colossians 3:3). A person who has the right relationship with God lives a life as natural as breathing wherever he goes. The lives that have been the greatest blessing to you are the lives of those people who themselves were unaware of having been a blessing.

DESTINED TO BE HOLY

"... it is written, 'Be holy, for I am holy' "
(1 Peter 1:16).

We must continually remind ourselves of the purpose of life. We are not destined to happiness, nor to health, but to holiness. Today we have far too many desires and interests, and our lives are being consumed and wasted by them. Many of them may be right, noble, and good, and may later be fulfilled, but in the meantime God must cause their importance to us to decrease. The only thing that truly matters is whether a person will accept the God who will make him holy. At all costs, a person must have the right relationship with God.

Do I believe I need to be holy? Do I believe that God can come into me and make me holy? If through your preaching you convince me that I am unholy, I then resent your preaching. The preaching of the gospel awakens an intense resentment because it is designed to reveal my unholiness, but it also awakens an intense yearning and desire within me. God has only one intended destiny for mankind—holiness. His only goal is to produce saints. God is not some eternal blessing-machine for people to use, and He did not come to save us out of pity—He came to save us because He created us to be holy. Atonement through the Cross of Christ means that God can put me back into perfect oneness with Himself through the death of Jesus Christ, without a trace of anything coming between us any longer.

Never tolerate, because of sympathy for yourself or for others, any practice that is not in keeping with a holy God. Holiness means absolute purity of your walk before God, the words coming from your mouth, and every thought in your mind—placing every detail of your life under the scrutiny of God Himself. Holiness is not simply what God gives me, but what God has given me that is being exhibited in my life.

A LIFE OF PURE
AND HOLY SACRIFICE

**"He who believes in Me . . . out of his heart
will flow . . ."** (John 7:38).

Jesus did not say, "He who believes in Me will realize all the blessings of the fullness of God," but, in essence, "He who believes in Me will have everything he receives escape out of him." Our Lord's teaching was always *anti*-self-realization. His purpose is not the development of a person—His purpose is to make a person exactly like Himself, and the Son of God is characterized by self-expenditure. If we believe in Jesus, it is not what we gain but what He pours through us that really counts. God's purpose is not simply to make us beautiful, plump grapes, but to make us grapes so that He may squeeze the sweetness out of us. Our spiritual life cannot be measured by success as the world measures it, but only by what God pours through us—and we cannot measure that at all.

When Mary of Bethany "broke the flask . . . of very costly oil . . . and poured it on [Jesus'] head," it was an act for which no one else saw any special occasion; in fact, ". . . there were some who . . . said, 'Why was this fragrant oil wasted?' " (Mark 14:3-4). But Jesus commended Mary for her extravagant act of devotion, and said, ". . . wherever this gospel is preached . . . what this woman has done will also be told as a memorial to her" (Mark 14:9). Our Lord is filled with overflowing joy whenever He sees any of us doing what Mary did—not being bound by a particular set of rules, but being totally surrendered to Him. God poured out the life of His Son "that the world through Him might be saved" (John 3:17). Are we prepared to pour out our lives for Him?

"He who believes in Me . . . out of his heart will flow rivers of living water"—and hundreds of other lives will be continually refreshed. Now is the time for us to break "the flask" of our lives, to stop seeking our own satisfaction, and to pour out our lives before Him. Our Lord is asking who of us will do it for Him?

POURING OUT THE
WATER OF SATISFACTION

"He would not drink it, but poured it out to the LORD" (2 Samuel 23:16).

What has been like "water from the well of Bethlehem" to you recently—love, friendship, or maybe some spiritual blessing (23:16)? Have you taken whatever it may be, even at the risk of damaging your own soul, simply to satisfy yourself? If you have, then you cannot pour it out "to the LORD." You can never set apart for God something that you desire for yourself to achieve your own satisfaction. If you try to satisfy yourself with a blessing from God, it will corrupt you. You must sacrifice it, pouring it out to God—something that your common sense says is an absurd waste.

How can I pour out "to the LORD" natural love and spiritual blessings? There is only one way—I must make a determination in my mind to do so. There are certain things other people do that could never be received by someone who does not know God, because it is humanly impossible to repay them. As soon as I realize that something is too wonderful for me, that I am not worthy to receive it, and that it is not meant for a human being at all, I must pour it out "to the LORD." Then these very things that have come to me will be poured out as "rivers of living water" all around me (John 7:38). And until I pour these things out to God, they actually endanger those I love, as well as myself, because they will be turned into lust. Yes, we can be lustful in things that are not sordid and vile. Even love must be transformed by being poured out "to the LORD."

If you have become bitter and sour, it is because when God gave you a blessing you hoarded it. Yet if you had poured it out to Him, you would have been the sweetest person on earth. If you are always keeping blessings to yourself and never learning to pour out anything "to the LORD," other people will never have their vision of God expanded through you.

His!

"They were Yours, You gave them to Me . . ."
(John 17:6).

A missionary is someone in whom the Holy Spirit has brought about this realization: "You are not your own" (1 Corinthians 6:19). To say, "I am not my own," is to have reached a high point in my spiritual stature. The true nature of that life in actual everyday confusion is evidenced by the deliberate giving up of myself to another Person through a sovereign decision, and that Person is Jesus Christ. The Holy Spirit interprets and explains the nature of Jesus to me to make me one with my Lord, not that I might simply become a trophy for His showcase. Our Lord never sent any of His disciples out on the basis of what He had done for them. It was not until after the resurrection, when the disciples had perceived through the power of the Holy Spirit who Jesus really was, that He said, "Go" (Matthew 28:19; also see Luke 24:49 and Acts 1:8).

"If anyone comes to Me and does not hate his father and mother, wife and children, brothers and sisters, yes, and his own life also, he cannot be My disciple" (Luke 14:26). He was not saying that this person cannot be good and upright, but that he cannot be someone over whom Jesus can write the word *Mine*. Any one of the relationships our Lord mentions in this verse can compete with our relationship with Him. I may prefer to belong to my mother, or to my wife, or to myself, but if that is the case, then, Jesus said, "[You] cannot be My disciple." This does not mean that I will not be saved, but it does mean that I cannot be entirely *His.*

Our Lord makes His disciple His very own possession, becoming responsible for him. ". . . you shall be witnesses to Me . . ." (Acts 1:8). The desire that comes into a disciple is not one of *doing* anything for Jesus, but of *being* a perfect delight to Him. The missionary's secret is truly being able to say, "I am His, and He is accomplishing His work and His purposes through me."

Be entirely His!

WATCHING WITH JESUS

"Stay here and watch with Me" (Matthew 26:38).

Watch with Me." Jesus was saying, in effect, "Watch with no private point of view at all, but watch solely and entirely with Me." In the early stages of our Christian life, we do not watch *with* Jesus, we watch *for* Him. We do not watch with Him through the revealed truth of the Bible even in the circumstances of our own lives. Our Lord is trying to introduce us to identification with Himself through a particular "Gethsemane" experience of our own. But we refuse to go, saying, "No, Lord, I can't see the meaning of this, and besides, it's very painful." And how can we possibly watch with Someone who is so incomprehensible? How are we going to understand Jesus sufficiently to watch with Him in His Gethsemane, when we don't even know why He is suffering? We don't know how to watch with Him—we are only used to the idea of Jesus watching with us.

The disciples loved Jesus Christ to the limit of their natural capacity, but they did not fully understand His purpose. In the Garden of Gethsemane they slept as a result of their own sorrow, and at the end of three years of the closest and most intimate relationship of their lives they "all . . . forsook Him and fled" (26:56).

"They were all filled with the Holy Spirit . . ." (Acts 2:4). "They" refers to the same people, but something wonderful has happened between these two events—our Lord's death, resurrection, and ascension—and the disciples have now been invaded and "filled with the Holy Spirit." Our Lord had said, "You shall receive power when the Holy Spirit has come upon you . . ." (Acts 1:8). This meant that they learned to watch *with* Him the rest of their lives.

THE FAR-REACHING RIVERS OF LIFE

"He who believes in Me . . . out of his heart will flow rivers of living water" (John 7:38).

A river reaches places which its source never knows. And Jesus said that, if we have received His fullness, "rivers of living water" will flow out of us, reaching in blessing even "to the end of the earth" (Acts 1:8) regardless of how small the visible effects of our lives may appear to be. We have nothing to do with the outflow—"This is the work of God, that you *believe* . . ." (John 6:29). God rarely allows a person to see how great a blessing he is to others.

A river is victoriously persistent, overcoming all barriers. For a while it goes steadily on its course, but then comes to an obstacle. And for a while it is blocked, yet it soon makes a pathway around the obstacle. Or a river will drop out of sight for miles, only later to emerge again even broader and greater than ever. Do you see God using the lives of others, but an obstacle has come into your life and you do not seem to be of any use to God? Then keep paying attention to the Source, and God will either take you around the obstacle or remove it. The river of the Spirit of God overcomes all obstacles. Never focus your eyes on the obstacle or the difficulty. The obstacle will be a matter of total indifference to the river that will flow steadily through you if you will simply remember to stay focused on the Source. Never allow anything to come between you and Jesus Christ—not emotion nor experience—nothing must keep you from the one great sovereign Source.

Think of the healing and far-reaching rivers developing and nourishing themselves in our souls! God has been opening up wonderful truths to our minds, and every point He has opened up is another indication of the wider power of the river that He will flow through us. If you believe in Jesus, you will find that God has developed and nourished in you mighty, rushing rivers of blessing for others.

FOUNTAINS OF BLESSINGS

"The water that I shall give him will become in him a fountain of water springing up into everlasting life" (John 4:14).

The picture our Lord described here is not that of a simple stream of water, but an overflowing fountain. Continue to "be filled" (Ephesians 5:18) and the sweetness of your vital relationship to Jesus will flow as generously out of you as it has been given to you. If you find that His life is not springing up as it should, you are to blame—something is obstructing the flow. Was Jesus saying to stay focused on the Source so that you may be blessed personally? No, you are to focus on the Source so that out of you "will flow rivers of living water"—irrepressible life (John 7:38).

We are to be fountains through which Jesus can flow as "rivers of living water" in blessing to everyone. Yet some of us are like the Dead Sea, always receiving but never giving, because our relationship is not right with the Lord Jesus. As surely as we receive blessings from Him, He will pour out blessings through us. But whenever the blessings are not being poured out in the same measure they are received, there is a defect in our relationship with Him. Is there anything between you and Jesus Christ? Is there anything hindering your faith in Him? If not, then Jesus says that out of you "will flow rivers of living water." It is not a blessing that you pass on, or an experience that you share with others, but a river that continually flows through you. Stay at the Source, closely guarding your faith in Jesus Christ and your relationship to Him, and there will be a steady flow into the lives of others with no dryness or deadness whatsoever.

Is it excessive to say that rivers will flow out of one individual believer? Do you look at yourself and say, "But I don't see the rivers"? Through the history of God's work you will usually find that He has started with the obscure, the unknown, the ignored, but with those who have been steadfastly true to Jesus Christ.

DO IT YOURSELF

"... casting down arguments and every high thing that exalts itself against the knowledge of God ..." (2 Corinthians 10:5).

Determinedly Demolish Some Things. Deliverance from sin is not the same as deliverance from human nature. There are things in human nature, such as prejudices, that the saint can only destroy through sheer neglect. But there are other things that have to be destroyed through violence, that is, through God's divine strength imparted by His Spirit. There are some things over which we are not to fight, but only to "stand still, and see the salvation of the Lord ..." (Exodus 14:13). But every theory or thought that raises itself up as a fortified barrier "against the knowledge of God" is to be determinedly demolished by drawing on God's power, not through human effort or by compromise (see 2 Corinthians 10:4).

It is only when God has transformed our nature and we have entered into the experience of sanctification that the fight begins. The warfare is not against sin; we can never fight against sin—Jesus Christ conquered that in His redemption of us. The conflict is waged over turning our natural life into a spiritual life. This is never done easily, nor does God intend that it be so. It is accomplished only through a series of moral choices. God does not make us holy in the sense that He makes our character holy. He makes us holy in the sense that He has made us innocent before Him. And then we have to turn that innocence into holy character through the moral choices we make. These choices are continually opposed and hostile to the things of our natural life which have become so deeply entrenched—the very things that raise themselves up as fortified barriers "against the knowledge of God." We can either turn back, making ourselves of no value to the kingdom of God, or we can determinedly demolish these things, allowing Jesus to bring another son to glory (see Hebrews 2:10).

DO IT YOURSELF

"... bringing every thought into captivity to the obedience of Christ ..." (2 Corinthians 10:5).

Determinedly Discipline Other Things. This is another difficult aspect of the strenuous nature of sainthood. Paul said, according to the Moffatt translation of this verse, "... I take every project prisoner to make it obey Christ . . . ." So much Christian work today has never been disciplined, but has simply come into being by impulse! In our Lord's life every project was disciplined to the will of His Father. There was never the slightest tendency to follow the impulse of His own will as distinct from His Father's will—"the Son can do nothing of Himself . . . " (John 5:19). Then compare this with what we do—we take "every thought" or project that comes to us by impulse and jump into action immediately, instead of imprisoning and disciplining ourselves to obey Christ.

Practical work for Christians is greatly overemphasized today, and the saints who are "bringing every thought [and project] into captivity" are criticized and told that they are not determined, and that they lack zeal for God or zeal for the souls of others. But true determination and zeal are found in obeying God, not in the inclination to serve Him that arises from our own undisciplined human nature. It is inconceivable, but true nevertheless, that saints are not "bringing every thought [and project] into captivity," but are simply doing work for God that has been instigated by their own human nature, and has not been made spiritual through determined discipline.

We have a tendency to forget that a person is not only committed to Jesus Christ for salvation, but is also committed, responsible, and accountable to Jesus Christ's view of God, the world, and of sin and the devil. This means that each person must recognize the responsibility to "be transformed by the renewing of [his] mind. . . ." (Romans 12:2).

SEPTEMBER 9

MISSIONARY WEAPONS

"When you were under the fig tree, I saw you"
(John 1:48).

Worshiping in Everyday Occasions. We presume that we would be ready for battle if confronted with a great crisis, but it is not the crisis that builds something within us—it simply reveals what we are made of already. Do you find yourself saying, "If God calls me to battle, of course I will rise to the occasion"? Yet you won't rise to the occasion unless you have done so on God's training ground. If you are not doing the task that is closest to you now, which God has engineered into your life, when the crisis comes, instead of being fit for battle, you will be revealed as being unfit. Crises always reveal a person's true character.

A private relationship of worshiping God is the greatest essential element of spiritual fitness. The time will come, as Nathanael experienced in this passage, that a private "fig-tree" life will no longer be possible. Everything will be out in the open, and you will find yourself to be of no value there if you have not been worshiping in everyday occasions in your own home. If your worship is right in your private relationship with God, then when He sets you free, you will be ready. It is in the unseen life, which only God saw, that you have become perfectly fit. And when the strain of the crisis comes, you can be relied upon by God.

Are you saying, "But I can't be expected to live a sanctified life in my present circumstances; I have no time for prayer or Bible study right now; besides, my opportunity for battle hasn't come yet, but when it does, of course I will be ready"? No, you will not. If you have not been worshiping in everyday occasions, when you get involved in God's work, you will not only be useless yourself but also a hindrance to those around you.

God's training ground, where the missionary weapons are found, is the hidden, personal, worshiping life of the saint.

MISSIONARY WEAPONS

"If I then, your Lord and Teacher, have washed your feet, you also ought to wash one another's feet" (John 13:14).

Ministering in Everyday Opportunities. Ministering in everyday opportunities that surround us does not mean that we select our own surroundings—it means being God's very special choice to be available for use in any of the seemingly random surroundings which He has engineered for us. The very character we exhibit in our present surroundings is an indication of what we will be like in other surroundings.

The things Jesus did were the most menial of everyday tasks, and this is an indication that it takes all of God's power in me to accomplish even the most common tasks in His way. Can I use a towel as He did? Towels, dishes, sandals, and all the other ordinary things in our lives reveal what we are made of more quickly than anything else. It takes God Almighty Incarnate in us to do the most menial duty as it ought to be done.

Jesus said, "I have given you an example, that you should do as I have done to you" (13:15). Notice the kind of people that God brings around you, and you will be humiliated once you realize that this is actually His way of revealing to you the kind of person you have been to Him. Now He says we should exhibit to those around us exactly what He has exhibited to us.

Do you find yourself responding by saying, "Oh, I will do all that once I'm out on the mission field"? Talking in this way is like trying to produce the weapons of war while in the trenches of the battlefield—you will be killed while trying to do it.

We have to go the "second mile" with God (see Matthew 5:41). Yet some of us become worn out in the first ten steps. Then we say, "Well, I'll just wait until I get closer to the next big crisis in my life." But if we do not steadily minister in everyday opportunities, we will do nothing when the crisis comes.

GOING THROUGH
SPIRITUAL CONFUSION

"Jesus answered and said, 'You do not know what you ask'" (Matthew 20:22).

There are times in your spiritual life when there is confusion, and the way out of it is not simply to say that you should not be confused. It is not a matter of right and wrong, but a matter of God taking you through a way that you temporarily do not understand. And it is only by going through the spiritual confusion that you will come to the understanding of what God wants for you.

The Shrouding of His Friendship (see Luke 11:5-8). Jesus gave the illustration here of a man who appears not to care for his friend. He was saying, in effect, that is how the heavenly Father will appear to you at times. You will think that He is an unkind friend, but remember—He is not. The time will come when everything will be explained. There seems to be a cloud on the friendship of the heart, and often even love itself has to wait in pain and tears for the blessing of fuller fellowship and oneness. When God appears to be completely shrouded, will you hang on with confidence in Him?

The Shadow on His Fatherhood (see Luke 11:11-13). Jesus said that there are times when your Father will appear as if He were an unnatural father—as if He were callous and indifferent—but remember, He is not. "Everyone who asks receives . . ." (Luke 11:10). If all you see is a shadow on the face of the Father right now, hang on to the fact that He will ultimately give you clear understanding and will fully justify Himself in everything that He has allowed into your life.

The Strangeness of His Faithfulness (see Luke 18:1-8). "When the Son of Man comes, will He really find faith on the earth?" (Luke 18:8). Will He find the kind of faith that counts on Him in spite of the confusion? Stand firm in faith, believing that what Jesus said is true, although in the meantime you do not understand what God is doing. He has bigger issues at stake than the particular things you are asking of Him right now.

AFTER SURRENDER—
THEN WHAT?

"I have finished the work which You have given Me to do" (John 17:4).

True surrender is not simply surrender of our external life but surrender of our will—and once that is done, surrender is complete. The greatest crisis we ever face is the surrender of our will. Yet God never forces a person's will into surrender, and He never begs. He patiently waits until that person willingly yields to Him. And once that battle has been fought, it never needs to be fought again.

Surrender for Deliverance. "Come to Me . . . and I will give you rest" (Matthew 11:28). It is only after we have begun to experience what salvation really means that we surrender our will to Jesus for rest. Whatever is causing us a sense of uncertainty is actually a call to our will—"Come to Me." And it is a voluntary coming.

Surrender for Devotion. "If anyone desires to come after Me, let him deny himself . . . " (Matthew 16:24). The surrender here is of my *self* to Jesus, with His rest at the heart of my being. He says, "If you want to be My disciple, you must give up your right to yourself to Me." And once this is done, the remainder of your life will exhibit nothing but the evidence of this surrender, and you never need to be concerned again with what the future may hold for you. Whatever your circumstances may be, Jesus is totally sufficient (see 2 Corinthians 12:9 and Philippians 4:19).

Surrender for Death. ". . . another will gird you . . ." (John 21:18; also see verse 19). Have you learned what it means to be girded for death? Beware of some surrender that you make to God in an ecstatic moment in your life, because you are apt to take it back again. True surrender is a matter of being "united together [with Jesus] in the likeness of His death" (Romans 6:5) until nothing ever appeals to you that did not appeal to Him.

And after you surrender—then what? Your entire life should be characterized by an eagerness to maintain unbroken fellowship and oneness with God.

ARGUMENTS OR OBEDIENCE?

"... the simplicity that is in Christ"
(2 Corinthians 11:3).

Simplicity is the secret to seeing things clearly. A saint does not *think* clearly until a long time passes, but a saint ought to *see* clearly without any difficulty. You cannot think through spiritual confusion to make things clear; to make things clear, you must obey. In intellectual matters you can think things out, but in spiritual matters you will only think yourself into further wandering thoughts and more confusion. If there is something in your life upon which God has put His pressure, then obey Him in that matter. Bring all your "arguments and ... every thought into captivity to the obedience of Christ" regarding the matter, and everything will become as clear as daylight to you (2 Corinthians 10:5). Your reasoning capacity will come later, but reasoning is not how we see. We see like children, and when we try to be wise we see nothing (see Matthew 11:25).

Even the very smallest thing that we allow in our lives that is not under the control of the Holy Spirit is completely sufficient to account for spiritual confusion, and spending all of our time thinking about it will still never make it clear. Spiritual confusion can only be conquered through obedience. As soon as we obey, we have discernment. This is humiliating, because when we are confused we know that the reason lies in the state of our mind. But when our natural power of sight is devoted and submitted in obedience to the Holy Spirit, it becomes the very power by which we perceive God's will, and our entire life is kept in simplicity.

WHAT TO RENOUNCE

"We have renounced the hidden things of shame . . ." (2 Corinthians 4:2).

Have you "renounced the hidden things of shame" in your life—the things that your sense of honor or pride will not allow to come into the light? You can easily hide them. Is there a thought in your heart about anyone that you would not like to be brought into the light? Then renounce it as soon as it comes to mind—renounce everything in its entirety until there is no hidden dishonesty or craftiness about you at all. Envy, jealousy, and strife don't necessarily arise from your old nature of sin, but from the flesh which was used for these kinds of things in the past (see Romans 6:19 and 1 Peter 4:1-3). You must maintain continual watchfulness so that nothing arises in your life that would cause you shame.

". . . not walking in craftiness. . ." (2 Corinthians 4:2). This means not resorting to something simply to make your own point. This is a terrible trap. You know that God will allow you to work in only one way—the way of truth. Then be careful never to catch people through the other way—the way of deceit. If you act deceitfully, God's blight and ruin will be upon you. What may be craftiness for you, may not be for others—God has called you to a higher standard. Never dull your sense of being your utmost for His highest—your best for His glory. For you, doing certain things would mean craftiness coming into your life for a purpose other than what is the highest and best, and it would dull the motivation that God has given you. Many people have turned back because they are afraid to look at things from God's perspective. The greatest spiritual crisis comes when a person has to move a little farther on in his faith than the beliefs he has already accepted.

Praying to God in Secret

"When you pray, go into your room, and when you have shut your door, pray to your Father who is in the secret place . . ." (Matthew 6:6).

The primary thought in the area of religion is—keep your eyes on God, not on people. Your motivation should not be the desire to be known as a praying person. Find an inner room in which to pray where no one even knows you are praying, shut the door, and talk to God in secret. Have no motivation other than to know your Father in heaven. It is impossible to carry on your life as a disciple without definite times of secret prayer.

"When you pray, do not use vain repetitions . . ." (6:7). God does not hear us because we pray earnestly—He hears us solely on the basis of redemption. God is never impressed by our earnestness. Prayer is not simply getting things from God—that is only the most elementary kind of prayer. Prayer is coming into perfect fellowship and oneness with God. If the Son of God has been formed in us through regeneration (see Galatians 4:19), then He will continue to press on beyond our common sense and will change our attitude about the things for which we pray.

"Everyone who *asks* receives . . ." (Matthew 7:8). We pray religious nonsense without even involving our will, and then we say that God did not answer—but in reality we have never *asked* for anything. Jesus said, ". . . you will ask what you *desire* . . ." (John 15:7). Asking means that our will must be involved. Whenever Jesus talked about prayer, He spoke with wonderful childlike simplicity. Then we respond with our critical attitude, saying, "Yes, but even Jesus said that we must *ask*." But remember that we have to ask things of God that are in keeping with the God whom Jesus Christ revealed.

IS THERE GOOD IN TEMPTATION?

"No temptation has overtaken you except such as is common to man . . ." (1 Corinthians 10:13).

The word *temptation* has come to mean something bad to us today, but we tend to use the word in the wrong way. Temptation itself is not sin; it is something we are bound to face simply by virtue of being human. Not to be tempted would mean that we were already so shameful that we would be beneath contempt. Yet many of us suffer from temptations we should never have to suffer, simply because we have refused to allow God to lift us to a higher level where we would face temptations of another kind.

A person's inner nature, what he possesses in the inner, spiritual part of his being, determines what he is tempted by on the outside. The temptation fits the true nature of the person being tempted and reveals the possibilities of his nature. Every person actually determines or sets the level of his own temptation, because temptation will come to him in accordance with the level of his controlling, inner nature.

Temptation comes to me, suggesting a possible shortcut to the realization of my highest goal—it does not direct me toward what I understand to be evil, but toward what I understand to be good. Temptation is something that confuses me for a while, and I don't know whether something is right or wrong. When I yield to it, I have made lust a god, and the temptation itself becomes the proof that it was only my own fear that prevented me from falling into the sin earlier.

Temptation is not something we can escape; in fact, it is essential to the well-rounded life of a person. Beware of thinking that you are tempted as no one else—what you go through is the common inheritance of the human race, not something that no one has ever before endured. God does not save us from temptations—He sustains us in the midst of them (see Hebrews 2:18 and 4:15–16).

His Temptation and Ours

"We do not have a High Priest who cannot sympathize with our weaknesses, but was in all points tempted as we are, yet without sin" (Hebrews 4:15).

Until we are born again, the only kind of temptation we understand is the kind mentioned in James 1:14, "Each one is tempted when he is drawn away by his own desires and enticed." But through regeneration we are lifted into another realm where there are other temptations to face, namely, the kind of temptations our Lord faced. The temptations of Jesus had no appeal to us as unbelievers because they were not at home in our human nature. Our Lord's temptations and ours are in different realms until we are born again and become His brothers. The temptations of Jesus are not those of a mere man, but the temptations of God as Man. Through regeneration, the Son of God is formed in us (see Galatians 4:19), and in our physical life He has the same setting that He had on earth. Satan does not tempt us just to make us do wrong things—he tempts us to make us lose what God has put into us through regeneration, namely, the possibility of being of value to God. He does not come to us on the premise of tempting us to sin, but on the premise of shifting our point of view, and only the Spirit of God can detect this as a temptation of the devil.

Temptation means a test of the possessions held within the inner, spiritual part of our being by a power outside us and foreign to us. This makes the temptation of our Lord explainable. After Jesus' baptism, having accepted His mission of being the One "who takes away the sin of the world" (John 1:29) He "was led up by the Spirit into the wilderness" (Matthew 4:1) and into the testing devices of the devil. Yet He did not become weary or exhausted. He went through the temptation "without sin," and He retained all the possessions of His spiritual nature completely intact.

ARE YOU GOING ON
WITH JESUS?

"You are those who have continued with Me in My trials" (Luke 22:28).

It is true that Jesus Christ is with us through our temptations, but are we going on with Him through His temptations? Many of us turn back from going on with Jesus from the very moment we have an experience of what He can do. Watch when God changes your circumstances to see whether you are going on with Jesus, or siding with the world, the flesh, and the devil. We wear His name, but are we going on with Him? "From that time many of His disciples went back and walked with Him no more" (John 6:66).

The temptations of Jesus continued throughout His earthly life, and they will continue throughout the life of the Son of God in us. Are we going on with Jesus in the life we are living right now?

We have the idea that we ought to shield ourselves from some of the things God brings around us. May it never be! It is God who engineers our circumstances, and whatever they may be we must see that we face them while continually abiding with Him in His temptations. They are *His* temptations, not temptations to us, but temptations to the life of the Son of God in us. Jesus Christ's honor is at stake in our bodily lives. Are we remaining faithful to the Son of God in everything that attacks His life in us?

Are you going on with Jesus? The way goes through Gethsemane, through the city gate, and on "outside the camp" (Hebrews 13:13). The way is lonely and goes on until there is no longer even a trace of a footprint to follow—but only the voice saying, *"Follow Me"* (Matthew 4:19).

THE DIVINE
COMMANDMENT OF LIFE

"... be perfect, just as your Father in heaven is perfect" (Matthew 5:48).

Our Lord's exhortation to us in verses 38–48 is to be generous in our behavior toward everyone. Beware of living according to your natural affections in your spiritual life. Everyone has natural affections—some people we like and others we don't like. Yet we must never let those likes and dislikes rule our Christian life. "If we walk in the light as He is in the light, we have fellowship with one another" (1 John 1:7), even those toward whom we have no affection.

The example our Lord gave us here is not that of a good person, or even of a good Christian, but of God Himself. "... be perfect, just as your Father in heaven is perfect." In other words, simply show to the other person what God has shown to you. And God will give you plenty of real life opportunities to prove whether or not you are "perfect, just as your Father in heaven is perfect." Being a disciple means deliberately identifying yourself with God's interests in other people. Jesus says, "A new commandment I give to you, that you love one another; as I have loved you, that you also love one another. By this all will know that you are My disciples, if you have love for one another" (John 13:34–35).

The true expression of Christian character is not in good-doing, but in God-likeness. If the Spirit of God has transformed you within, you will exhibit divine characteristics in your life, not just good human characteristics. God's life in us expresses itself as *God's* life, not as human life trying to be godly. The secret of a Christian's life is that the supernatural becomes natural in him as a result of the grace of God, and the experience of this becomes evident in the practical, everyday details of life, not in times of intimate fellowship with God. And when we come in contact with things that create confusion and a flurry of activity, we find to our own amazement that we have the power to stay wonderfully poised even in the center of it all.

THE MISSIONARY'S
PREDESTINED PURPOSE

"Now the LORD says, who formed Me from the womb to be His Servant . . ." (Isaiah 49:5).

The first thing that happens after we recognize our election by God in Christ Jesus is the destruction of our preconceived ideas, our narrow-minded thinking, and all of our other allegiances—we are turned solely into servants of God's own purpose. The entire human race was created to glorify God and to enjoy Him forever. Sin has diverted the human race onto another course, but it has not altered God's purpose to the slightest degree. And when we are born again we are brought into the realization of God's great purpose for the human race, namely, that He created us for Himself. This realization of our election by God is the most joyful on earth, and we must learn to rely on this tremendous creative purpose of God. The first thing God will do is force the interests of the whole world through the channel of our hearts. The love of God, and even His very nature, is introduced into us. And we see the nature of Almighty God purely focused in John 3:16—"*For God so loved the world . . . .*"

We must continually keep our soul open to the fact of God's creative purpose, and never confuse or cloud it with our own intentions. If we do, God will have to force our intentions aside no matter how much it may hurt. A missionary is created for the purpose of being God's servant, one in whom God is glorified. Once we realize that it is through the salvation of Jesus Christ that we are made perfectly fit for the purpose of God, we will understand why Jesus Christ is so strict and relentless in His demands. He demands absolute righteousness from His servants, because He has put into them the very nature of God.

Beware lest you forget God's purpose for your life.

THE MISSIONARY'S MASTER AND TEACHER

"You call Me Teacher and Lord, and you say well, for so I am. . . . I say to you, a servant is not greater than his master . . ." (John 13:13, 16).

To have a master and teacher is not the same thing as being mastered and taught. Having a master and teacher means that there is someone who knows me better than I know myself, who is closer than a friend, and who understands the remotest depths of my heart and is able to satisfy them fully. It means having someone who has made me secure in the knowledge that he has met and solved all the doubts, uncertainties, and problems in my mind. To have a master and teacher is this and nothing less—". . . for One is your Teacher, the Christ . . ." (Matthew 23:8).

Our Lord never takes measures to make me do what He wants. Sometimes I wish God would master and control me to make me do what He wants, but He will not. And at other times I wish He would leave me alone, and He does not.

"You call Me Teacher and Lord . . ."—but *is* He? *Teacher, Master,* and *Lord* have little place in our vocabulary. We prefer the words *Savior, Sanctifier,* and *Healer.* The only word that truly describes the experience of being mastered is *love,* and we know little about love as God reveals it in His Word. The way we use the word *obey* is proof of this. In the Bible, obedience is based on a relationship between equals; for example, that of a son with his father. Our Lord was not simply God's servant— He was His Son. ". . . *though He was a Son,* yet He learned obedience. . ." (Hebrews 5:8). If we are consciously aware that we are being mastered, that idea itself is proof that we have no master. If that is our attitude toward Jesus, we are far away from having the relationship He wants with us. He wants us in a relationship where He is so easily our Master and Teacher that we have no conscious awareness of it—a relationship where all we know is that we are His to obey.

The Missionary's Goal

**"He . . . said to them, 'Behold, we are going
up to Jerusalem . . . ' " (Luke 18:31).**

In our natural life our ambitions change as we grow,
but in the Christian life the goal is given at the very
beginning, and the beginning and the end are exactly
the same, namely, our Lord Himself. We start with Christ
and we end with Him—". . . till we all come . . . to the
measure of the stature of the fullness of Christ . . ."
(Ephesians 4:13), not simply to our own idea of what the
Christian life should be. The goal of the missionary is to
do God's will, not to be useful or to win the lost. A missionary *is* useful and he *does* win the lost, but that is not
his goal. His goal is to do the will of his Lord.

In our Lord's life, Jerusalem was the place where He
reached the culmination of His Father's will upon the
cross, and unless we go there with Jesus we will have no
friendship or fellowship with Him. Nothing ever diverted our Lord on His way to Jerusalem. He never hurried
through certain villages where He was persecuted, or lin-
gered in others where He was blessed. Neither gratitude
nor ingratitude turned our Lord even the slightest degree
away from His purpose to go "up to Jerusalem."

"A disciple is not above his teacher, nor a servant
above his master" (Matthew 10:24). In other words, the
same things that happened to our Lord will happen to
us on our way to our "Jerusalem." There will be works of
God exhibited through us, people will get blessed, and
one or two will show gratitude while the rest will show
total ingratitude, but nothing must divert us from going
"up to [our] Jerusalem."

". . . there they crucified Him . . ." (Luke 23:33). That
is what happened when our Lord reached Jerusalem,
and that event is the doorway to our salvation. The
saints, however, do not end in crucifixion; by the Lord's
grace they end in glory. In the meantime our watchword
should be summed up by each of us saying, "I too go 'up
to Jerusalem.' "

THE "GO" OF PREPARATION

"If you bring your gift to the altar, and there remember that your brother has something against you, leave your gift there before the altar, and go your way. First be reconciled to your brother, and then come and offer your gift" (Matthew 5:23-24).

I t is easy for us to imagine that we will suddenly come to a point in our lives where we are fully prepared, but preparation is not suddenly accomplished. In fact, it is a process that must be steadily maintained. It is dangerous to become settled and complacent in our present level of experience. The Christian life requires preparation *and* more preparation.

The sense of sacrifice in the Christian life is readily appealing to a new Christian. From a human standpoint, the one thing that attracts us to Jesus Christ is our sense of the heroic, and a close examination of us by our Lord's words suddenly puts this tide of enthusiasm to the test. ". . . *go* your way. First be reconciled to your brother. . . ." The "go" of preparation is to allow the Word of God to examine you closely. Your sense of heroic sacrifice is not good enough. The thing the Holy Spirit will detect in you is your nature that can never work in His service. And no one but God can detect that nature in you. Do you have anything to hide from God? If you do, then let God search you with His light. If there is sin in your life, don't just *admit* it—*confess* it. Are you willing to obey your Lord and Master, whatever the humiliation to your right to yourself may be?

Never disregard a conviction that the Holy Spirit brings to you. If it is important enough for the Spirit of God to bring it to your mind, it is the very thing He is detecting in you. You were looking for some big thing to give up, while God is telling you of some tiny thing that must go. But behind that tiny thing lies the stronghold of obstinacy, and you say, "I will not give up my right to myself"—the very thing that God intends you to give up if you are to be a disciple of Jesus Christ.

The "Go" of Relationship

"Whoever compels you to go one mile, go with him two" (Matthew 5:41).

Our Lord's teaching can be summed up in this: the relationship that He demands for us is an impossible one unless He has done a supernatural work in us. Jesus Christ demands that His disciple does not allow even the slightest trace of resentment in his heart when faced with tyranny and injustice. No amount of enthusiasm will ever stand up to the strain that Jesus Christ will put upon His servant. Only one thing will bear the strain, and that is a personal relationship with Jesus Christ Himself—a relationship that has been examined, purified, and tested until only one purpose remains and I can truly say, "I am here for God to send me where He will." Everything else may become blurred, but this relationship with Jesus Christ must never be.

The Sermon on the Mount is not some unattainable goal; it is a statement of what will happen in me when Jesus Christ has changed my nature by putting His own nature in me. Jesus Christ is the only One who can fulfill the Sermon on the Mount.

If we are to be disciples of Jesus, we must be made disciples supernaturally. And as long as we consciously maintain the determined purpose to be His disciples, we can be sure that we are not disciples. Jesus says, "You did not choose Me, but *I chose you . . .*" (John 15:16). That is the way the grace of God begins. It is a constraint we can never escape; we can disobey it, but we can never start it or produce it ourselves. We are drawn to God by a work of His supernatural grace, and we can never trace back to find where the work began. Our Lord's making of a disciple is supernatural. He does not build on any natural capacity of ours at all. God does not ask us to do the things that are naturally easy for us—He only asks us to do the things that we are perfectly fit to do through His grace, and that is where the cross we must bear will always come.

The "Go" of Reconciliation

"If you . . . remember that your brother has something against you . . ." (Matthew 5:23).

This verse says, "If you bring your gift to the altar, and there remember that your brother has something against you . . . ." It is not saying, "If you search and find something because of your unbalanced sensitivity," but, "If you . . . remember . . . ." In other words, if something is brought to your conscious mind by the Spirit of God—"First be reconciled to your brother, and then come and offer your gift" (5:24). Never object to the intense sensitivity of the Spirit of God in you when He is instructing you down to the smallest detail.

"First be reconciled to your brother . . . ." Our Lord's directive is simple—"First be reconciled . . . ." He says, in effect, "Go back the way you came—the way indicated to you by the conviction given to you at the altar; have an attitude in your mind and soul toward the person who has something against you that makes reconciliation as natural as breathing." Jesus does not mention the other person—He says for *you* to go. It is not a matter of your rights. The true mark of the saint is that he can waive his own rights and obey the Lord Jesus.

". . . and then come and offer your gift." The process of reconciliation is clearly marked. First we have the heroic spirit of self-sacrifice, then the sudden restraint by the sensitivity of the Holy Spirit, and then we are stopped at the point of our conviction. This is followed by obedience to the Word of God, which builds an attitude or state of mind that places no blame on the one with whom you have been in the wrong. And finally there is the glad, simple, unhindered offering of your gift to God.

THE "GO" OF RENUNCIATION

"... someone said to Him, 'Lord, I will follow You wherever You go' " (Luke 9:57).

Our Lord's attitude toward this man was one of severe discouragement, "for He knew what was in man" (John 2:25). We would have said, "I can't imagine why He lost the opportunity of winning that man! Imagine being so cold to him and turning him away so discouraged!" Never apologize for your Lord. The words of the Lord hurt and offend until there is nothing left to be hurt or offended. Jesus Christ had no tenderness whatsoever toward anything that was ultimately going to ruin a person in his service to God. Our Lord's answers were not based on some whim or impulsive thought, but on the knowledge of "what was in man." If the Spirit of God brings to your mind a word of the Lord that hurts you, you can be sure that there is something in you that He wants to hurt to the point of its death.

Luke 9:58. These words destroy the argument of serving Jesus Christ because it is a pleasant thing to do. And the strictness of the rejection that He demands of me allows for nothing to remain in my life but my Lord, myself, and a sense of desperate hope. He says that I must let everyone else come or go, and that I must be guided solely by my relationship to Him. And He says, ". . . the Son of Man has nowhere to lay His head."

Luke 9:59. This man did not want to disappoint Jesus, nor did he want to show a lack of respect for his father. We put our sense of loyalty to our relatives ahead of our loyalty to Jesus Christ, forcing Him to take last place. When your loyalties conflict, always obey Jesus Christ whatever the cost.

Luke 9:61. The person who says, "Lord, I will follow You, but . . .," is the person who is intensely ready to go, but never goes. This man had reservations about going. The exacting call of Jesus has no room for good-byes; good-byes, as we often use them, are pagan, not Christian, because they divert us from the call. Once the call of God comes to you, start going and never stop.

THE "GO" OF
UNCONDITIONAL IDENTIFICATION

> "Jesus . . . said to him, 'One thing you lack:
> Go your way, sell whatever you have and give
> to the poor . . . and come, take up the cross,
> and follow Me' " (Mark 10:21).

The rich young ruler had the controlling passion to
be perfect. When he saw Jesus Christ, he wanted
to be like Him. Our Lord never places anyone's
personal holiness above everything else when He calls
a disciple. Jesus' primary consideration is my absolute
annihilation of my right to myself and my identification
with Him, which means having a relationship with Him
in which there are no other relationships. Luke 14:26 has
nothing to do with salvation or sanctification, but deals
solely with unconditional identification with Jesus Christ.
Very few of us truly know what is meant by the absolute
"go" of unconditional identification with, and abandonment and surrender to, Jesus.

"Then Jesus, looking at him, loved him . . ." (Mark
10:21). This look of Jesus will require breaking your
heart away forever from allegiance to any other person or
thing. Has Jesus ever looked in this way at you? This look
of Jesus transforms, penetrates, and captivates. Where
you are soft and pliable with God is where the Lord has
looked at you. If you are hard and vindictive, insistent on
having your own way, and always certain that the other
person is more likely to be in the wrong than you are,
then there are whole areas of your nature that have never
been transformed by His gaze.

"One thing you lack. . . ." From Jesus Christ's perspective, oneness with Him, with nothing between, is the
only good thing.

". . . sell whatever you have. . . ." I must humble
myself until I am merely a living person. I must essen-
tially renounce possessions of all kinds, not for salvation
(for only one thing saves a person and that is absolute
reliance in faith upon Jesus Christ), but to follow Jesus.
". . . come . . . and follow Me." And the road is the way
He went.

THE AWARENESS OF THE CALL

"... for necessity is laid upon me; yes,
woe is me if I do not preach the gospel!"
(1 Corinthians 9:16).

We are inclined to forget the deeply spiritual and supernatural touch of God. If you are able to tell exactly where you were when you received the call of God and can explain all about it, I question whether you have truly been called. The call of God does not come like that; it is much more supernatural. The realization of the call in a person's life may come like a clap of thunder or it may dawn gradually. But however quickly or slowly this awareness comes, it is always accompanied with an undercurrent of the supernatural—something that is inexpressible and produces a "glow." At any moment the sudden awareness of this incalculable, supernatural, surprising call that has taken hold of your life may break through—"I chose you ..." (John 15:16). The call of God has nothing to do with salvation and sanctification. You are not called to preach the gospel because you are sanctified; the call to preach the gospel is infinitely different. Paul describes it as a compulsion that was placed upon him.

If you have ignored, and thereby removed, the great supernatural call of God in your life, take a review of your circumstances. See where you have put your own ideas of service or your particular abilities ahead of the call of God. Paul said, "... woe is me if I do not preach the gospel!" He had become aware of the call of God, and his compulsion to "preach the gospel" was so strong that nothing else was any longer even a competitor for his strength.

If a man or woman is called of God, it doesn't matter how difficult the circumstances may be. God orchestrates every force at work for His purpose in the end. If you will agree with God's purpose, He will bring not only your conscious level but also all the deeper levels of your life, which you yourself cannot reach, into perfect harmony.

THE ASSIGNING OF THE CALL

"I now rejoice in my sufferings for you, and fill up in my flesh what is lacking in the afflictions of Christ, for the sake of His body, which is the church . . ." (Colossians 1:24).

We take our own spiritual consecration and try to make it into a call of God, but when we get right with Him He brushes all this aside. Then He gives us a tremendous, riveting pain to fasten our attention on something that we never even dreamed could be His call for us. And for one radiant, flashing moment we see His purpose, and we say, "Here am I! Send me" (Isaiah 6:8).

This call has nothing to do with personal sanctification, but with being made broken bread and poured-out wine. Yet God can never make us into wine if we object to the fingers He chooses to use to crush us. We say, "If God would only use His own fingers, and make me broken bread and poured-out wine in a special way, then I wouldn't object!" But when He uses someone we dislike, or some set of circumstances to which we said we would never submit, to crush us, then we object. Yet we must never try to choose the place of our own martyrdom. If we are ever going to be made into wine, we will have to be crushed—you cannot drink grapes. Grapes become wine only when they have been squeezed.

I wonder what finger and thumb God has been using to squeeze you? Have you been as hard as a marble and escaped? If you are not ripe yet, and if God *had* squeezed you anyway, the wine produced would have been remarkably bitter. To be a holy person means that the elements of our natural life experience the very presence of God as they are providentially broken in His service. We have to be placed into God and brought into agreement with Him before we can be broken bread in His hands. Stay right with God and let Him do as He likes, and you will find that He is producing the kind of bread and wine that will benefit His other children.

The Place of Exaltation

". . . Jesus took . . . them up on a high mountain apart by themselves . . ." (Mark 9:2).

We have all experienced times of exaltation on the mountain, when we have seen things from God's perspective and have wanted to stay there. But God will never allow us to stay there. The true test of our spiritual life is in exhibiting the power to descend from the mountain. If we only have the power to go up, something is wrong. It is a wonderful thing to be on the mountain with God, but a person only gets there so that he may later go down and lift up the demon-possessed people in the valley (see 9:14–18). We are not made for the mountains, for sunrises, or for the other beautiful attractions in life—those are simply intended to be moments of inspiration. We are made for the valley and the ordinary things of life, and that is where we have to prove our stamina and strength. Yet our spiritual selfishness always wants repeated moments on the mountain. We feel that we could talk and live like perfect angels, if we could only stay on the mountaintop. Those times of exaltation are exceptional and they have their meaning in our life with God, but we must beware to prevent our spiritual selfishness from wanting to make them the only time.

We are inclined to think that everything that happens is to be turned into useful teaching. In actual fact, it is to be turned into something even better than teaching, namely, character. The mountaintop is not meant to *teach* us anything, it is meant to *make* us something. There is a terrible trap in always asking, "What's the use of this experience?" We can never measure spiritual matters in that way. The moments on the mountaintop are rare moments, and they are meant for something in God's purpose.

THE PLACE OF HUMILIATION

"If You can do anything, have compassion on us and help us" (Mark 9:22).

After every time of exaltation, we are brought down with a sudden rush into things as they really are, where it is neither beautiful, poetic, nor thrilling. The height of the mountaintop is measured by the dismal drudgery of the valley, but it is in the valley that we have to live for the glory of God. We *see* His glory on the mountain, but we never *live* for His glory there. It is in the place of humiliation that we find our true worth to God—that is where our faithfulness is revealed. Most of us can do things if we are always at some heroic level of intensity, simply because of the natural selfishness of our own hearts. But God wants us to be at the drab everyday level, where we live in the valley according to our personal relationship with Him. Peter thought it would be a wonderful thing for them to remain on the mountain, but Jesus Christ took the disciples down from the mountain and into the valley, where the true meaning of the vision was explained (see 9:5-6, 14-23).

"If you can do anything . . . ." It takes the valley of humiliation to remove the skepticism from us. Look back at your own experience and you will find that until you learned who Jesus really was, you were a skillful skeptic about His power. When you were on the mountaintop you could believe anything, but what about when you were faced with the facts of the valley? You may be able to give a testimony regarding your sanctification, but what about the thing that is a humiliation to you right now? The last time you were on the mountain with God, you saw that all the power in heaven and on earth belonged to Jesus—will you be skeptical now, simply because you are in the valley of humiliation?

THE PLACE OF MINISTRY

"He said to them, 'This kind [of unclean spirit] can come out by nothing but prayer and fasting' " (Mark 9:29).

H is disciples asked Him privately, 'Why could we not cast it out?' " (9:28). The answer lies in a personal relationship with Jesus Christ. "This kind can come out by nothing but" concentrating on Him, and then doubling and redoubling that concentration on Him. We can remain powerless forever, as the disciples were in this situation, by trying to do God's work without concentrating on His power, and by following instead the ideas that we draw from our own nature. We actually slander and dishonor God by our very eagerness to serve Him without knowing Him.

When you are brought face to face with a difficult situation and nothing happens externally, you can still know that freedom and release will be given because of your continued concentration on Jesus Christ. Your duty in service and ministry is to see that there is nothing between Jesus and yourself. Is there anything between you and Jesus even now? If there is, you must get through it, not by ignoring it as an irritation, or by going up and over it, but by facing it and getting through it into the presence of Jesus Christ. Then that very problem itself, and all that you have been through in connection with it, will glorify Jesus Christ in a way that you will never know until you see Him face to face.

We must be able to "mount up with wings like eagles" (Isaiah 40:31), but we must also know how to come down. The power of the saint lies in the coming down and in the living that is done in the valley. Paul said, "I can do all things through Christ who strengthens me" (Philippians 4:13) and what he was referring to were mostly humiliating things. And yet it is in our power to refuse to be humiliated and to say, "No, thank you, I much prefer to be on the mountaintop with God." Can I face things as they actually are in the light of the reality of Jesus Christ, or do things as they really are destroy my faith in Him, and put me into a panic?

OCTOBER 3

THE VISION AND THE REALITY

". . . to those who are . . . called to be saints . . ." (1 Corinthians 1:2).

Thank God for being able to see all that you have not yet been. You have had the vision, but you are not yet to the reality of it by any means. It is when we are in the valley, where we prove whether we will be the choice ones, that most of us turn back. We are not quite prepared for the bumps and bruises that must come if we are going to be turned into the shape of the vision. We have seen what we are not, and what God wants us to be, but are we willing to be battered into the shape of the vision to be used by God? The beatings will always come in the most common, everyday ways and through common, everyday people.

There are times when we do know what God's purpose is; whether we will let the vision be turned into actual character depends on us, not on God. If we prefer to relax on the mountaintop and live in the memory of the vision, then we will be of no real use in the ordinary things of which human life is made. We have to learn to live in reliance upon what we saw in the vision, not simply live in ecstatic delight and conscious reflection upon God. This means living the realities of our lives in the light of the vision until the truth of the vision is actually realized in us. Every bit of our training is in that direction. Learn to thank God for making His demands known.

Our little "I am" always sulks and pouts when God says *do*. Let your little "I am" be shriveled up in God's wrath and indignation—"I AM WHO I AM . . . has sent me to you" (Exodus 3:14). He must dominate. Isn't it piercing to realize that God not only knows where we live, but also knows the gutters into which we crawl! He will hunt us down as fast as a flash of lightning. No human being knows human beings as God does.

THE NATURE OF DEGENERATION

"Just as through one man sin entered the world, and death through sin, and thus death spread to all men, because all sinned . . ." (Romans 5:12).

The Bible does not say that God punished the human race for one man's sin, but that the nature of sin, namely, my claim to my right to myself, entered into the human race through one man. But it also says that another Man took upon Himself the sin of the human race and put it away—an infinitely more profound revelation (see Hebrews 9:26). The nature of sin is not immorality and wrongdoing, but the nature of self-realization which leads us to say, "I am my own god." This nature may exhibit itself in proper morality or in improper immorality, but it always has a common basis—my claim to my right to myself. When our Lord faced either people with all the forces of evil in them, or people who were clean-living, moral, and upright, He paid no attention to the moral degradation of one, nor any attention to the moral attainment of the other. He looked at something we do not see, namely, the nature of man (see John 2:25).

Sin is something I am born with and cannot touch—only God touches sin through redemption. It is through the Cross of Christ that God redeemed the entire human race from the possibility of damnation through the heredity of sin. God nowhere holds a person responsible for having the heredity of sin, and does not condemn anyone because of it. Condemnation comes when I realize that Jesus Christ came to deliver me from this heredity of sin, and yet I refuse to let Him do so. From that moment I begin to get the seal of damnation. "This is the condemnation [and the critical moment], that the light has come into the world, and men loved darkness rather than light . . . " (John 3:19).

THE NATURE OF REGENERATION

"When it pleased God . . . to reveal His Son in me . . ." (Galatians 1:15–16).

I f Jesus Christ is going to regenerate me, what is the problem He faces? It is simply this—I have a heredity in which I had no say or decision; I am not holy, nor am I likely to be; and if all Jesus Christ can do is tell me that I must be holy, His teaching only causes me to despair. But if Jesus Christ is truly a regenerator, someone who can put His own heredity of holiness into me, then I can begin to see what He means when He says that I have to be holy. Redemption means that Jesus Christ can put into anyone the hereditary nature that was in Himself, and all the standards He gives us are based on that nature—*His teaching is meant to be applied to the life which He puts within us.* The proper action on my part is simply to agree with God's verdict on sin as judged on the Cross of Christ.

The New Testament teaching about regeneration is that when a person is hit by his own sense of need, God will put the Holy Spirit into his spirit, and his personal spirit will be energized by the Spirit of the Son of God— ". . . until Christ is formed in you" (Galatians 4:19). The moral miracle of redemption is that God can put a new nature into me through which I can live a totally new life. When I finally reach the edge of my need and know my own limitations, then Jesus says, "Blessed are you . . ." (Matthew 5:11). But I must get to that point. God cannot put into me, the responsible moral person that I am, the nature that was in Jesus Christ unless I am aware of my need for it.

Just as the nature of sin entered into the human race through one man, the Holy Spirit entered into the human race through another Man (see Romans 5:12-19). And redemption means that I can be delivered from the heredity of sin, and that through Jesus Christ I can receive a pure and spotless heredity, namely, the Holy Spirit.

THE NATURE OF RECONCILIATION

"He made Him who knew no sin to be sin for us, that we might become the righteousness of God in Him" (2 Corinthians 5:21).

S in is a fundamental relationship—it is not wrong *doing*, but wrong *being*—it is deliberate and determined independence from God. The Christian faith bases everything on the extreme, self-confident nature of sin. Other faiths deal with *sins*—the Bible alone deals with *sin*. The first thing Jesus Christ confronted in people was the heredity of sin, and it is because we have ignored this in our presentation of the gospel that the message of the gospel has lost its sting and its explosive power.

The revealed truth of the Bible is not that Jesus Christ took on Himself our fleshly sins, but that He took on Himself the heredity of sin that no man can even touch. God made His own Son "to be sin" that He might make the sinner into a saint. It is revealed throughout the Bible that our Lord took on Himself the sin of the world through *identification with us*, not through *sympathy for us*. He deliberately took on His own shoulders, and endured in His own body, the complete, cumulative sin of the human race. "He made Him who knew no sin *to be sin for us* . . ." and by so doing He placed salvation for the entire human race solely on the basis of redemption. Jesus Christ reconciled the human race, putting it back to where God designed it to be. And now anyone can experience that reconciliation, being brought into oneness with God, on the basis of what our Lord has done on the cross.

A man cannot redeem himself—redemption is the work of God, and is absolutely finished and complete. And its application to individual people is a matter of their own individual action or response to it. A distinction must always be made between the revealed truth of redemption and the actual conscious experience of salvation in a person's life.

COMING TO JESUS

"Come to Me . . ." (Matthew 11:28).

I sn't it humiliating to be told that we must come to Jesus! Think of the things about which we will not come to Jesus Christ. If you want to know how real you are, test yourself by these words—"Come to Me. . . ." In every dimension in which you are not real, you will argue or evade the issue altogether rather than come; you will go through sorrow rather than come; and you will do anything rather than come the last lap of the race of seemingly unspeakable foolishness and say, "Just as I am, I come." As long as you have even the least bit of spiritual disrespect, it will always reveal itself in the fact that you are expecting God to tell you to do something very big, and yet all He is telling you to do is to "Come. . . ."

"Come to Me. . . ." When you hear those words, you will know that something must happen in you before you can come. The Holy Spirit will show you what you have to do, and it will involve anything that will uproot whatever is preventing you from getting through to Jesus. And you will never get any further until you are willing to do that very thing. The Holy Spirit will search out that one immovable stronghold within you, but He cannot budge it unless you are willing to let Him do so.

How often have you come to God with your requests and gone away thinking, "I've really received what I wanted this time!" And yet you go away with nothing, while all the time God has stood with His hands outstretched not only to take you but also for you to take Him. Just think of the invincible, unconquerable, and untiring patience of Jesus, who lovingly says, *"Come to Me. . . ."*

BUILDING ON
THE ATONEMENT

**". . . present . . . your members as instruments
of righteousness to God" (Romans 6:13).**

I cannot save and sanctify myself; I cannot make atonement for sin; I cannot redeem the world; I cannot right what is wrong, purify what is impure, or make holy what is unholy. That is all the sovereign work of God. Do I have faith in what Jesus Christ has done? He has made the perfect atonement for sin. Am I in the habit of constantly realizing it? The greatest need we have is not to *do* things, but to *believe* things. The redemption of Christ is not an experience, it is the great act of God which He has performed through Christ, and I have to build my faith on it. If I construct my faith on my own experience, I produce the most unscriptural kind of life—an isolated life, with my eyes focused solely on my own holiness. Beware of that human holiness that is not based on the atonement of the Lord. It has no value for anything except a life of isolation—it is useless to God and a nuisance to man. Measure every kind of experience you have by our Lord Himself. We cannot do anything pleasing to God unless we deliberately build on the foundation of the atonement by the Cross of Christ.

The atonement of Jesus must be exhibited in practical, unassuming ways in my life. Every time I obey, the absolute deity of God is on my side, so that the grace of God and my natural obedience are in perfect agreement. Obedience means that I have completely placed my trust in the atonement, and my obedience is immediately met by the delight of the supernatural grace of God.

Beware of the human holiness that denies the reality of the natural life—it is a fraud. Continually bring yourself to the trial or test of the atonement and ask, "Where is the discernment of the atonement in this, and in that?"

How Will I Know?

"Jesus answered and said, 'I thank You, Father . . . that You have hidden these things from the wise and prudent and have revealed them to babes' " (Matthew 11:25).

We do not grow into a spiritual relationship step by step—we either have a relationship or we do not. God does not continue to cleanse us more and more from sin—"But if we walk in the light," we *are* cleansed "from all sin" (1 John 1:7). It is a matter of obedience, and once we obey, the relationship is instantly perfected. But if we turn away from obedience for even one second, darkness and death are immediately at work again.

All of God's revealed truths are sealed until they are opened to us through obedience. You will never open them through philosophy or thinking. But once you obey, a flash of light comes immediately. Let God's truth work into you by immersing yourself in it, not by worrying into it. The only way you can get to know the truth of God is to stop trying to find out and by being born again. If you obey God in the first thing He shows you, then He instantly opens up the next truth to you. You could read volumes on the work of the Holy Spirit, when five minutes of total, uncompromising obedience would make things as clear as sunlight. Don't say, "I suppose I will understand these things someday!" You can understand them now. And it is not study that brings understanding to you, but obedience. Even the smallest bit of obedience opens heaven, and the deepest truths of God immediately become yours. Yet God will never reveal more truth about Himself to you, until you have obeyed what you know already. Beware of becoming one of the "wise and prudent." "If anyone wills to do His will, he shall know . . ." (John 7:17).

GOD'S SILENCE—THEN WHAT?

"When He heard that he was sick, He stayed two more days in the place where He was" (John 11:6).

Has God trusted you with His silence—a silence that has great meaning? God's silences are actually His answers. Just think of those days of absolute silence in the home at Bethany! Is there anything comparable to those days in your life? Can God trust you like that, or are you still asking Him for a visible answer? God will give you the very blessings you ask if you refuse to go any further without them, but His silence is the sign that He is bringing you into an even more wonderful understanding of Himself. Are you mourning before God because you have not had an audible response? When you cannot hear God, you will find that He has trusted you in the most intimate way possible—with absolute silence, not a silence of despair, but one of pleasure, because He saw that you could withstand an even bigger revelation. If God has given you a silence, then praise Him—He is bringing you into the mainstream of His purposes. The actual evidence of the answer in time is simply a matter of God's sovereignty. Time is nothing to God. For a while you may have said, "I asked God to give me bread, but He gave me a stone instead" (see Matthew 7:9). He did not give you a stone, and today you find that He gave you the "bread of life" (John 6:35).

A wonderful thing about God's silence is that His stillness is contagious—it gets into you, causing you to become perfectly confident so that you can honestly say, "I know that God has heard me." His silence is the very proof that He has. As long as you have the idea that God will always bless you in answer to prayer, He will do it, but He will never give you the grace of His silence. If Jesus Christ is bringing you into the understanding that prayer is for the glorifying of His Father, then He will give you the first sign of His intimacy—silence.

GETTING INTO GOD'S STRIDE

"Enoch walked with God . . ." (Genesis 5:24).

The true test of a person's spiritual life and character is not what he does in the extraordinary moments of life, but what he does during the ordinary times when there is nothing tremendous or exciting happening. A person's worth is revealed in his attitude toward the ordinary things of life when he is not under the spotlight (see John 1:35-37 and 3:30). It is painful work to get in step with God and to keep pace with Him—it means getting your second wind spiritually. In learning to walk with God, there is always the difficulty of getting into His stride, but once we have done so, the only characteristic that exhibits itself is the very life of God Himself. The individual person is merged into a personal oneness with God, and God's stride and His power alone are exhibited.

It is difficult to get into stride with God, because as soon as we start walking with Him we find that His pace has surpassed us before we have even taken three steps. He has different ways of doing things, and we have to be trained and disciplined in His ways. It was said of Jesus—"He will not fail nor be discouraged . . ." (Isaiah 42:4) because He never worked from His own individual standpoint, but always worked from the standpoint of His Father. And we must learn to do the same. Spiritual truth is learned through the atmosphere that surrounds us, not through intellectual reasoning. It is God's Spirit that changes the atmosphere of our way of looking at things, and then things begin to be possible which before were impossible. Getting into God's stride means nothing less than oneness with Him. It takes a long time to get there, but keep at it. Don't give up because the pain is intense right now—get on with it, and before long you will find that you have a new vision and a new purpose.

INDIVIDUAL DISCOURAGEMENT AND PERSONAL GROWTH

"... when Moses was grown ... he went out
to his brethren and looked at their burdens"
(Exodus 2:11).

Moses saw the oppression of his people and felt
certain that he was the one to deliver them, and
in the righteous indignation of his own spirit
he started to right their wrongs. After he launched his
first strike for God and for what was right, God allowed
Moses to be driven into empty discouragement, sending
him into the desert to feed sheep for forty years. At the
end of that time, God appeared to Moses and said to
him, " '... bring My people ... out of Egypt.' But Moses
said to God, 'Who am I that I should go ... ?' " (Exodus
3:10-11). In the beginning Moses had realized that he
was the one to deliver the people, but he had to be
trained and disciplined by God first. He was right in his
individual perspective, but he was not the person for the
work until he had learned true fellowship and oneness
with God.

We may have the vision of God and a very clear
understanding of what God wants, and yet when we
start to do it, there comes to us something equivalent to
Moses' forty years in the wilderness. It's as if God had
ignored the entire thing, and when we are thoroughly
discouraged, God comes back and revives His call to us.
And then we begin to tremble and say, "Who am I that I
should go ... ?" We must learn that God's great stride is
summed up in these words—"I AM WHO I AM ... has
sent me to you" (Exodus 3:14). We must also learn that
our individual effort for God shows nothing but disrespect for Him—our individuality is to be rendered radiant through a personal relationship with God, so that He
may be "well pleased" (Matthew 3:17). We are focused on
the right individual perspective of things; we have the
vision and can say, "I know this is what God wants me to
do." But we have not yet learned to get into God's stride.
If you are going through a time of discouragement, there
is a time of great personal growth ahead.

OCTOBER 13

THE KEY TO THE MISSIONARY'S WORK

"Jesus came and spoke to them, saying, 'All authority has been given to Me in heaven and on earth. Go therefore and make disciples of all the nations . . .' " (Matthew 28:18–19).

The key to the missionary's work is the authority of Jesus Christ, not the needs of the lost. We are inclined to look on our Lord as one who assists us in our endeavors for God. Yet our Lord places Himself as the absolute sovereign and supreme Lord over His disciples. He does not say that the lost will never be saved if we don't go—He simply says, "Go therefore and make disciples of all the nations . . . ." He says, "Go on the basis of the revealed truth of My sovereignty, teaching and preaching out of your living experience of Me."

"Then the eleven disciples went . . . to the mountain which Jesus had appointed for them" (28:16). If I want to know the universal sovereignty of Christ, I must know Him myself. I must take time to worship the One whose name I bear. Jesus says, "Come to Me . . ."—that is the place to meet Jesus—"all you who labor and are heavy laden . . ." (Matthew 11:28)—and how many missionaries are! We completely dismiss these wonderful words of the universal Sovereign of the world, but they are the words of Jesus to His disciples meant for here and now.

"Go therefore . . . ." To "go" simply means to live. Acts 1:8 is the description of *how* to go. Jesus did not say in this verse, "*Go* into Jerusalem, Judea, and Samaria," but, ". . . you shall *be witnesses* to Me in [all these places]." He takes upon Himself the work of sending us.

"If you abide in Me, and My words abide in you . . ." (John 15:7)—that is the way to keep *going*. Where we are placed is then a matter of indifference to us, because God sovereignly engineers our *goings*.

"None of these things move me; nor do I count my life dear to myself, so that I may finish my race with joy, and the ministry which I received from the Lord Jesus . . ." (Acts 20:24). That is how to keep going until we are gone from this life.

THE KEY TO THE MISSIONARY'S MESSAGE

"He Himself is the propitiation for our sins, and not for ours only but also for the whole world" (1 John 2:2).

The key to the missionary's message is the propitiation of Christ Jesus—His sacrifice for us that completely satisfied the wrath of God. Look at any other aspect of Christ's work, whether it is healing, saving, or sanctifying, and you will see that there is nothing limitless about those. But—"The Lamb of God who takes away the sin of the world!"—that is limitless (John 1:29). The missionary's message is the limitless importance of Jesus Christ as the propitiation for our sins, and a missionary is someone who is immersed in the truth of that revelation.

The real key to the missionary's message is the "remissionary" aspect of Christ's life, not His kindness, His goodness, or even His revealing of the fatherhood of God to us. ". . . repentance and *remission* of sins should be preached . . . to all nations . . ." (Luke 24:47). The greatest message of limitless importance is that "He Himself is the propitiation for our sins . . . ." The missionary's message is not nationalistic, favoring nations or individuals; it is "for the whole world." When the Holy Spirit comes into me, He does not consider my partialities or preferences; He simply brings me into oneness with the Lord Jesus.

A missionary is someone who is bound by marriage to the stated mission and purpose of his Lord and Master. He is not to proclaim his own point of view, but is only to proclaim "the Lamb of God." It is easier to belong to a faction that simply tells what Jesus Christ has done for me, and easier to become a devotee of divine healing, or of a special type of sanctification, or of the baptism of the Holy Spirit. But Paul did not say, "Woe is me if I do not preach what Christ has done for me," but, ". . . woe is me if I do not preach the gospel!" (1 Corinthians 9:16). And this is the gospel—"the Lamb of God who takes away the sin of the world!"

OCTOBER 15

THE KEY TO THE MASTER'S ORDERS

"Pray the Lord of the harvest to send out laborers into His harvest" (Matthew 9:38).

The key to the missionary's difficult task is in the hand of God, and that key is prayer, not work—that is, not work as the word is commonly used today, which often results in the shifting of our focus away from God. The key to the missionary's difficult task is also not the key of common sense, nor is it the key of medicine, civilization, education, or even evangelization. The key is in following the Master's orders—the key is prayer. "Pray the Lord of the harvest . . . ." In the natural realm, prayer is not practical but absurd. We have to realize that prayer is foolish from the commonsense point of view.

From Jesus Christ's perspective, there are no nations, but only *the world*. How many of us pray without regard to the persons, but with regard to only one Person—Jesus Christ? He owns the harvest that is produced through distress and through conviction of sin. This is the harvest for which we have to pray that laborers be sent out to reap. We stay busy at work, while people all around us are ripe and ready to be harvested; we do not reap even one of them, but simply waste our Lord's time in over-energized activities and programs. Suppose a crisis were to come into your father's or your brother's life—are you there as a laborer to reap the harvest for Jesus Christ? Is your response, "Oh, but I have a special work to do!" No Christian has a special work to do. A Christian is called to be Jesus Christ's own, "a servant [who] is not greater than his master" (John 13:16), and someone who does not dictate to Jesus Christ what he intends to do. Our Lord calls us to no special work—He calls us to Himself. "Pray the Lord of the harvest," and He will engineer your circumstances to send you out as His laborer.

THE KEY OF THE
GREATER WORK

"... I say to you, he who believes in Me, ...
greater works than these he will do, because I
go to My Father" (John 14:12).

Prayer does not equip us for greater works—prayer
is the greater work. Yet we think of prayer as some
commonsense exercise of our higher powers that
simply prepares us for God's work. In the teachings
of Jesus Christ, prayer is the working of the miracle
of redemption in me, which produces the miracle of
redemption in others, through the power of God. The
way fruit remains firm is through prayer, but remember
that it is prayer based on the agony of Christ in redemption, not on my own agony. We must go to God as His
child, because only a child gets his prayers answered; a
"wise" man does not (see Matthew 11:25).

Prayer is *the* battle, and it makes no difference where
you are. However God may engineer your circumstances,
your duty is to pray. Never allow yourself this thought, "I
am of no use where I am," because you certainly cannot
be used where you have not yet been placed. Wherever
God has placed you and whatever your circumstances,
you should pray, continually offering up prayers to Him.
And He promises, "Whatever you ask in My name, that I
will do ..." (14:13). Yet we refuse to pray unless it thrills
or excites us, which is the most intense form of spiritual
selfishness. We must learn to work according to God's
direction, and He says to *pray*. "Pray the Lord of the
harvest to send out laborers into His harvest" (Matthew
9:38).

There is nothing thrilling about a laboring person's
work, but it is the laboring person who makes the ideas
of the genius possible. And it is the laboring saint who
makes the ideas of his Master possible. When you labor
at prayer, from God's perspective there are always results.
What an astonishment it will be to see, once the veil is
finally lifted, all the souls that have been reaped by you,
simply because you have been in the habit of taking your
orders from Jesus Christ.

OCTOBER 17

THE KEY TO THE
MISSIONARY'S DEVOTION

**". . . they went forth for His name's sake . . ."
(3 John 7).**

Our Lord told us how our love for Him is to exhibit itself when He asked, "Do you love Me?" (John 21:17). And then He said, "Feed My sheep." In effect, He said, "Identify *yourself* with My interests in other people," not, "Identify *Me* with *your* interests in other people." First Corinthians 13:4-8 shows us the characteristics of this love—it is actually the love *of* God expressing itself. The true test of my love for Jesus is a very practical one, and all the rest is sentimental talk.

Faithfulness to Jesus Christ is the supernatural work of redemption that has been performed in me by the Holy Spirit—"the love of God has been poured out in our hearts by the Holy Spirit . . ." (Romans 5:5). And it is that love in me that effectively works through me and comes in contact with everyone I meet. I remain faithful to His name, even though the commonsense view of my life may seemingly deny that, and may appear to be declaring that He has no more power than the morning mist.

The key to the missionary's devotion is that he is attached to nothing and to no one except our Lord Himself. It does not mean simply being detached from the external things surrounding us. Our Lord was amazingly in touch with the ordinary things of life, but He had an inner detachment except toward God. External detachment is often an actual indication of a secret, growing, inner attachment to the things we stay away from externally.

The duty of a faithful missionary is to concentrate on keeping his soul completely and continually open to the nature of the Lord Jesus Christ. The men and women our Lord sends out on His endeavors are ordinary human people, but people who are controlled by their devotion to Him, which has been brought about through the work of the Holy Spirit.

OCTOBER 18

THE UNHEEDED SECRET

"Jesus answered, 'My kingdom is not of this world' " (John 18:36).

The great enemy of the Lord Jesus Christ today is the idea of practical work that has no basis in the New Testament but comes from the systems of the world. This work insists upon endless energy and activities, but no private life with God. The emphasis is put on the wrong thing. Jesus said, "The kingdom of God does not come with observation . . . . For indeed, the kingdom of God is within you" (Luke 17:20-21). It is a hidden, obscure thing. An active Christian worker too often lives to be seen by others, while it is the innermost, personal area that reveals the power of a person's life.

We must get rid of the plague of the spirit of this religious age in which we live. In our Lord's life there was none of the pressure and the rushing of tremendous activity that we regard so highly today, and a disciple is to be like His Master. The central point of the kingdom of Jesus Christ is a personal relationship with Him, not public usefulness to others.

It is not the practical activities that are the strength of this Bible Training College—its entire strength lies in the fact that here you are immersed in the truths of God to soak in them before Him. You have no idea of where or how God is going to engineer your future circumstances, and no knowledge of what stress and strain is going to be placed on you either at home or abroad. And if you waste your time in overactivity, instead of being immersed in the great fundamental truths of God's redemption, then you will snap when the stress and strain do come. But if this time of soaking before God is being spent in getting rooted and grounded in Him, which may appear to be impractical, then you will remain true to Him whatever happens.

IS GOD'S WILL MY WILL?

"This is the will of God, your sanctification . . ."
(1 Thessalonians 4:3).

Sanctification is not a question of whether God is willing to sanctify me—is it *my* will? Am I willing to let God do in me everything that has been made possible through the atonement of the Cross of Christ? Am I willing to let Jesus become sanctification to me, and to let His life be exhibited in my human flesh? (see 1 Corinthians 1:30). Beware of saying, "Oh, I am longing to be sanctified." No, you are not. Recognize your need, but stop longing and make it a matter of action. Receive Jesus Christ to become sanctification for you by absolute, unquestioning faith, and the great miracle of the atonement of Jesus will become real in you.

All that Jesus made possible becomes mine through the free and loving gift of God on the basis of what Christ accomplished on the cross. And my attitude as a saved and sanctified soul is that of profound, humble holiness (there is no such thing as proud holiness). It is a holiness based on agonizing repentance, a sense of inexpressible shame and degradation, and also on the amazing realization that the love of God demonstrated itself to me while I cared nothing about Him (see Romans 5:8). He completed everything for my salvation and sanctification. No wonder Paul said that nothing "shall be able to separate us from the love of God which is in Christ Jesus our Lord" (Romans 8:39).

Sanctification makes me one with Jesus Christ, and in Him one with God, and it is accomplished only through the magnificent atonement of Christ. Never confuse the effect with the cause. The effect in me is obedience, service, and prayer, and is the outcome of inexpressible thanks and adoration for the miraculous sanctification that has been brought about in me because of the atonement through the Cross of Christ.

OCTOBER 20

IMPULSIVENESS OR DISCIPLESHIP?

"But you, beloved, building yourselves up on your most holy faith . . ." (Jude 20).

There was nothing of the nature of impulsive or thoughtless action about our Lord, but only a calm strength that never got into a panic. Most of us develop our Christianity along the lines of our own nature, not along the lines of God's nature. Impulsiveness is a trait of the natural life, and our Lord always ignores it, because it hinders the development of the life of a disciple. Watch how the Spirit of God gives a sense of restraint to impulsiveness, suddenly bringing us a feeling of self-conscious foolishness, which makes us instantly want to vindicate ourselves. Impulsiveness is all right in a child, but is disastrous in a man or woman—an impulsive adult is always a spoiled person. Impulsiveness needs to be trained into intuition through discipline.

Discipleship is built entirely on the supernatural grace of God. Walking on water is easy to someone with impulsive boldness, but walking on dry land as a disciple of Jesus Christ is something altogether different. Peter walked on the water to go to Jesus, but he "followed Him at a distance" on dry land (Mark 14:54). We do not need the grace of God to withstand crises—human nature and pride are sufficient for us to face the stress and strain magnificently. But it does require the supernatural grace of God to live twenty-four hours of every day as a saint, going through drudgery, and living an ordinary, unnoticed, and ignored existence as a disciple of Jesus. It is ingrained in us that we have to do exceptional things for God—but we do not. We have to be exceptional in the ordinary things of life, and holy on the ordinary streets, among ordinary people—and this is not learned in five minutes.

THE WITNESS OF THE SPIRIT

"The Spirit Himself bears witness with our spirit . . ." (Romans 8:16).

We are in danger of getting into a bargaining spirit with God when we come to Him—we want the witness of the Spirit before we have done what God tells us to do.

Why doesn't God reveal Himself to you? He cannot. It is not that He will not, but He cannot, because you are in the way as long as you won't abandon yourself to Him in total surrender. Yet once you do, immediately God witnesses to Himself—He cannot witness to you, but He instantly witnesses to His own nature in you. If you received the witness of the Spirit before the reality and truth that comes from obedience, it would simply result in sentimental emotion. But when you act on the basis of redemption, and stop the disrespectfulness of debating with God, He immediately gives His witness. As soon as you abandon your own reasoning and arguing, God witnesses to what He has done, and you are amazed at your total disrespect in having kept Him waiting. If you are debating as to whether or not God can deliver from sin, then either let Him do it or tell Him that He cannot. Do not quote this or that person to Him. Simply obey Matthew 11:28, "Come to Me, all you who labor and are heavy laden . . . ." *Come*, if you are weary, and *ask*, if you know you are evil (see Luke 11:9–13).

The Spirit of God witnesses to the redemption of our Lord, and to nothing else. He cannot witness to our reason. We are inclined to mistake the simplicity that comes from our natural commonsense decisions for the witness of the Spirit, but the Spirit witnesses only to His own nature, and to the work of redemption, never to our reason. If we are trying to make Him witness to our reason, it is no wonder that we are in darkness and uncertainty. Throw it all overboard, trust in Him, and He will give you the witness of the Spirit.

NOTHING OF THE OLD LIFE!

"If anyone is in Christ, he is a new creation; old things have passed away; behold, all things have become new" (2 Corinthians 5:17).

Our Lord never tolerates our prejudices—He is directly opposed to them and puts them to death. We tend to think that God has some special interest in our particular prejudices, and are very sure that He will never deal with us as He has to deal with others. We even say to ourselves, "God has to deal with other people in a very strict way, but of course He knows that my prejudices are all right." But we must learn that God accepts nothing of the old life! Instead of being on the side of our prejudices, He is deliberately removing them from us. It is part of our moral education to see our prejudices put to death by His providence, and to watch how He does it. God pays no respect to anything we bring to Him. There is only one thing God wants of us, and that is our unconditional surrender.

When we are born again, the Holy Spirit begins to work His new creation in us, and there will come a time when there is nothing remaining of the old life. Our old gloomy outlook disappears, as does our old attitude toward things, and "all things are of God" (5:18). How are we going to get a life that has no lust, no self-interest, and is not sensitive to the ridicule of others? How will we have the type of love that "is kind . . . is not provoked, [and] thinks no evil"? (1 Corinthians 13:4-5). The only way is by allowing nothing of the old life to remain, and by having only simple, perfect trust in God—such a trust that we no longer want God's blessings, but only want God Himself. Have we come to the point where God can withdraw His blessings from us without our trust in Him being affected? Once we truly see God at work, we will never be concerned again about the things that happen, because we are actually trusting in our Father in heaven, whom the world cannot see.

THE PROPER PERSPECTIVE

"Thanks be to God who always leads us in triumph in Christ . . ." (2 Corinthians 2:14).

The proper perspective of a servant of God must not simply be as near to the highest as he can get, but it must be *the* highest. Be careful that you vigorously maintain God's perspective, and remember that it must be done every day, little by little. Don't think on a finite level. No outside power can touch the proper perspective.

The proper perspective to maintain is that we are here for only one purpose—to be captives marching in the procession of Christ's triumphs. We are not on display in God's showcase—we are here to exhibit only one thing—the "captivity [of our lives] to the obedience of Christ" (2 Corinthians 10:5). How small all the other perspectives are! For example, the ones that say, "I am standing all alone, battling for Jesus," or, "I have to maintain the cause of Christ and hold down this fort for Him." But Paul said, in essence, "I am in the procession of a conqueror, and it doesn't matter what the difficulties are, for I am always led in triumph." Is this idea being worked out practically in us? Paul's secret joy was that God took him as a blatant rebel against Jesus Christ, and made him a captive—and that became his purpose. It was Paul's joy to be a captive of the Lord, and he had no other interest in heaven or on earth. It is a shameful thing for a Christian to talk about getting the victory. We should belong so completely to the Victor that it is always His victory, and "we are more than conquerors through Him . . ." (Romans 8:37).

"We are to God the fragrance of Christ . . ." (2 Corinthians 2:15). We are encompassed with the sweet aroma of Jesus, and wherever we go we are a wonderful refreshment to God.

SUBMITTING TO GOD'S PURPOSE

"I have become all things to all men, that I might by all means save some" (1 Corinthians 9:22).

A Christian worker has to learn how to be God's man or woman of great worth and excellence in the midst of a multitude of meager and worthless things. Never protest by saying, "If only I were somewhere else!" All of God's people are ordinary people who have been made extraordinary by the purpose He has given them. Unless we have the right purpose intellectually in our minds and lovingly in our hearts, we will very quickly be diverted from being useful to God. We are not workers for God by choice. Many people deliberately choose to be workers, but they have no purpose of God's almighty grace or His mighty Word in them. Paul's whole heart, mind, and soul were consumed with the great purpose of what Jesus Christ came to do, and he never lost sight of that one thing. We must continually confront ourselves with one central fact—". . . Jesus Christ and Him crucified" (1 Corinthians 2:2).

"I chose you . . ." (John 15:16). Keep these words as a wonderful reminder in your theology. It is not that you have gotten God, but that He has gotten you. God is at work bending, breaking, molding, and doing exactly as He chooses. And why is He doing it? He is doing it for only one purpose—that He may be able to say, "This is My man, and this is My woman." We have to be in God's hand so that He can place others on the Rock, Jesus Christ, just as He has placed us.

Never choose to be a worker, but once God has placed His call upon you, woe be to you if you "turn aside . . . to the right or the left . . ." (Deuteronomy 28:14). He will do with you what He never did before His call came to you, and He will do with you what He is not doing with other people. Let Him have His way.

WHAT IS A MISSIONARY?

"Jesus said to them again, '. . . As the Father has sent Me, I also send you' " (John 20:21).

A missionary is someone sent by Jesus Christ just as He was sent by God. The great controlling factor is not the needs of people, but the command of Jesus. The source of our inspiration in our service for God is behind us, not ahead of us. The tendency today is to put the inspiration out in front—to sweep everything together in front of us and make it conform to our definition of success. But in the New Testament the inspiration is put behind us, and is the Lord Jesus Himself. The goal is to be true to Him—to carry out *His* plans.

Personal attachment to the Lord Jesus and to His perspective is the one thing that must not be overlooked. In missionary work the great danger is that God's call will be replaced by the needs of the people, to the point that human sympathy for those needs will absolutely overwhelm the meaning of being sent by Jesus. The needs are so enormous, and the conditions so difficult, that every power of the mind falters and fails. We tend to forget that the one great reason underneath all missionary work is not primarily the elevation of the people, their education, nor their needs, but is first and foremost the command of Jesus Christ—"Go therefore and make disciples of all the nations . . ." (Matthew 28:19).

When looking back on the lives of men and women of God, the tendency is to say, "What wonderfully keen and intelligent wisdom they had, and how perfectly they understood all that God wanted!" But the keen and intelligent mind behind them was the mind of God, not human wisdom at all. We give credit to human wisdom when we should give credit to the divine guidance of God being exhibited through childlike people who were "foolish" enough to trust God's wisdom and His supernatural equipment.

THE METHOD OF MISSIONS

"Go therefore and make disciples of all the
nations . . ." (Matthew 28:19).

Jesus Christ did not say, "Go and save souls" (the salvation of souls is the supernatural work of God), but He said, "Go . . . make disciples of all the nations . . . ." Yet you cannot make disciples unless you are a disciple yourself. When the disciples returned from their first mission, they were filled with joy because even the demons were subject to them. But Jesus said, in effect, "Don't rejoice in successful service—the great secret of joy is that you have the right relationship with Me" (see Luke 10:17-20). The missionary's great essential is remaining true to the call of God, and realizing that his one and only purpose is to disciple men and women to Jesus. Remember that there is a passion for souls that does not come from God, but from our desire to make converts to our point of view.

The challenge to the missionary does not come from the fact that people are difficult to bring to salvation, that backsliders are difficult to reclaim, or that there is a barrier of callous indifference. No, the challenge comes from the perspective of the missionary's own personal relationship with Jesus Christ—"Do you believe that I am able to do this?" (Matthew 9:28). Our Lord unwaveringly asks us that question, and it confronts us in every individual situation we encounter. The one great challenge to us is—do I know my risen Lord? Do I know the power of His indwelling Spirit? Am I wise enough in God's sight, but foolish enough according to the wisdom of the world, to trust in what Jesus Christ has said? Or am I abandoning the great supernatural position of limitless confidence in Christ Jesus, which is really God's only call for a missionary? If I follow any other method, I depart altogether from the methods prescribed by our Lord—"All authority has been given to Me . . . . *Go therefore* . . ." (Matthew 28:18-19).

JUSTIFICATION BY FAITH

"If when we were enemies we were reconciled to God through the death of His Son, much more, having been reconciled, we shall be saved by His life" (Romans 5:10).

I am not saved by believing—I simply realize I am saved by believing. And it is not repentance that saves me—repentance is only the sign that I realize what God has done through Christ Jesus. The danger here is putting the emphasis on the effect, instead of on the cause. Is it my obedience, consecration, and dedication that make me right with God? It is never that! I am made right with God because, prior to all of that, Christ died. When I turn to God and by belief accept what God reveals, the miraculous atonement by the Cross of Christ instantly places me into a right relationship with God. And as a result of the supernatural miracle of God's grace I stand justified, not because I am sorry for my sin, or because I have repented, but because of what Jesus has done. The Spirit of God brings justification with a shattering, radiant light, and I know that I am saved, even though I don't know how it was accomplished.

The salvation that comes from God is not based on human logic, but on the sacrificial death of Jesus. We can be born again solely because of the atonement of our Lord. Sinful men and women can be changed into new creations, not through their repentance or their belief, but through the wonderful work of God in Christ Jesus which preceded all of our experience (see 2 Corinthians 5:17-19). The unconquerable safety of justification and sanctification is God Himself. We do not have to accomplish these things ourselves—they have been accomplished through the atonement of the Cross of Christ. The supernatural becomes natural to us through the miracle of God, and there is the realization of what Jesus Christ has already done—*"It is finished!"* (John 19:30).

SUBSTITUTION

"He made Him who knew no sin to be sin for us, that we might become the righteousness of God in Him" (2 Corinthians 5:21).

The modern view of the death of Jesus is that He died for our sins out of sympathy for us. Yet the New Testament view is that He took our sin on Himself not because of sympathy, but because of His identification with us. He was *"made . . . to be sin . . . ."* Our sins are removed because of the death of Jesus, and the only explanation for His death is His obedience to His Father, not His sympathy for us. We are acceptable to God not because we have obeyed, nor because we have promised to give up things, but because of the death of Christ, and for no other reason. We say that Jesus Christ came to reveal the fatherhood and the lovingkindness of God, but the New Testament says that He came to take "away the sin of the world!" (John 1:29). And the revealing of the fatherhood of God is only to those to whom Jesus has been introduced as Savior. In speaking to the world, Jesus Christ never referred to Himself as One who revealed the Father, but He spoke instead of being a stumbling block (see John 15:22-24). John 14:9, where Jesus said, "He who has seen Me has seen the Father," was spoken to His disciples.

That Christ died for me, and therefore I am completely free from penalty, is never taught in the New Testament. What *is* taught in the New Testament is that "He died for all" (2 Corinthians 5:15)—not, "He died my death"—and that through identification with His death I can be freed from sin, and have His very righteousness imparted as a gift to me. The substitution which is taught in the New Testament is twofold—"For He made Him who knew no sin to be sin for us, *that we might become the righteousness of God in Him.*" The teaching is not Christ *for* me unless I am determined to have Christ formed *in* me (see Galatians 4:19).

FAITH

"Without faith it is impossible to please Him . . ." (Hebrews 11:6).

Faith in active opposition to common sense is mistaken enthusiasm and narrow-mindedness, and common sense in opposition to faith demonstrates a mistaken reliance on reason as the basis for truth. The life of faith brings the two of these into the proper relationship. Common sense and faith are as different from each each other as the natural life is from the spiritual, and as impulsiveness is from inspiration. Nothing that Jesus Christ ever said is common sense, but is revelation sense, and is complete, whereas common sense falls short. Yet faith must be tested and tried before it becomes real in your life. "We know that all things work together for good . . ." (Romans 8:28) so that no matter what happens, the transforming power of God's providence transforms perfect faith into reality. Faith always works in a personal way, because the purpose of God is to see that perfect faith is made real in His children.

For every detail of common sense in life, there is a truth God has revealed by which we can prove in our practical experience what we believe God to be. Faith is a tremendously active principle that always puts Jesus Christ first. The life of faith says, "Lord, You have said it, it appears to be irrational, but I'm going to step out boldly, trusting in Your Word" (for example, see Matthew 6:33). Turning intellectual faith into our personal possession is *always* a fight, not just sometimes. God brings us into particular circumstances to educate our faith, because the nature of faith is to make the object of our faith very real to us. Until we know Jesus, God is merely a concept, and we can't have faith in Him. But once we hear Jesus say, "He who has seen Me has seen the Father" (John 14:9) we immediately have something that is real, and our faith is limitless. Faith is the entire person in the right relationship with God through the power of the Spirit of Jesus Christ.

THE TRIAL OF FAITH

"If you have faith as a mustard seed . . . nothing will be impossible for you" (Matthew 17:20).

We have the idea that God rewards us for our faith, and it may be so in the initial stages. But we do not earn anything through faith— faith brings us into the right relationship with God and gives Him His opportunity to work. Yet God frequently has to knock the bottom out of your experience as His saint to get you in direct contact with Himself. God wants you to understand that it is a life of *faith*, not a life of emotional enjoyment of His blessings. The beginning of your life of faith was very narrow and intense, centered around a small amount of experience that had as much emotion as faith in it, and it was full of light and sweetness. Then God withdrew His conscious blessings to teach you to "walk by faith" (2 Corinthians 5:7). And you are worth much more to Him now than you were in your days of conscious delight with your thrilling testimony.

Faith by its very nature must be tested and tried. And the real trial of faith is not that we find it difficult to trust God, but that God's character must be proven as trustworthy in our own minds. Faith being worked out into reality must experience times of unbroken isolation. Never confuse the trial of faith with the ordinary discipline of life, because a great deal of what we call the trial of faith is the inevitable result of being alive. Faith, as the Bible teaches it, is faith in God coming against everything that contradicts Him—a faith that says, "I will remain true to God's character whatever He may do." The highest and the greatest expression of faith in the whole Bible is—"Though He slay me, yet will I trust Him" (Job 13:15).

"You Are Not Your Own"

"Do you not know that . . . you are not your own?" (1 Corinthians 6:19).

There is no such thing as a private life, or a place to hide in this world, for a man or woman who is intimately aware of and shares in the sufferings of Jesus Christ. God divides the private life of His saints and makes it a highway for the world on one hand and for Himself on the other. No human being can stand that unless he is identified with Jesus Christ. We are not sanctified for ourselves. We are called into intimacy with the gospel, and things happen that appear to have nothing to do with us. But God is getting us into fellowship with Himself. Let Him have His way. If you refuse, you will be of no value to God in His redemptive work in the world, but will be a hindrance and a stumbling block.

The first thing God does is get us grounded on strong reality and truth. He does this until our cares for ourselves individually have been brought into submission to His way for the purpose of His redemption. Why shouldn't we experience heartbreak? Through those doorways God is opening up ways of fellowship with His Son. Most of us collapse at the first grip of pain. We sit down at the door of God's purpose and enter a slow death through self-pity. And all the so-called Christian sympathy of others helps us to our deathbed. But God will not. He comes with the grip of the pierced hand of His Son, as if to say, "Enter into fellowship with Me; arise and shine." If God can accomplish His purposes in this world through a broken heart, then why not thank Him for breaking yours?

OBEDIENCE OR INDEPENDENCE?

**"If you love Me, keep My commandments"
(John 14:15).**

Our Lord never insists on our obedience. He stresses very definitely what we *ought* to do, but He never *forces* us to do it. We have to obey Him out of a oneness of spirit with Him. That is why whenever our Lord talked about discipleship, He prefaced it with an "If," meaning, "You do not need to do this unless you desire to do so." "*If* anyone desires to come after Me, let him deny himself . . ." (Luke 9:23). In other words, "To be My disciple, let him give up his right to himself to Me." Our Lord is not talking about our eternal position, but about our being of value to Him in this life here and now. That is why He sounds so stern (see Luke 14:26). Never try to make sense from these words by separating them from the One who spoke them.

The Lord does not give me rules, but He makes His standard very clear. If my relationship to Him is that of love, I will do what He says without hesitation. If I hesitate, it is because I love someone I have placed in competition with Him, namely, myself. Jesus Christ will not force me to obey Him, but I must. And as soon as I obey Him, I fulfill my spiritual destiny. My personal life may be crowded with small, petty happenings, altogether insignificant. But if I obey Jesus Christ in the seemingly random circumstances of life, they become pinholes through which I see the face of God. Then, when I stand face to face with God, I will discover that through my obedience thousands were blessed. When God's redemption brings a human soul to the point of obedience, it always produces. If I obey Jesus Christ, the redemption of God will flow through me to the lives of others, because behind the deed of obedience is the reality of Almighty God.

A Bondservant of Jesus

"I have been crucified with Christ; it is no longer I who live, but Christ lives in me . . ." (Galatians 2:20).

These words mean the breaking and collapse of my independence brought about by my own hands, and the surrendering of my life to the supremacy of the Lord Jesus. No one can do this for me, I must do it myself. God may bring me up to this point three hundred and sixty-five times a year, but He cannot push me through it. It means breaking the hard outer layer of my individual independence from God, and the liberating of myself and my nature into oneness with Him; not following my own ideas, but choosing absolute loyalty to Jesus. Once I am at that point, there is no possibility of misunderstanding. Very few of us know anything about loyalty to Christ or understand what He meant when He said, *". . . for My sake"* (Matthew 5:11). That is what makes a strong saint.

Has that breaking of my independence come? All the rest is religious fraud. The one point to decide is— will I give up? Will I surrender to Jesus Christ, placing no conditions whatsoever as to how the brokenness will come? I must be broken from my own understanding of myself. When I reach that point, immediately the reality of the supernatural identification with Jesus Christ takes place. And the witness of the Spirit of God is unmistakable—"I have been crucified with Christ . . . ."

The passion of Christianity comes from deliberately signing away my own rights and becoming a bondservant of Jesus Christ. Until I do that, I will not begin to be a saint.

One student a year who hears God's call would be sufficient for God to have called the Bible Training College into existence. This college has no value as an organization, not even academically. Its sole value for existence is for God to help Himself to lives. Will we allow Him to help Himself to us, or are we more concerned with our own ideas of what we are going to be?

THE AUTHORITY OF TRUTH

"Draw near to God and He will draw near to you" (James 4:8).

It is essential that you give people the opportunity to act on the truth of God. The responsibility must be left with the individual—you cannot act for him. It must be his own deliberate act, but the evangelical message should always lead him to action. Refusing to act leaves a person paralyzed, exactly where he was previously. But once he acts, he is never the same. It is the apparent folly of the truth that stands in the way of hundreds who have been convicted by the Spirit of God. Once I press myself into action, I immediately begin to live. Anything less is merely existing. The moments I truly live are the moments when I act with my entire will.

When a truth of God is brought home to your soul, never allow it to pass without acting on it internally in your will, not necessarily externally in your physical life. Record it with ink and with blood—work it into your life. The weakest saint who transacts business with Jesus Christ is liberated the second he acts and God's almighty power is available on his behalf. We come up to the truth of God, confess we are wrong, but go back again. Then we approach it again and turn back, until we finally learn we have no business going back. When we are confronted with such a word of truth from our redeeming Lord, we must move directly to transact business with Him. "Come to Me . . ." (Matthew 11:28). His word *come* means "to act." Yet the last thing we want to do is come. But everyone who does come knows that, at that very moment, the supernatural power of the life of God invades him. The dominating power of the world, the flesh, and the devil is now paralyzed; not by your act, but because your act has joined you to God and tapped you in to His redemptive power.

PARTAKERS OF HIS SUFFERINGS

"... but rejoice to the extent that you partake of Christ's sufferings ..." (1 Peter 4:13).

If you are going to be used by God, He will take you through a number of experiences that are not meant for you personally at all. They are designed to make you useful in His hands, and to enable you to understand what takes place in the lives of others. Because of this process, you will never be surprised by what comes your way. You say, "Oh, I can't deal with that person." Why can't you? God gave you sufficient opportunities to learn from Him about that problem; but you turned away, not heeding the lesson, because it seemed foolish to spend your time that way.

The sufferings of Christ were not those of ordinary people. He suffered "according to the will of God" (1 Peter 4:19), having a different point of view of suffering from ours. It is only through our relationship with Jesus Christ that we can understand what God is after in His dealings with us. When it comes to suffering, it is part of our Christian culture to want to know God's purpose beforehand. In the history of the Christian church, the tendency has been to avoid being identified with the sufferings of Jesus Christ. People have sought to carry out God's orders through a shortcut of their own. God's way is always the way of suffering—the way of the "long road home."

Are we partakers of Christ's sufferings? Are we prepared for God to stamp out our personal ambitions? Are we prepared for God to destroy our individual decisions by supernaturally transforming them? It will mean not knowing why God is taking us that way, because knowing would make us spiritually proud. We never realize at the time what God is putting us through—we go through it more or less without understanding. Then suddenly we come to a place of enlightenment, and realize—"God has strengthened me and I didn't even know it!"

INTIMATE THEOLOGY

"Do you believe this?" (John 11:26).

Martha believed in the power available to Jesus Christ; she believed that if He had been there He could have healed her brother; she also believed that Jesus had a special intimacy with God, and that whatever He asked of God, God would do. But—she needed a closer personal intimacy with Jesus. Martha's theology had its fulfillment in the future. But Jesus continued to attract and draw her in until her belief became an intimate possession. It then slowly emerged into a personal inheritance—"Yes, Lord, I believe that You are the Christ . . ." (11:27).

Is the Lord dealing with you in the same way? Is Jesus teaching you to have a personal intimacy with Himself? Allow Him to drive His question home to you— "Do you believe *this?*" Are you facing an area of doubt in your life? Have you come, like Martha, to a crossroads of overwhelming circumstances where your theology is about to become a very personal belief? This happens only when a personal problem brings the awareness of our personal need.

To believe is to commit. In the area of intellectual learning I commit myself mentally, and reject anything not related to that belief. In the realm of personal belief I commit myself morally to my convictions and refuse to compromise. But in intimate personal belief I commit myself spiritually to Jesus Christ and make a determination to be dominated by Him alone.

Then, when I stand face to face with Jesus Christ and He says to me, "Do you believe this?" I find that faith is as natural as breathing. And I am staggered when I think how foolish I have been in not trusting Him earlier.

THE UNDETECTED SACREDNESS OF CIRCUMSTANCES

"We know that all things work together for good to those who love God . . ." (Romans 8:28).

The circumstances of a saint's life are ordained of God. In the life of a saint there is no such thing as chance. God by His providence brings you into circumstances that you can't understand at all, but the Spirit of God understands. God brings you to places, among people, and into certain conditions to accomplish a definite purpose through the intercession of the Spirit in you. Never put yourself in front of your circumstances and say, "I'm going to be my own providence here; I will watch this closely, or protect myself from that." All your circumstances are in the hand of God, and therefore you don't ever have to think they are unnatural or unique. Your part in intercessory prayer is not to agonize over how to intercede, but to use the everyday circumstances and people God puts around you by His providence to bring them before His throne, and to allow the Spirit in you the opportunity to intercede for them. In this way God is going to touch the whole world with His saints.

Am I making the Holy Spirit's work difficult by being vague and unsure, or by trying to do His work for Him? I must do the human side of intercession—utilizing the circumstances in which I find myself and the people who surround me. I must keep my conscious life as a sacred place for the Holy Spirit. Then as I lift different ones to God through prayer, the Holy Spirit intercedes for them.

Your intercessions can never be mine, and my intercessions can never be yours, ". . . but the Spirit Himself makes intercession" in each of our lives (Romans 8:26). And without that intercession, the lives of others would be left in poverty and in ruin.

THE UNRIVALED POWER OF PRAYER

"We do not know what we should pray for as we ought, but the Spirit Himself makes intercession for us with groanings which cannot be uttered" (Romans 8:26).

We realize that we are energized by the Holy Spirit for prayer; and we know what it is to pray in accordance with the Spirit; but we don't often realize that the Holy Spirit Himself prays prayers in us which we cannot utter ourselves. When we are born again of God and are indwelt by the Spirit of God, He expresses for us the unutterable.

"He," the Holy Spirit in you, "makes intercession for the saints according to the will of God" (8:27). And God searches your heart, not to know what your conscious prayers are, but to find out what the prayer of the Holy Spirit is.

The Spirit of God uses the nature of the believer as a temple in which to offer His prayers of intercession. ". . . your body is the temple of the Holy Spirit . . ." (1 Corinthians 6:19). When Jesus Christ cleansed the temple, ". . . He would not allow anyone to carry wares through the temple" (Mark 11:16). The Spirit of God will not allow you to use your body for your own convenience. Jesus ruthlessly cast out everyone who bought and sold in the temple, and said, "My house shall be called a house of prayer . . . . But you have made it a 'den of thieves' " (Mark 11:17).

Have we come to realize that our "body is the temple of the Holy Spirit"? If so, we must be careful to keep it undefiled for Him. We have to remember that our conscious life, even though only a small part of our total person, is to be regarded by us as a "temple of the Holy Spirit." He will be responsible for the unconscious part which we don't know, but we must pay careful attention to and guard the conscious part for which we are responsible.

SACRED SERVICE

"I now rejoice in my sufferings for you, and fill up in my flesh what is lacking in the afflictions of Christ . . ." (Colossians 1:24).

The Christian worker has to be a sacred "go-between." He must be so closely identified with his Lord and the reality of His redemption that Christ can continually bring His creating life through him. I am not referring to the strength of one individual's personality being superimposed on another, but the real presence of Christ coming through every aspect of the worker's life. When we preach the historical facts of the life and death of our Lord as they are conveyed in the New Testament, our words are made sacred. God uses these words, on the basis of His redemption, to create something in those who listen which otherwise could never have been created. If we simply preach the effects of redemption in the human life instead of the revealed, divine truth regarding Jesus Himself, the result is not new birth in those who listen. The result is a refined religious lifestyle, and the Spirit of God cannot witness to it because such preaching is in a realm other than His. We must make sure that we are living in such harmony with God that as we proclaim His truth He can create in others those things which He alone can do.

When we say, "What a wonderful personality, what a fascinating person, and what wonderful insight!" then what opportunity does the gospel of God have through all of that? It cannot get through, because the attraction is to the messenger and not the message. If a person attracts through his personality, that becomes his appeal. If, however, he is identified with the Lord Himself, then the appeal becomes what Jesus Christ can do. The danger is to glory in men, yet Jesus says we are to lift up only *Him* (see John 12:32).

FELLOWSHIP IN THE GOSPEL

". . . fellow laborer in the gospel of Christ . . ."
(1 Thessalonians 3:2).

After sanctification, it is difficult to state what your purpose in life is, because God has moved you into His purpose through the Holy Spirit. He is using you now for His purposes throughout the world as He used His Son for the purpose of our salvation. If you seek great things for yourself, thinking, "God has called me for this and for that," you barricade God from using you. As long as you maintain your own personal interests and ambitions, you cannot be completely aligned or identified with God's interests. This can only be accomplished by giving up all of your personal plans once and for all, and by allowing God to take you directly into His purpose for the world. Your understanding of your ways must also be surrendered, because they are now the ways of the Lord.

I must learn that the purpose of my life belongs to God, not me. God is using me from His great personal perspective, and all He asks of me is that I trust Him. I should never say, "Lord, this causes me such heartache." To talk that way makes me a stumbling block. When I stop telling God what I want, He can freely work His will in me without any hindrance. He can crush me, exalt me, or do anything else He chooses. He simply asks me to have absolute faith in Him and His goodness. Self-pity is of the devil, and if I wallow in it I cannot be used by God for His purpose in the world. Doing this creates for me my own cozy "world within the world," and God will not be allowed to move me from it because of my fear of being "frost-bitten."

THE SUPREME CLIMB

"He said, 'Take now your son . . .' " (Genesis 22:2).

God's command is, "Take *now*," not later. It is incredible how we debate! We know something is right, but we try to find excuses for not doing it immediately. If we are to climb to the height God reveals, it can never be done later—it must be done now. And the sacrifice must be worked through our will before we actually perform it.

"So Abraham rose early in the morning . . . and went to the place of which God had told him" (22:3). Oh, the wonderful simplicity of Abraham! When God spoke, he did not "confer with flesh and blood" (Galatians 1:16). Beware when you want to "confer with flesh and blood" or even your own thoughts, insights, or understandings—anything that is not based on your personal relationship with God. These are all things that compete with and hinder obedience to God.

Abraham did not choose what the sacrifice would be. Always guard against self-chosen service for God. Self-sacrifice may be a disease that impairs your service. If God has made your cup sweet, drink it with grace; or even if He has made it bitter, drink it in communion with Him. If the providential will of God means a hard and difficult time for you, go through it. But never decide the place of your own martyrdom, as if to say, "I will only go to there, but no farther." God chose the test for Abraham, and Abraham neither delayed nor protested, but steadily obeyed. If you are not living in touch with God, it is easy to blame Him or pass judgment on Him. You must go through the trial before you have any right to pronounce a verdict, because by going through the trial you learn to know God better. God is working in us to reach His highest goals until His purpose and our purpose become one.

THE CHANGED LIFE

"If anyone is in Christ, he is a new creation; old things have passed away; behold, all things have become new" (2 Corinthians 5:17).

What understanding do you have of the salvation of your soul? The work of salvation means that in your real life things are dramatically changed. You no longer look at things in the same way. Your desires are new and the old things have lost their power to attract you. One of the tests for determining if the work of salvation in your life is genuine is—has God changed the things that really matter to you? If you still yearn for the old things, it is absurd to talk about being born from above—you are deceiving yourself. If you are born again, the Spirit of God makes the change very evident in your real life and thought. And when a crisis comes, you are the most amazed person on earth at the wonderful difference there is in you. There is no possibility of imagining that *you* did it. It is this complete and amazing change that is the very evidence that you are saved.

What difference has my salvation and sanctification made? For instance, can I stand in the light of 1 Corinthians 13, or do I squirm and evade the issue? True salvation, worked out in me by the Holy Spirit, frees me completely. And as long as I "walk in the light as He is in the light" (1 John 1:7), God sees nothing to rebuke because His life is working itself into every detailed part of my being, not on the conscious level, but even deeper than my consciousness.

FAITH OR EXPERIENCE?

"... the Son of God, who loved me and gave Himself for me" (Galatians 2:20).

We should battle through our moods, feelings, and emotions into absolute devotion to the Lord Jesus. We must break out of our own little world of experience into abandoned devotion to Him. Think who the New Testament says Jesus Christ is, and then think of the despicable meagerness of the miserable faith we exhibit by saying, "I haven't had this experience or that experience"! Think what faith in Jesus Christ claims and provides—He can present us faultless before the throne of God, inexpressibly pure, absolutely righteous, and profoundly justified. Stand in absolute adoring faith "in Christ Jesus, who became for us wisdom from God—and righteousness and sanctification and redemption ..." (1 Corinthians 1:30). How dare we talk of making a sacrifice for the Son of God! We are saved from hell and total destruction, and then we talk about making sacrifices!

We must continually focus and firmly place our faith in Jesus Christ—not a "prayer meeting" Jesus Christ, or a "book" Jesus Christ, but the New Testament Jesus Christ, who is God Incarnate, and who ought to strike us dead at His feet. Our faith must be in the One from whom our salvation springs. Jesus Christ wants our absolute, unrestrained devotion to Himself. We can never *experience* Jesus Christ, or selfishly bind Him in the confines of our own hearts. Our faith must be built on strong determined confidence in Him.

It is because of our trusting in experience that we see the steadfast impatience of the Holy Spirit against unbelief. All of our fears are sinful, and we create our own fears by refusing to nourish ourselves in our faith. How can anyone who is identified with Jesus Christ suffer from doubt or fear! Our lives should be an absolute hymn of praise resulting from perfect, irrepressible, triumphant belief.

DISCOVERING DIVINE DESIGN

"As for me, being on the way, the Lord led me . . ." (Genesis 24:27).

We should be so one with God that we don't need to ask continually for guidance. Sanctification means that we are made the children of God. A child's life is normally obedient, until he chooses disobedience. But as soon as he chooses to disobey, an inherent inner conflict is produced. On the spiritual level, inner conflict is the warning of the Spirit of God. When He warns us in this way, we must stop at once and be renewed in the spirit of our mind to discern God's will (see Romans 12:2). If we are born again by the Spirit of God, our devotion to Him is hindered, or even stopped, by continually asking Him to guide us here and there. ". . . the Lord led me . . ." and on looking back we see the presence of an amazing design. If we are born of God we will see His guiding hand and give Him the credit.

We can all see God in exceptional things, but it requires the growth of spiritual discipline to see God in every detail. Never believe that the so-called random events of life are anything less than God's appointed order. Be ready to discover His divine designs anywhere and everywhere.

Beware of being obsessed with consistency to your own convictions instead of being devoted to God. If you are a saint and say, "I will never do this or that," in all probability this will be exactly what God will require of you. There was never a more inconsistent being on this earth than our Lord, but He was never inconsistent with His Father. The important consistency in a saint is not to a principle but to the divine life. It is the divine life that continually makes more and more discoveries about the divine mind. It is easier to be an excessive fanatic than it is to be consistently faithful, because God causes an amazing humbling of our religious conceit when we are faithful to Him.

"What Is That to You?"

"Peter . . . said to Jesus, 'But Lord, what about this man?' Jesus said to him, '. . . what is that to you? You follow Me' " (John 21:21–22).

One of the hardest lessons to learn comes from our stubborn refusal to refrain from interfering in other people's lives. It takes a long time to realize the danger of being an amateur providence, that is, interfering with God's plan for others. You see someone suffering and say, "He will not suffer, and I will make sure that he doesn't." You put your hand right in front of God's permissive will to stop it, and then God says, "What is that to you?" Is there stagnation in your spiritual life? Don't allow it to continue, but get into God's presence and find out the reason for it. You will possibly find it is because you have been interfering in the life of another—proposing things you had no right to propose, or advising when you had no right to advise. When you do have to give advice to another person, God will advise through you with the direct understanding of His Spirit. Your part is to maintain the right relationship with God so that His discernment can come through you continually for the purpose of blessing someone else.

Most of us live only within the level of consciousness—consciously serving and consciously devoted to God. This shows immaturity and the fact that we're not yet living the real Christian life. Maturity is produced in the life of a child of God on the unconscious level, until we become so totally surrendered to God that we are not even aware of being used by Him. When we are consciously aware of being used as broken bread and poured-out wine, we have yet another level to reach—a level where all awareness of ourselves and of what God is doing through us is completely eliminated. A saint is never consciously a saint—a saint is consciously dependent on God.

STILL HUMAN!

". . . whatever you do, do all to the glory of God" (1 Corinthians 10:31).

In the Scriptures, the great miracle of the incarnation slips into the ordinary life of a child; the great miracle of the transfiguration fades into the demon-possessed valley below; the glory of the resurrection descends into a breakfast on the seashore. This is not an anticlimax, but a great revelation of God.

We have a tendency to look for wonder in our experience, and we mistake heroic actions for real heroes. It's one thing to go through a crisis grandly, yet quite another to go through every day glorifying God when there is no witness, no limelight, and no one paying even the remotest attention to us. If we are not looking for halos, we at least want something that will make people say, "What a wonderful man of prayer he is!" or, "What a great woman of devotion she is!" If you are properly devoted to the Lord Jesus, you have reached the lofty height where no one would ever notice you personally. All that is noticed is the power of God coming through you all the time.

We want to be able to say, "Oh, I have had a wonderful call from God!" But to do even the most humbling tasks to the glory of God takes the Almighty God Incarnate working in us. To be utterly unnoticeable requires God's Spirit in us making us absolutely humanly His. The true test of a saint's life is not successfulness but faithfulness on the human level of life. We tend to set up success in Christian work as our purpose, but our purpose should be to display the glory of God in human life, to live a life "hidden with Christ in God" in our everyday human conditions (Colossians 3:3). Our human relationships are the very conditions in which the ideal life of God should be exhibited.

THE ETERNAL GOAL

"By Myself I have sworn, says the LORD, because you have done this thing . . . I will bless you . . ." (Genesis 22:16-17).

Abraham, at this point, has reached the place where he is in touch with the very nature of God. He now understands the reality of God.

> My goal is God Himself . . .
> At any cost, dear Lord, by any road.

"At any cost . . . by any road" means submitting to God's way of bringing us to the goal.

There is no possibility of questioning God when He speaks, if He speaks to His own nature in me. Prompt obedience is the only result. When Jesus says, "Come," I simply come; when He says, "Let go," I let go; when He says, "Trust God in this matter," I trust. This work of obedience is the evidence that the nature of God is in me.

God's revelation of Himself to me is influenced by my character, not by God's character.

> 'Tis because I am ordinary,
> Thy ways so often look ordinary to me.

It is through the discipline of obedience that I get to the place where Abraham was and I see who God is. God will never be real to me until I come face to face with Him in Jesus Christ. Then I will know and can boldly proclaim, "In all the world, my God, there is none but Thee, there is none but Thee."

The promises of God are of no value to us until, through obedience, we come to understand the nature of God. We may read some things in the Bible every day for a year and they may mean nothing to us. Then, because we have been obedient to God in some small detail, we suddenly see what God means and His nature is instantly opened up to us. "All the promises of God in Him are Yes, and in Him Amen . . ." (2 Corinthians 1:20). Our "Yes" must be born of obedience; when by obedience we ratify a promise of God by saying, "Amen," or, "So be it." That promise becomes ours.

WINNING INTO FREEDOM

"If the Son makes you free, you shall be free indeed" (John 8:36).

I f there is even a trace of individual self-satisfaction left in us, it always says, "I can't surrender," or "I can't be free." But the spiritual part of our being never says "I can't"; it simply soaks up everything around it. Our spirit hungers for more and more. It is the way we are built. We are designed with a great capacity for God, but sin, our own individuality, and wrong thinking keep us from getting to Him. God delivers us from sin—we have to deliver ourselves from our individuality. This means offering our natural life to God and sacrificing it to Him, so He may transform it into spiritual life through our obedience.

God pays no attention to our natural individuality in the development of our spiritual life. His plan runs right through our natural life. We must see to it that we aid and assist God, and not stand against Him by saying, "I can't do that." God will not discipline us; we must discipline ourselves. God will not bring our "arguments . . . and every thought into captivity to the obedience of Christ" (2 Corinthians 10:5)—we have to do it. Don't say, "Oh, Lord, I suffer from wandering thoughts." *Don't* suffer from wandering thoughts. Stop listening to the tyranny of your individual natural life and win freedom into the spiritual life.

"If the Son makes you free . . . ." Do not substitute *Savior* for *Son* in this passage. The *Savior* has set us free from sin, but this is the freedom that comes from being set free from myself *by the Son.* It is what Paul meant in Galatians 2:20 when he said, "I have been crucified with Christ . . . ." His individuality had been broken and his spirit had been united with his Lord; not just merged into Him, but made one with Him. ". . . you shall be free indeed"—free to the very core of your being; free from the inside to the outside. We tend to rely on our own energy, instead of being energized by the power that comes from identification with Jesus.

NOVEMBER 18

"WHEN HE HAS COME"

"When He has come, He will convict the world of sin . . ." (John 16:8).

Very few of us know anything about conviction of sin. We know the experience of being disturbed because we have done wrong things. But conviction of sin by the Holy Spirit blots out every relationship on earth and makes us aware of only one—"Against You, You only, have I sinned . . ." (Psalm 51:4). When a person is convicted of sin in this way, he knows with every bit of his conscience that God would not dare to forgive him. If God did forgive him, then this person would have a stronger sense of justice than God. God does forgive, but it cost the breaking of His heart with grief in the death of Christ to enable Him to do so. The great miracle of the grace of God is that He forgives sin, and it is the death of Jesus Christ alone that enables the divine nature to forgive and to remain true to itself in doing so. It is shallow nonsense to say that God forgives us because He is love. Once we have been convicted of sin, we will never say this again. The love of God means Calvary—nothing less! The love of God is spelled out on the Cross and nowhere else. The only basis for which God can forgive me is the Cross of Christ. It is there that His conscience is satisfied.

Forgiveness doesn't merely mean that I am saved from hell and have been made ready for heaven (no one would accept forgiveness on that level). Forgiveness means that I am forgiven into a newly created relationship which identifies me with God in Christ. The miracle of redemption is that God turns me, the unholy one, into the standard of Himself, the Holy One. He does this by putting into me a new nature, the nature of Jesus Christ.

THE FORGIVENESS OF GOD

"In Him we have . . . the forgiveness of sins . . ." (Ephesians 1:7).

Beware of the pleasant view of the fatherhood of God: God is so kind and loving that of course He will forgive us. That thought, based solely on emotion, cannot be found anywhere in the New Testament. The only basis on which God can forgive us is the tremendous tragedy of the Cross of Christ. To base our forgiveness on any other ground is unconscious blasphemy. The only ground on which God can forgive our sin and reinstate us to His favor is through the Cross of Christ. There is no other way! Forgiveness, which is so easy for us to accept, cost the agony at Calvary. We should never take the forgiveness of sin, the gift of the Holy Spirit, and our sanctification in simple faith, and then forget the enormous cost to God that made all of this ours.

Forgiveness is the divine miracle of grace. The cost to God was the Cross of Christ. To forgive sin, while remaining a holy God, this price had to be paid. Never accept a view of the fatherhood of God if it blots out the atonement. The revealed truth of God is that without the atonement He cannot forgive—He would contradict His nature if He did. The only way we can be forgiven is by being brought back to God through the atonement of the Cross. God's forgiveness is possible only in the supernatural realm.

Compared with the miracle of the forgiveness of sin, the experience of sanctification is small. Sanctification is simply the wonderful expression or evidence of the forgiveness of sins in a human life. But the thing that awakens the deepest fountain of gratitude in a human being is that God has forgiven his sin. Paul never got away from this. Once you realize all that it cost God to forgive you, you will be held as in a vise, constrained by the love of God.

"IT IS FINISHED!"

"I have finished the work which You have given Me to do" (John 17:4).

The death of Jesus Christ is the fulfillment in history of the very mind and intent of God. There is no place for seeing Jesus Christ as a martyr. His death was not something that happened *to* Him—something that might have been prevented. His death was the very reason He came.

Never build your case for forgiveness on the idea that God is our Father and He will forgive us because He loves us. That contradicts the revealed truth of God in Jesus Christ. It makes the Cross unnecessary, and the redemption "much ado about nothing." God forgives sin only because of the death of Christ. God could forgive people in no other way than by the death of His Son, and Jesus is exalted as Savior because of His death. "We see Jesus . . . *for the suffering of death* crowned with glory and honor . . ." (Hebrews 2:9). The greatest note of triumph ever sounded in the ears of a startled universe was that sounded on the Cross of Christ—"*It is finished!*" (John 19:30). That is the final word in the redemption of humankind.

Anything that lessens or completely obliterates the holiness of God, through a false view of His love, contradicts the truth of God as revealed by Jesus Christ. Never allow yourself to believe that Jesus Christ stands with us, and against God, out of pity and compassion, or that He became a curse for us out of sympathy for us. Jesus Christ became a curse for us by divine decree. Our part in realizing the tremendous meaning of His curse is the conviction of sin. Conviction is given to us as a gift of shame and repentance; it is the great mercy of God. Jesus Christ hates the sin in people, and Calvary is the measure of His hatred.

SHALLOW AND PROFOUND

"Whether you eat or drink, or whatever you do, do all to the glory of God" (1 Corinthians 10:31).

Beware of allowing yourself to think that the shallow aspects of life are not ordained by God; they are ordained by Him equally as much as the profound. We sometimes refuse to be shallow, not out of our deep devotion to God but because we wish to impress other people with the fact that we are not shallow. This is a sure sign of spiritual pride. We must be careful, for this is how contempt for others is produced in our lives. And it causes us to be a walking rebuke to other people because they are more shallow than we are. Beware of posing as a profound person—God became a baby.

To be shallow is not a sign of being sinful, nor is shallowness an indication that there is no depth to your life at all—the ocean has a shore. Even the shallow things of life, such as eating and drinking, walking and talking, are ordained by God. These are all things our Lord did. He did them as the Son of God, and He said, "A disciple is not above his teacher . . ." (Matthew 10:24).

We are safeguarded by the shallow things of life. We have to live the surface, commonsense life in a common-sense way. Then when God gives us the deeper things, they are obviously separated from the shallow concerns. Never show the depth of your life to anyone but God. We are so nauseatingly serious, so desperately interested in our own character and reputation, we refuse to behave like Christians in the shallow concerns of life.

Make a determination to take no one seriously except God. You may find that the first person you must be the most critical with, as being the greatest fraud you have ever known, is yourself.

THE DISTRACTION OF CONTEMPT

"**Have mercy on us, O LORD, have mercy on us! For we are exceedingly filled with contempt**" (Psalm 123:3).

What we must beware of is not damage to our belief in God but damage to our Christian disposition or state of mind. "Take heed to your spirit, that you do not deal treacherously" (Malachi 2:16). Our state of mind is powerful in its effects. It can be the enemy that penetrates right into our soul and distracts our mind from God. There are certain attitudes we should never dare to indulge. If we do, we will find they have distracted us from faith in God. Until we get back into a quiet mood before Him, our faith is of no value, and our confidence in the flesh and in human ingenuity is what rules our lives.

Beware of "the cares of this world . . ." (Mark 4:19). They are the very things that produce the wrong attitudes in our soul. It is incredible what enormous power there is in simple things to distract our attention away from God. Refuse to be swamped by "the cares of this world."

Another thing that distracts us is our passion for vindication. St. Augustine prayed, "O Lord, deliver me from this lust of always vindicating myself." Such a need for constant vindication destroys our soul's faith in God. Don't say, "I must explain myself," or, "I must get people to understand." Our Lord never explained anything—He left the misunderstandings or misconceptions of others to correct themselves.

When we discern that other people are not growing spiritually and allow that discernment to turn to criticism, we block our fellowship with God. God never gives us discernment so that we may criticize, but that we may intercede.

DIRECTION OF FOCUS

"Behold, as the eyes of servants look to the
hand of their masters . . . , so our eyes look to
the LORD our God . . ." (Psalm 123:2).

This verse is a description of total reliance on God.
Just as the eyes of a servant are riveted on his
master, our eyes should be directed to and focused
on God. This is how knowledge of His countenance is
gained and how God reveals Himself to us (see Isaiah
53:1). Our spiritual strength begins to be drained when
we stop lifting our eyes to Him. Our stamina is sapped,
not so much through external troubles surrounding us
but through problems in our thinking. We wrongfully
think, "I suppose I've been stretching myself a little too
much, standing too tall and trying to look like God
instead of being an ordinary humble person." We have to
realize that no effort can be too high.

For example, you came to a crisis in your life, took
a stand for God, and even had the witness of the Spirit
as a confirmation that what you did was right. But now,
maybe weeks or years have gone by, and you are slowly
coming to the conclusion—"Well, maybe what I did
showed too much pride or was superficial. Was I taking
a stand a bit too high for me?" Your "rational" friends
come and say, "Don't be silly. We knew when you first
talked about this spiritual awakening that it was a passing impulse, that you couldn't hold up under the strain.
And anyway, God doesn't expect you to endure." You
respond by saying, "Well, I suppose I was expecting too
much." That sounds humble to say, but it means that
your reliance on God is gone, and you are now relying
on worldly opinion. The danger comes when, no longer
relying on God, you neglect to focus your eyes on Him.
Only when God brings you to a sudden stop will you
realize that you have been the loser. Whenever there is a
spiritual drain in your life, correct it immediately. Realize
that something has been coming between you and God,
and change or remove it at once.

THE SECRET OF
SPIRITUAL CONSISTENCY

"God forbid that I should boast except in the cross of our Lord Jesus Christ . . ." (Galatians 6:14).

When a person is newly born again, he seems inconsistent due to his unrelated emotions and the state of the external things or circumstances in his life. The apostle Paul had a strong and steady underlying consistency in his life. Consequently, he could let his external life change without internal distress because he was rooted and grounded in God. Most of us are not consistent spiritually because we are more concerned about being consistent externally. In the external expression of things, Paul lived in the basement, while his critics lived on the upper level. And these two levels do not begin to touch each other. But Paul's consistency was down deep in the fundamentals. The great basis of his consistency was the agony of God in the redemption of the world, namely, the Cross of Christ.

State your beliefs to yourself again. Get back to the foundation of the Cross of Christ, doing away with any belief not based on it. In secular history the Cross is an infinitesimally small thing, but from the biblical perspective it is of more importance than all the empires of the world. If we get away from dwelling on the tragedy of God on the Cross in our preaching, our preaching produces nothing. It will not transmit the energy of God to man; it may be interesting, but it will have no power. However, when we preach the Cross, the energy of God is released. ". . . it pleased God through the foolishness of the message preached to save those who believe. . . . we preach Christ crucified . . ." (1 Corinthians 1:21, 23).

THE FOCAL POINT OF
SPIRITUAL POWER

". . . except in the cross of our Lord Jesus
Christ . . ." (Galatians 6:14).

I f you want to know the power of God (that is, the
resurrection life of Jesus) in your human flesh, you
must dwell on the tragedy of God. Break away from
your personal concern over your own spiritual condition,
and with a completely open spirit consider the tragedy of
God. Instantly the power of God will be in you. "Look
to *Me* . . ." (Isaiah 45:22). Pay attention to the external
Source and the internal power will be there. We lose
power because we don't focus on the right thing. The
effect of the Cross is salvation, sanctification, healing,
etc., but we are not to preach any of these. We are to
preach "Jesus Christ and Him crucified" (1 Corinthians
2:2). The proclaiming of Jesus will do its own work.
Concentrate on God's focal point in your preaching, and
even if your listeners seem to pay it no attention, they will
never be the same again. If I share my own words, they
are of no more importance than your words are to me.
But if we share the truth of God with one another, we
will encounter it again and again. We have to focus on
the great point of spiritual power—the Cross. If we stay in
contact with that center of power, its energy is released in
our lives. In holiness movements and spiritual experience
meetings, the focus tends to be put not on the Cross of
Christ but on the effects of the Cross.

The feebleness of the church is being criticized
today, and the criticism is justified. One reason for
the feebleness is that there has not been this focus on
the true center of spiritual power. We have not dwelt
enough on the tragedy of Calvary or on the meaning of
redemption.

THE CONSECRATION OF SPIRITUAL POWER

". . . by whom the world has been crucified to me, and I to the world" (Galatians 6:14).

If I dwell on the Cross of Christ, I do not simply become inwardly devout and solely interested in my own holiness—I become strongly focused on Jesus Christ's interests. Our Lord was not a recluse nor a fanatical holy man practicing self-denial. He did not physically cut Himself off from society, but He was inwardly disconnected all the time. He was not aloof, but He lived in another world. In fact, He was so much in the common everyday world that the religious people of His day accused Him of being a glutton and a drunkard. Yet our Lord never allowed anything to interfere with His consecration of spiritual power.

It is not genuine consecration to think that we can refuse to be used of God now in order to store up our spiritual power for later use. That is a hopeless mistake. The Spirit of God has set a great many people free from their sin, yet they are experiencing no fullness in their lives—no true sense of freedom. The kind of religious life we see around the world today is entirely different from the vigorous holiness of the life of Jesus Christ. "I do not pray that You should take them out of the world, but that You should keep them from the evil one" (John 17:15). We are to be *in* the world but not *of* it—to be separated internally, not externally (see John 17:16).

We must never allow anything to interfere with the consecration of our spiritual power. Consecration (being dedicated to God's service) is our part; sanctification (being set apart from sin and being made holy) is God's part. We must make a deliberate determination to be interested only in what God is interested. The way to make that determination, when faced with a perplexing problem, is to ask yourself, "Is this the kind of thing in which Jesus Christ is interested, or is it something in which the spirit that is diametrically opposed to Jesus is interested?"

THE RICHES OF THE DESTITUTE

The gospel of the grace of God awakens an intense longing in human souls and an equally intense resentment, because the truth that it reveals is not palatable or easy to swallow. There is a certain pride in people that causes them to give and give, but to come and accept a gift is another thing. I will give my life to martyrdom; I will dedicate my life to service—I will do anything. But do not humiliate me to the level of the most hell-deserving sinner and tell me that all I have to do is accept the gift of salvation through Jesus Christ.

We have to realize that we cannot earn or win anything from God through our own efforts. We must either receive it as a gift or do without it. The greatest spiritual blessing we receive is when we come to the knowledge that we are destitute. Until we get there, our Lord is powerless. He can do nothing for us as long as we think we are sufficient in and of ourselves. We must enter into His kingdom through the door of destitution. As long as we are "rich," particularly in the area of pride or independence, God can do nothing for us. It is only when we get hungry spiritually that we receive the Holy Spirit. The gift of the essential nature of God is placed and made effective in us by the Holy Spirit. He imparts to us the quickening life of Jesus, making us truly alive. He takes that which was "beyond" us and places it "within" us. And immediately, once "the beyond" has come "within," it rises up to "the above," and we are lifted into the kingdom where Jesus lives and reigns (see John 3:5).

THE SUPREMACY OF
JESUS CHRIST

"He will glorify Me . . ." (John 16:14).

The holiness movements of today have none of the rugged reality of the New Testament about them. There is nothing about them that needs the death of Jesus Christ. All that is required is a pious atmosphere, prayer, and devotion. This type of experience is not supernatural nor miraculous. It did not cost the sufferings of God, nor is it stained with "the blood of the Lamb" (Revelation 12:11). It is not marked or sealed by the Holy Spirit as being genuine, and it has no visual sign that causes people to exclaim with awe and wonder, "That is the work of God Almighty!" Yet the New Testament is about the work of God and nothing else.

The New Testament example of the Christian experience is that of a personal, passionate devotion to the Person of Jesus Christ. Every other kind of so-called Christian experience is detached from the Person of Jesus. There is no regeneration—no being born again into the kingdom in which Christ lives and reigns supreme. There is only the idea that He is our pattern. In the New Testament Jesus Christ is the Savior long before He is the pattern. Today He is being portrayed as the figurehead of a religion—a mere example. He is that, but He is infinitely more. He is salvation itself; He *is* the gospel of God!

Jesus said, ". . . when He, the Spirit of truth, has come, . . . He will glorify Me . . ." (John 16:13–14). When I commit myself to the revealed truth of the New Testament, I receive from God the gift of the Holy Spirit, who then begins interpreting to me what Jesus did. The Spirit of God does in me internally all that Jesus Christ did for me externally.

"BY THE GRACE OF GOD I AM WHAT I AM"

"By the grace of God I am what I am, and His grace toward me was not in vain . . ."
(1 Corinthians 15:10).

The way we continually talk about our own inabilities is an insult to our Creator. To complain over our incompetence is to accuse God falsely of having overlooked us. Get into the habit of examining from God's perspective those things that sound so humble to men. You will be amazed at how unbelievably inappropriate and disrespectful they are to Him. We say things such as, "Oh, I shouldn't claim to be sanctified; I'm not a saint." But to say that before God means, "No, Lord, it is impossible for You to save and sanctify me; there are opportunities I have not had and so many imperfections in my brain and body; no, Lord, it isn't possible." That may sound wonderfully humble to others, but before God it is an attitude of defiance.

Conversely, the things that sound humble before God may sound exactly the opposite to people. To say, "Thank God, I know I am saved and sanctified," is in God's eyes the purest expression of humility. It means you have so completely surrendered yourself to God that you know He is true. Never worry about whether what you say sounds humble before others or not. But always be humble before God, and allow Him to be your all in all.

There is only one relationship that really matters, and that is your personal relationship to your personal Redeemer and Lord. If you maintain that at all costs, letting everything else go, God will fulfill His purpose through your life. One individual life may be of priceless value to God's purposes, and yours may be that life.

THE LAW AND THE GOSPEL

"Whoever shall keep the whole law, and yet stumble in one point, he is guilty of all" (James 2:10).

The moral law does not consider our weaknesses as human beings; in fact, it does not take into account our heredity or infirmities. It simply demands that we be absolutely moral. The moral law never changes, either for the highest of society or for the weakest in the world. It is enduring and eternally the same. The moral law, ordained by God, does not make itself weak to the weak by excusing our shortcomings. It remains absolute for all time and eternity. If we are not aware of this, it is because we are less than alive. Once we do realize it, our life immediately becomes a fatal tragedy. "I was alive once without the law, but when the commandment came, sin revived and I died" (Romans 7:9). The moment we realize this, the Spirit of God convicts us of sin. Until a person gets there and sees that there is no hope, the Cross of Christ remains absurd to him. Conviction of sin always brings a fearful, confining sense of the law. It makes a person hopeless—". . . *sold under sin*" (Romans 7:14). I, a guilty sinner, can never work to get right with God—it is impossible. There is only one way by which I can get right with God, and that is through the death of Jesus Christ. I must get rid of the underlying idea that I can ever be right with God because of my obedience. Who of us could ever obey God to absolute perfection!

We only begin to realize the power of the moral law once we see that it comes with a condition and a promise. But God never coerces us. Sometimes we wish He would make us be obedient, and at other times we wish He would leave us alone. Whenever God's will is in complete control, He removes all pressure. And when we deliberately choose to obey Him, He will reach to the remotest star and to the ends of the earth to assist us with all of His almighty power.

CHRISTIAN PERFECTION

"Not that I have already attained, or am already perfect . . . " (Philippians 3:12).

It is a trap to presume that God wants to make us perfect specimens of what He can do—God's purpose is to make us one with Himself. The emphasis of holiness movements tends to be that God is producing specimens of holiness to put in His museum. If you accept this concept of personal holiness, your life's determined purpose will not be for God, but for what you call the evidence of God in your life. How can we say, "It could never be God's will for me to be sick"? If it was God's will to bruise His own Son (Isaiah 53:10), why shouldn't He bruise you? What shines forth and reveals God in your life is not your relative consistency to an idea of what a saint should be, but your genuine, living relationship with Jesus Christ, and your unrestrained devotion to Him whether you are well or sick.

Christian perfection is not, and never can be, human perfection. Christian perfection is the perfection of a relationship with God that shows itself to be true even amid the seemingly unimportant aspects of human life. When you obey the call of Jesus Christ, the first thing that hits you is the pointlessness of the things you have to do. The next thought that strikes you is that other people seem to be living perfectly consistent lives. Such lives may leave you with the idea that God is unnecessary—that through your own human effort and devotion you can attain God's standard for your life. In a fallen world this can never be done. I am called to live in such a perfect relationship with God that my life produces a yearning for God in the lives of others, not admiration for myself. Thoughts about myself hinder my usefulness to God. God's purpose is not to perfect me to make me a trophy in His showcase; He is getting me to the place where He can use me. Let Him do what He wants.

"NOT BY MIGHT NOR BY POWER"

> "My speech and my preaching were not with persuasive words of human wisdom, but in demonstration of the Spirit and of power . . ." (1 Corinthians 2:4).

If in preaching the gospel you substitute your knowledge of the way of salvation for confidence in the power of the gospel, you hinder people from getting to reality. Take care to see while you proclaim your knowledge of the way of salvation, that you yourself are rooted and grounded by faith in God. Never rely on the clearness of your presentation, but as you give your explanation make sure that you are relying on the Holy Spirit. Rely on the certainty of God's redemptive power, and He will create His own life in people.

Once you are rooted in reality, nothing can shake you. If your faith is in experiences, anything that happens is likely to upset that faith. But nothing can ever change God or the reality of redemption. Base your faith on that, and you are as eternally secure as God Himself. Once you have a personal relationship with Jesus Christ, you will never be moved again. That is the meaning of sanctification. God disapproves of our human efforts to cling to the concept that sanctification is merely an experience, while forgetting that even our sanctification must also be sanctified (see John 17:19). I must deliberately give my sanctified life to God for His service, so that He can use me as His hands and His feet.

THE LAW OF OPPOSITION

"To him who overcomes . . ." (Revelation 2:7).

Life without war is impossible in the natural or the supernatural realm. It is a fact that there is a continuing struggle in the physical, mental, moral, and spiritual areas of life.

Health is the balance between the physical parts of my body and all the things and forces surrounding me. To maintain good health I must have sufficient internal strength to fight off the things that are external. Everything outside my physical life is designed to cause my death. The very elements that sustain me while I am alive work to decay and disintegrate my body once it is dead. If I have enough inner strength to fight, I help to produce the balance needed for health. The same is true of the mental life. If I want to maintain a strong and active mental life, I have to fight. This struggle produces the mental balance called thought.

Morally it is the same. Anything that does not strengthen me morally is the enemy of virtue within me. Whether I overcome, thereby producing virtue, depends on the level of moral excellence in my life. But we must fight to be moral. Morality does not happen by accident; moral virtue is acquired.

And spiritually it is also the same. Jesus said, "In the world you will have tribulation . . ." (John 16:33). This means that anything which is not spiritual leads to my downfall. Jesus went on to say, ". . . but be of good cheer, I have overcome the world." I must learn to fight against and overcome the things that come against me, and in that way produce the balance of holiness. Then it becomes a delight to meet opposition.

Holiness is the balance between my nature and the law of God as expressed in Jesus Christ.

"THE TEMPLE OF THE HOLY SPIRIT"

". . . only in regard to the throne will I be greater than you" (Genesis 41:40).

I am accountable to God for the way I control my body under His authority. Paul said he did not "set aside the grace of God"—make it ineffective (Galatians 2:21). The grace of God is absolute and limitless, and the work of salvation through Jesus is complete and finished forever. I am not being saved—I am saved. Salvation is as eternal as God's throne, but I must put to work or use what God has placed within me. To "work out [my] own salvation" (Philippians 2:12) means that I am responsible for using what He has given me. It also means that I must exhibit in my own body the life of the Lord Jesus, not mysteriously or secretly, but openly and boldly. "I discipline my body and bring it into subjection . . ." (1 Corinthians 9:27). Every Christian can have his body under absolute control for God. God has given us the responsibility to rule over all "the temple of the Holy Spirit," including our thoughts and desires (1 Corinthians 6:19). We are responsible for these, and we must never give way to improper ones. But most of us are much more severe in our judgment of others than we are in judging ourselves. We make excuses for things in ourselves, while we condemn things in the lives of others simply because we are not naturally inclined to do them.

Paul said, "I beseech you . . . that you present your bodies a living sacrifice . . ." (Romans 12:1). What I must decide is whether or not I will agree with my Lord and Master that my body will indeed be His temple. Once I agree, all the rules, regulations, and requirements of the law concerning the body are summed up for me in this revealed truth—my body is "the temple of the Holy Spirit."

"MY RAINBOW IN THE CLOUD"

"I set My rainbow in the cloud, and it shall be for the sign of the covenant between Me and the earth" (Genesis 9:13).

It is the will of God that human beings should get into a right-standing relationship with Him, and His covenants are designed for this purpose. Why doesn't God save me? He has accomplished and provided for my salvation, but I have not yet entered into a relationship with Him. Why doesn't God do everything we ask? He has done it. The point is—will I step into that covenant relationship? All the great blessings of God are finished and complete, but they are not mine until I enter into a relationship with Him on the basis of His covenant.

Waiting for God to act is fleshly unbelief. It means that I have no faith in Him. I wait for Him to do something in me so I may trust in that. But God won't do it, because that is not the basis of the God-and-man relationship. Man must go beyond the physical body and feelings in his covenant with God, just as God goes beyond Himself in reaching out with His covenant to man. It is a question of faith in God—a very rare thing. We only have faith in our feelings. I don't believe God until He puts something tangible in my hand, so that I know I have it. Then I say, "Now I believe." There is no faith exhibited in that. God says, "*Look to Me*, and be saved . . ." (Isaiah 45:22).

When I have really transacted business with God on the basis of His covenant, letting everything else go, there is no sense of personal achievement—no human ingredient in it at all. Instead, there is a complete overwhelming sense of being brought into union with God, and my life is transformed and radiates peace and joy.

REPENTANCE

"Godly sorrow produces repentance leading to salvation . . ." (2 Corinthians 7:10).

Conviction of sin is best described in the words:
My sins, my sins, my Savior,
How sad on Thee they fall.
Conviction of sin is one of the most uncommon things that ever happens to a person. It is the beginning of an understanding of God. Jesus Christ said that when the Holy Spirit came He would convict people of sin (see John 16:8). And when the Holy Spirit stirs a person's conscience and brings him into the presence of God, it is not that person's relationship with others that bothers him but his relationship with God—"Against You, You only, have I sinned, and done this evil in your sight . . ." (Psalm 51:4). The wonders of conviction of sin, forgiveness, and holiness are so interwoven that it is only the forgiven person who is truly holy. He proves he is forgiven by being the opposite of what he was previously, by the grace of God. Repentance always brings a person to the point of saying, "I have sinned." The surest sign that God is at work in his life is when he says that and means it. Anything less is simply sorrow for having made foolish mistakes—a reflex action caused by self-disgust.

The entrance into the kingdom of God is through the sharp, sudden pains of repentance colliding with man's respectable "goodness." Then the Holy Spirit, who produces these struggles, begins the formation of the Son of God in the person's life (see Galatians 4:19). This new life will reveal itself in conscious repentance followed by unconscious holiness, never the other way around. The foundation of Christianity is repentance. Strictly speaking, a person cannot repent when he chooses—repentance is a gift of God. The old Puritans used to pray for "the gift of tears." If you ever cease to understand the value of repentance, you allow yourself to remain in sin. Examine yourself to see if you have forgotten how to be truly repentant.

The Impartial Power of God

"By one offering He has perfected forever those who are being sanctified" (Hebrews 10:14).

We trample the blood of the Son of God underfoot if we think we are forgiven because we are sorry for our sins. The only reason for the forgiveness of our sins by God, and the infinite depth of His promise to forget them, is the death of Jesus Christ. Our repentance is merely the result of our personal realization of the atonement by the Cross of Christ, which He has provided for us. ". . . Christ Jesus . . . became for us wisdom from God—and righteousness and sanctification and redemption . . ." (1 Corinthians 1:30). Once we realize that Christ has become all this for us, the limitless joy of God begins in us. And wherever the joy of God is not present, the death sentence is still in effect.

No matter who or what we are, God restores us to right standing with Himself only by means of the death of Jesus Christ. God does this, not because Jesus pleads with Him to do so but because He died. It cannot be earned, just accepted. All the pleading for salvation which deliberately ignores the Cross of Christ is useless. It is knocking at a door other than the one which Jesus has already opened. We protest by saying, "But I don't want to come that way. It is too humiliating to be received as a sinner." God's response, through Peter, is, ". . . there is no other name . . . by which we must be saved" (Acts 4:12). What at first appears to be heartlessness on God's part is actually the true expression of His heart. There is unlimited entrance His way. "In Him we have redemption through His blood . . ." (Ephesians 1:7). To identify with the death of Jesus Christ means that we must die to everything that was never a part of Him.

God is just in saving bad people only as He makes them good. Our Lord does not pretend we are all right when we are all wrong. The atonement by the Cross of Christ is the propitiation God uses to make unholy people holy.

December 8

THE OPPOSITION
OF THE NATURAL

"Those who are Christ's have crucified the flesh with its passions and desires" (Galatians 5:24).

The natural life itself is not sinful. But we must abandon sin, having nothing to do with it in any way whatsoever. Sin belongs to hell and to the devil. I, as a child of God, belong to heaven and to God. It is not a question of giving up sin, but of giving up my right to myself, my natural independence, and my self-will. This is where the battle has to be fought. The things that are right, noble, and good from the natural standpoint are the very things that keep us from being God's best. Once we come to understand that natural moral excellence opposes or counteracts surrender to God, we bring our soul into the center of its greatest battle. Very few of us would debate over what is filthy, evil, and wrong, but we do debate over what is good. It is the good that opposes the best. The higher up the scale of moral excellence a person goes, the more intense the opposition to Jesus Christ. "Those who are Christ's have crucified the flesh . . . ." The cost to your natural life is not just one or two things, but everything. Jesus said, "If anyone desires to come after Me, let him deny *himself* . . ." (Matthew 16:24). That is, he must deny his right to himself, and he must realize who Jesus Christ is before he will bring himself to do it. Beware of refusing to go to the funeral of your own independence.

The natural life is not spiritual, and it can be made spiritual only through sacrifice. If we do not purposely sacrifice the natural, the supernatural can never become natural to us. There is no high or easy road. Each of us has the means to accomplish it entirely in his own hands. It is not a question of praying, but of sacrificing, and thereby performing His will.

THE OFFERING OF THE NATURAL

"It is written that Abraham had two sons: the one by a bondwoman, the other by a free-woman" (Galatians 4:22).

Paul was not dealing with sin in this chapter of Galatians, but with the relation of the natural to the spiritual. The natural can be turned into the spiritual only through sacrifice. Without this a person will lead a divided life. Why did God demand that the natural must be sacrificed? God did not demand it. It is not God's perfect will, but His permissive will. God's perfect will was for the natural to be changed into the spiritual through obedience. Sin is what made it necessary for the natural to be sacrificed.

Abraham had to offer up Ishmael before he offered up Isaac (see Genesis 21:8-14). Some of us are trying to offer up spiritual sacrifices to God before we have sacrificed the natural. The only way we can offer a spiritual sacrifice to God is to "present [our] bodies a living sacrifice . . ." (Romans 12:1). Sanctification means more than being freed from sin. It means the deliberate commitment of myself to the God of my salvation, and being willing to pay whatever it may cost.

If we do not sacrifice the natural to the spiritual, the natural life will resist and defy the life of the Son of God in us and will produce continual turmoil. This is always the result of an undisciplined spiritual nature. We go wrong because we stubbornly refuse to discipline ourselves physically, morally, or mentally. We excuse ourselves by saying, "Well, I wasn't taught to be disciplined when I was a child." Then discipline yourself now! If you don't, you will ruin your entire personal life for God.

God is not actively involved with our natural life as long as we continue to pamper and gratify it. But once we are willing to put it out in the desert and are determined to keep it under control, God will be with it. He will then provide wells and oases and fulfill all His promises for the natural (see Genesis 21:15-19).

INDIVIDUALITY

> "Jesus said to His disciples, 'If anyone desires to come after Me, let him deny himself . . .' " (Matthew 16:24).

Individuality is the hard outer layer surrounding the inner spiritual life. Individuality shoves others aside, separating and isolating people. We see it as the primary characteristic of a child, and rightly so. When we confuse individuality with the spiritual life, we remain isolated. This shell of individuality is God's created natural covering designed to protect the spiritual life. But our individuality must be yielded to God so that our spiritual life may be brought forth into fellowship with Him. Individuality counterfeits spirituality, just as lust counterfeits love. God designed human nature for Himself, but individuality corrupts that human nature for its own purposes.

The characteristics of individuality are independence and self-will. We hinder our spiritual growth more than any other way by continually asserting our individuality. If you say, "I can't believe," it is because your individuality is blocking the way; individuality can never believe. But our spirit cannot help believing. Watch yourself closely when the Spirit of God is at work in you. He pushes you to the limits of your individuality where a choice must be made. The choice is either to say, "I will not surrender," or to surrender, breaking the hard shell of individuality, which allows the spiritual life to emerge. The Holy Spirit narrows it down every time to one thing (see Matthew 5:23-24). It is your individuality that refuses to "be reconciled to your brother" (5:24). God wants to bring you into union with Himself, but unless you are willing to give up your right to yourself, He cannot. ". . . let him deny himself . . ."—deny his independent right to himself. Then the real life—the spiritual life—is allowed the opportunity to grow.

DECEMBER 11

PERSONALITY

". . . that they may be one just as We are one . . ." (John 17:22).

Personality is the unique, limitless part of our life that makes us distinct from everyone else. It is too vast for us even to comprehend. An island in the sea may be just the top of a large mountain, and our personality is like that island. We don't know the great depths of our being, therefore we cannot measure ourselves. We start out thinking we can, but soon realize that there is really only one Being who fully understands us, and that is our Creator.

Personality is the characteristic mark of the inner, spiritual man, just as individuality is the characteristic of the outer, natural man. Our Lord can never be described in terms of individuality and independence, but only in terms of His total Person—"I and My Father are one" (John 10:30). Personality merges, and you only reach your true identity once you are merged with another person. When love or the Spirit of God come upon a person, he is transformed. He will then no longer insist on maintaining his individuality. Our Lord never referred to a person's individuality or his isolated position, but spoke in terms of the total person—". . . that they may be one just as We are one . . . ." Once your rights to yourself are surrendered to God, your true personal nature begins responding to God immediately. Jesus Christ brings freedom to your total person, and even your individuality is transformed. The transformation is brought about by love—personal devotion to Jesus. Love is the overflowing result of one person in true fellowship with another.

DECEMBER 12

INTERCESSORY PRAYER

". . . men always ought to pray and not lose heart" (Luke 18:1).

You cannot truly intercede through prayer if you do not believe in the reality of redemption. Instead, you will simply be turning intercession into useless sympathy for others, which will serve only to increase the contentment they have for remaining out of touch with God. True intercession involves bringing the person, or the circumstance that seems to be crashing in on you, before God, until you are changed by His attitude toward that person or circumstance. Intercession means to "fill up . . . [with] what is lacking in the afflictions of Christ" (Colossians 1:24), and this is precisely why there are so few intercessors. People describe intercession by saying, "It is putting yourself in someone else's place." That is not true! Intercession is putting yourself in God's place; it is having His mind and His perspective.

As an intercessor, be careful not to seek too much information from God regarding the situation you are praying about, because you may be overwhelmed. If you know too much, more than God has ordained for you to know, you can't pray; the circumstances of the people become so overpowering that you are no longer able to get to the underlying truth.

Our work is to be in such close contact with God that we may have His mind about everything, but we shirk that responsibility by substituting doing for interceding. And yet intercession is the only thing that has no drawbacks, because it keeps our relationship completely open with God.

What we must avoid in intercession is praying for someone to be simply "patched up." We must pray that person completely through into contact with the very life of God. Think of the number of people God has brought across our path, only to see us drop them! When we pray on the basis of redemption, God creates something He can create in no other way than through intercessory prayer.

THE GREAT LIFE

"Peace I leave with you, My peace I give to you; not as the world gives do I give to you. Let not your heart be troubled . . ." (John 14:27).

Whenever we experience something difficult in our personal life, we are tempted to blame God. But we are the ones in the wrong, not God. Blaming God is evidence that we are refusing to let go of some disobedience somewhere in our lives. But as soon as we let go, everything becomes as clear as daylight to us. As long as we try to serve two masters, ourselves and God, there will be difficulties combined with doubt and confusion. Our attitude must be one of complete reliance on God. Once we get to that point, there is nothing easier than living the life of a saint. We encounter difficulties when we try to usurp the authority of the Holy Spirit for our own purposes.

God's mark of approval, whenever you obey Him, is peace. He sends an immeasurable, deep peace; not a natural peace, "as the world gives," but the peace of Jesus. Whenever peace does not come, wait until it does, or seek to find out why it is not coming. If you are acting on your own impulse, or out of a sense of the heroic, to be seen by others, the peace of Jesus will not exhibit itself. This shows no unity with God or confidence in Him. The spirit of simplicity, clarity, and unity is born through the Holy Spirit, not through your decisions. God counters our self-willed decisions with an appeal for simplicity and unity.

My questions arise whenever I cease to obey. When I do obey God, problems come, not between me and God, but as a means to keep my mind examining with amazement the revealed truth of God. But any problem that comes between God and myself is the result of disobedience. Any problem that comes while I obey God (and there will be many), increases my overjoyed delight, because I know that my Father knows and cares, and I can watch and anticipate how He will unravel my problems.

"APPROVED TO GOD"

"Be diligent to present yourself approved to God, a worker who does not need to be ashamed, rightly dividing the word of truth" (2 Timothy 2:15).

I f you cannot express yourself well on each of your beliefs, work and study until you can. If you don't, other people may miss out on the blessings that come from knowing the truth. Strive to re-express a truth of God to yourself clearly and understandably, and God will use that same explanation when you share it with someone else. But you must be willing to go through God's winepress where the grapes are crushed. You must struggle, experiment, and rehearse your words to express God's truth clearly. Then the time will come when that very expression will become God's wine of strength to someone else. But if you are not diligent and say, "I'm not going to study and struggle to express this truth in my own words; I'll just borrow my words from someone else," then the words will be of no value to you or to others. Try to state to yourself what you believe to be the absolute truth of God, and you will be allowing God the opportunity to pass it on through you to someone else.

Always make it a practice to stir your own mind thoroughly to think through what you have easily believed. Your position is not really yours until you make it yours through suffering and study. The author or speaker from whom you learn the most is not the one who teaches you something you didn't know before, but the one who helps you take a truth with which you have quietly struggled, give it expression, and speak it clearly and boldly.

WRESTLING BEFORE GOD

"Take up the whole armor of God . . . praying always . . ." (Ephesians 6:13, 18).

You must learn to wrestle *against* the things that hinder your communication with God, and wrestle in prayer *for* other people; but to wrestle *with* God in prayer is unscriptural. If you ever do wrestle with God, you will be crippled for the rest of your life. If you grab hold of God and wrestle with Him, as Jacob did, simply because He is working in a way that doesn't meet with your approval, you force Him to put you out of joint (see Genesis 32:24-25). Don't become a cripple by wrestling with the ways of God, but be someone who wrestles before God with the things of this world, because "we are more than conquerors through Him . . ." (Romans 8:37). Wrestling before God makes an impact in His kingdom. If you ask me to pray for you, and I am not complete in Christ, my prayer accomplishes nothing. But if I am complete in Christ, my prayer brings victory all the time. Prayer is effective only when there is completeness—"take up the whole armor of God . . . ."

Always make a distinction between God's perfect will and His permissive will, which He uses to accomplish His divine purpose for our lives. God's perfect will is unchangeable. It is with His permissive will, or the various things that He allows into our lives, that we must wrestle before Him. It is our reaction to these things allowed by His permissive will that enables us to come to the point of seeing His perfect will for us. "We know that all things work together for good to those who love God . . ." (Romans 8:28)—to those who remain true to God's perfect will—His calling in Christ Jesus. God's permissive will is the testing He uses to reveal His true sons and daughters. We should not be spineless and automatically say, "Yes, it is the Lord's will." We don't have to fight or wrestle *with* God, but we must wrestle before God *with things*. Beware of lazily giving up. Instead, put up a glorious fight and you will find yourself empowered with His strength.

REDEMPTION—CREATING THE NEED IT SATISFIES

"The natural man does not receive the things of the Spirit of God, for they are foolishness to him . . ." (1 Corinthians 2:14).

The gospel of God creates the sense of need for the gospel. Is the gospel hidden to those who are servants already? No, Paul said, "But even if our gospel is veiled, it is veiled to those who are perishing, whose minds the god of this age has blinded, who do not believe . . ." (2 Corinthians 4:3-4). The majority of people think of themselves as being completely moral, and have no sense of need for the gospel. It is God who creates this sense of need in a human being, but that person remains totally unaware of his need until God makes Himself evident. Jesus said, "Ask, and it will be given to you . . ." (Matthew 7:7). But God cannot give until a man asks. It is not that He wants to withhold something from us, but that is the plan He has established for the way of redemption. Through our asking, God puts His process in motion, creating something in us that was nonexistent until we asked. The inner reality of redemption is that it creates all the time. And as redemption creates the life of God in us, it also creates the things which belong to that life. The only thing that can possibly satisfy the need is what created the need. This is the meaning of redemption—it creates and it satisfies.

Jesus said, "And I, if I am lifted up from the earth, will draw all peoples to Myself" (John 12:32). When we preach our own experiences, people may be interested, but it awakens no real sense of need. But once Jesus Christ is "lifted up," the Spirit of God creates an awareness of the need for Him. The creative power of the redemption of God works in the souls of men only through the preaching of the gospel. It is never the sharing of personal experiences that saves people, but the truth of redemption. "The words that I speak to you are spirit, and they are life" (John 6:63).

TEST OF FAITHFULNESS

"We know that all things work together for good to those who love God . . ." (Romans 8:28).

It is only a faithful person who truly believes that God sovereignly controls his circumstances. We take our circumstances for granted, saying God is in control, but not really believing it. We act as if the things that happen were completely controlled by people. To be faithful in every circumstance means that we have only one loyalty, or object of our faith—the Lord Jesus Christ. God may cause our circumstances to suddenly fall apart, which may bring the realization of our unfaithfulness to Him for not recognizing that He had ordained the situation. We never saw what He was trying to accomplish, and that exact event will never be repeated in our life. This is where the test of our faithfulness comes. If we will just learn to worship God even during the difficult circumstances, He will change them for the better very quickly if He so chooses.

Being faithful to Jesus Christ is the most difficult thing we try to do today. We will be faithful to our work, to serving others, or to anything else; just don't ask us to be faithful to Jesus Christ. Many Christians become very impatient when we talk about faithfulness to Jesus. Our Lord is dethroned more deliberately by Christian workers than by the world. We treat God as if He were a machine designed only to bless us, and we think of Jesus as just another one of the workers.

The goal of faithfulness is not that we will do work for God, but that He will be free to do His work through us. God calls us to His service and places tremendous responsibilities on us. He expects no complaining on our part and offers no explanation on His part. God wants to use us as He used His own Son.

THE FOCUS OF OUR MESSAGE

**"I did not come to bring peace but a sword"
(Matthew 10:34).**

Never be sympathetic with a person whose situation causes you to conclude that God is dealing harshly with him. God can be more tender than we can conceive, and every once in a while He gives us the opportunity to deal firmly with someone so that He may be viewed as the tender One. If a person cannot go to God, it is because he has something secret which he does not intend to give up—he may admit his sin, but would no more give up that thing than he could fly under his own power. It is impossible to deal sympathetically with people like that. We must reach down deep in their lives to the root of the problem, which will cause hostility and resentment toward the message. People want the blessing of God, but they can't stand something that pierces right through to the heart of the matter.

If you are sensitive to God's way, your message as His servant will be merciless and insistent, cutting to the very root. Otherwise, there will be no healing. We must drive the message home so forcefully that a person cannot possibly hide, but must apply its truth. Deal with people where they are, until they begin to realize their true need. Then hold high the standard of Jesus for their lives. Their response may be, "We can never be that." Then drive it home with, "Jesus Christ says you must." "But how can we be?" "You can't, unless you have a new Spirit" (see Luke 11:13).

There must be a sense of need created before your message is of any use. Thousands of people in this world profess to be happy without God. But if we could be truly happy and moral without Jesus, then why did He come? He came because that kind of happiness and peace is only superficial. Jesus Christ came to "bring . . . a sword" through every kind of peace that is not based on a personal relationship with Himself.

THE RIGHT KIND OF HELP

"And I, if I am lifted up . . . will draw all peoples to Myself" (John 12:32).

Very few of us have any understanding of the reason why Jesus Christ died. If sympathy is all that human beings need, then the Cross of Christ is an absurdity and there is absolutely no need for it. What the world needs is not "a little bit of love," but major surgery.

When you find yourself face to face with a person who is spiritually lost, remind yourself of Jesus Christ on the cross. If that person can get to God in any other way, then the Cross of Christ is unnecessary. If you think you are helping lost people with your sympathy and understanding, you are a traitor to Jesus Christ. You must have a right-standing relationship with Him yourself, and pour your life out in helping others in His way—not in a human way that ignores God. The theme of the world's religion today is to serve in a pleasant, nonconfrontational manner.

But our only priority must be to present Jesus Christ crucified—to lift Him up all the time (see 1 Corinthians 2:2). Every belief that is not firmly rooted in the Cross of Christ will lead people astray. If the worker himself believes in Jesus Christ and is trusting in the reality of redemption, his words will be compelling to others. What is extremely important is for the worker's simple relationship with Jesus Christ to be strong and growing. His usefulness to God depends on that, and that alone.

The calling of a New Testament worker is to expose sin and to reveal Jesus Christ as Savior. Consequently, he cannot always be charming and friendly, but must be willing to be stern to accomplish major surgery. We are sent by God to lift up Jesus Christ, not to give wonderfully beautiful speeches. We must be willing to examine others as deeply as God has examined us. We must also be sharply intent on sensing those Scripture passages that will drive the truth home, and then not be afraid to apply them.

EXPERIENCE OR GOD'S REVEALED TRUTH?

"We have received . . . the Spirit who is from God, that we might know the things that have been freely given to us by God" (1 Corinthians 2:12).

My experience is not what makes redemption real—redemption *is* reality. Redemption has no real meaning for me until it is worked out through my conscious life. When I am born again, the Spirit of God takes me beyond myself and my experiences, and identifies me with Jesus Christ. If I am left only with my personal experiences, I am left with something not produced by redemption. But experiences produced by redemption prove themselves by leading me beyond myself, to the point of no longer paying any attention to experiences as the basis of reality. Instead, I see that only the reality itself produced the experiences. My experiences are not worth anything unless they keep me at the Source of truth—Jesus Christ.

If you try to hold back the Holy Spirit within you, with the desire of producing more inner spiritual experiences, you will find that He will break the hold and take you again to the historic Christ. Never support an experience which does not have God as its Source and faith in God as its result. If you do, your experience is anti-Christian, no matter what visions or insights you may have had. Is Jesus Christ Lord of your experiences, or do you place your experiences above Him? Is any experience dearer to you than your Lord? You must allow Him to be Lord over you, and pay no attention to any experience over which He is not Lord. Then there will come a time when God will make you impatient with your own experience, and you can truthfully say, "I do not care what I experience—I am sure of Him!"

Be relentless and hard on yourself if you are in the habit of talking about the experiences you have had. Faith based on experience is not faith; faith based on God's revealed truth is the only faith there is.

THE DRAWING OF THE FATHER

"No one can come to Me unless the Father who sent Me draws him . . ." (John 6:44).

When God begins to draw me to Himself, the problem of my will comes in immediately. Will I react positively to the truth that God has revealed? Will I come to Him? To discuss or deliberate over spiritual matters when God calls is inappropriate and disrespectful to Him. When God speaks, never discuss it with anyone as if to decide what your response may be (see Galatians 1:15–16). Belief is not the result of an intellectual act, but the result of an act of my will whereby I deliberately commit myself. But will I commit, placing myself completely and absolutely on God, and be willing to act solely on what He says? If I will, I will find that I am grounded on reality as certain as God's throne.

In preaching the gospel, always focus on the matter of the will. Belief must come from the *will* to believe. There must be a surrender of the will, not a surrender to a persuasive or powerful argument. I must deliberately step out, placing my faith in God and in His truth. And I must place no confidence in my own works, but only in God. Trusting in my own mental understanding becomes a hindrance to complete trust in God. I must be willing to ignore and leave my feelings behind. I must *will* to believe. But this can never be accomplished without my forceful, determined effort to separate myself from my old ways of looking at things. I must surrender myself completely to God.

Everyone has been created with the ability to reach out beyond his own grasp. But it is God who draws me, and my relationship to Him in the first place is an inner, personal one, not an intellectual one. I come into the relationship through the miracle of God and through my own will to believe. Then I begin to get an intelligent appreciation and understanding of the wonder of the transformation in my life.

SHARING IN THE ATONEMENT

"God forbid that I should boast except in the cross of our Lord Jesus Christ . . ." (Galatians 6:14).

The gospel of Jesus Christ always forces a decision of our will. Have I accepted God's verdict on sin as judged on the Cross of Christ? Do I have even the slightest interest in the death of Jesus? Do I want to be identified with His death—to be completely dead to all interest in sin, worldliness, and self? Do I long to be so closely identified with Jesus that I am of no value for anything except Him and His purposes? The great privilege of discipleship is that I can commit myself under the banner of His Cross, and that means death to sin. You must get alone with Jesus and either decide to tell Him that you do not want sin to die out in you, or that at any cost you want to be identified with His death. When you act in confident faith in what our Lord did on the cross, a supernatural identification with His death takes place immediately. And you will come to know through a higher knowledge that your old life was "crucified with Him" (Romans 6:6). The proof that your old life is dead, having been "crucified with Christ" (Galatians 2:20), is the amazing ease with which the life of God in you now enables you to obey the voice of Jesus Christ.

Every once in a while our Lord gives us a glimpse of what we would be like if it were not for Him. This is a confirmation of what He said—". . . without Me you can do nothing" (John 15:5). That is why the underlying foundation of Christianity is personal, passionate devotion to the Lord Jesus. We mistake the joy of our first introduction into God's kingdom as His purpose for getting us there. Yet God's purpose in getting us into His kingdom is that we may realize all that identification with Jesus Christ means.

THE HIDDEN LIFE

". . . your life is hidden with Christ in God"
(Colossians 3:3).

The Spirit of God testifies to and confirms the simple, but almighty, security of the life that "is hidden with Christ in God." Paul continually brought this out in his New Testament letters. We talk as if living a sanctified life were the most uncertain and insecure thing we could do. Yet it is the most secure thing possible, because it has Almighty God in and behind it. The most dangerous and unsure thing is to try to live without God. For one who is born again, it is easier to live in a right-standing relationship with God than it is to go wrong, provided we heed God's warnings and "walk in the light" (1 John 1:7).

When we think of being delivered from sin, being "filled with the Spirit" (Ephesians 5:18), and "walk[ing] in the light," we picture the peak of a great mountain. We see it as very high and wonderful, but we say, "Oh, I could never live up there!" However, when we do get there through God's grace, we find it is not a mountain peak at all, but a plateau with plenty of room to live and to grow. "You enlarged my path under me, so my feet did not slip" (Psalm 18:36).

When you really see Jesus, I defy you to doubt Him. If you see Him when He says, "Let not your heart be troubled . . ." (John 14:27), I defy you to worry. It is virtually impossible to doubt when He is there. Every time you are in personal contact with Jesus, His words are real to you. "My peace I give to you . . ." (John 14:27)—a peace which brings an unconstrained confidence and covers you completely, from the top of your head to the soles of your feet. ". . . your life is hidden with Christ in God," and the peace of Jesus Christ that cannot be disturbed has been imparted to you.

HIS BIRTH AND OUR NEW BIRTH

" 'Behold, the virgin shall be with child, and bear a Son, and they shall call His name Immanuel,' which is translated, 'God with us'" (Matthew 1:23).

His Birth in History. ". . . that Holy One who is to be born will be called the Son of God (Luke 1:35). Jesus Christ was born *into* this world, not *from* it. He did not emerge out of history; He came into history from the outside. Jesus Christ is not the best human being the human race can boast of—He is a Being for whom the human race can take no credit at all. He is not man becoming God, but God Incarnate—God coming into human flesh from outside it. His life is the highest and the holiest entering through the most humble of doors. Our Lord's birth was an advent—the appearance of God in human form.

His Birth in Me. "My little children, for whom I labor in birth again until Christ is formed in you . . ." (Galatians 4:19). Just as our Lord came into human history from outside it, He must also come into me from outside. Have I allowed my personal human life to become a "Bethlehem" for the Son of God? I cannot enter the realm of the kingdom of God unless I am born again from above by a birth totally unlike physical birth. "You must be born again" (John 3:7). This is not a command, but a fact based on the authority of God. The evidence of the new birth is that I yield myself so completely to God that "Christ is formed" in me. And once "Christ is formed" in me, His nature immediately begins to work through me.

God Evident in the Flesh. This is what is made so profoundly possible for you and for me through the redemption of man by Jesus Christ.

"WALK IN THE LIGHT"

**"If we walk in the light as He is in the light
. . . the blood of Jesus Christ His Son cleanses
us from all sin" (1 John 1:7).**

To mistake freedom from sin only on the conscious level of our lives for complete deliverance from sin by the atonement through the Cross of Christ is a great error. No one fully knows what sin is until he is born again. Sin is what Jesus Christ faced at Calvary. The evidence that I have been delivered from sin is that I know the real nature of sin in me. For a person to really know what sin is requires the full work and deep touch of the atonement of Jesus Christ, that is, the imparting of His absolute perfection.

The Holy Spirit applies or administers the work of the atonement to us in the deep unconscious realm as well as in the conscious realm. And it is not until we truly perceive the unrivaled power of the Spirit in us that we understand the meaning of 1 John 1:7, which says, ". . . *the blood of Jesus Christ His Son cleanses us from all sin.*" This verse does not refer only to conscious sin, but also to the tremendously profound understanding of sin which only the Holy Spirit in me can accomplish.

I must "walk in the light as He is in the light . . ." —not in the light of my own conscience, but in God's light. If I will walk there, with nothing held back or hidden, then this amazing truth is revealed to me: ". . . the blood of Jesus Christ His Son cleanses [me] from all sin" so that God Almighty can see nothing to rebuke in me. On the conscious level it produces a keen, sorrowful knowledge of what sin really is. The love of God working in me causes me to hate, with the Holy Spirit's hatred for sin, anything that is not in keeping with God's holiness. To "walk in the light" means that everything that is of the darkness actually drives me closer to the center of the light.

WHERE THE BATTLE IS
WON OR LOST

" 'If you will return, O Israel,' says the
LORD . . ." (Jeremiah 4:1).

Our battles are first won or lost in the secret places
of our will in God's presence, never in full view
of the world. The Spirit of God seizes me and I
am compelled to get alone with God and fight the battle
before Him. Until I do this, I will lose every time. The
battle may take one minute or one year, but that will
depend on me, not God. However long it takes, I must
wrestle with it alone before God, and I must resolve to go
through the hell of renunciation or rejection before Him.
Nothing has any power over someone who has fought the
battle before God and won there.

I should never say, "I will wait until I get into difficult circumstances and then I'll put God to the test."
Trying to do that will not work. I must first get the issue
settled between God and myself in the secret places of
my soul, where no one else can interfere. Then I can go
ahead, knowing with certainty that the battle is won.
Lose it there, and calamity, disaster, and defeat before
the world are as sure as the laws of God. The reason the
battle is lost is that I fight it first in the external world.
Get alone with God, do battle before Him, and settle the
matter once and for all.

In dealing with other people, our stance should
always be to drive them toward making a decision of
their will. That is how surrendering to God begins.
Not often, but every once in a while, God brings us to a
major turning point—a great crossroads in our life. From
that point we either go toward a more and more slow,
lazy, and useless Christian life, or we become more and
more on fire, giving our utmost for *His* highest—our best
for *His* glory.

CONTINUOUS CONVERSION

". . . unless you are converted and become as little children, you will by no means enter the kingdom of heaven" (Matthew 18:3).

These words of our Lord refer to our initial conversion, but we should continue to turn to God as children, being continuously converted every day of our lives. If we trust in our own abilities, instead of God's, we produce consequences for which God will hold us responsible. When God through His sovereignty brings us into new situations, we should immediately make sure that our natural life submits to the spiritual, obeying the orders of the Spirit of God. Just because we have responded properly in the past is no guarantee that we will do so again. The response of the natural to the spiritual should be continuous conversion, but this is where we so often refuse to be obedient. No matter what our situation is, the Spirit of God remains unchanged and His salvation unaltered. But we must "put on the new man . . ." (Ephesians 4:24). God holds us accountable every time we refuse to convert ourselves, and He sees our refusal as willful disobedience. Our natural life must not rule—God must rule in us.

To refuse to be continuously converted puts a stumbling block in the growth of our spiritual life. There are areas of self-will in our lives where our pride pours contempt on the throne of God and says, "I won't submit." We deify our independence and self-will and call them by the wrong name. What God sees as stubborn weakness, we call strength. There are whole areas of our lives that have not yet been brought into submission, and this can only be done by this continuous conversion. Slowly but surely we can claim the whole territory for the Spirit of God.

DESERTER OR DISCIPLE?

"From that time many of His disciples went back and walked with Him no more" (John 6:66).

When God, by His Spirit through His Word, gives you a clear vision of His will, you must "walk in the light" of that vision (1 John 1:7). Even though your mind and soul may be thrilled by it, if you don't "walk in the light" of it you will sink to a level of bondage never envisioned by our Lord. Mentally disobeying the "heavenly vision" (Acts 26:19) will make you a slave to ideas and views that are completely foreign to Jesus Christ. Don't look at someone else and say, "Well, if he can have those views and prosper, why can't I?" You have to "walk in the light" of the vision that has been given to *you*. Don't compare yourself with others or judge them—that is between God and them. When you find that one of your favorite and strongly held views clashes with the "heavenly vision," do not begin to debate it. If you do, a sense of property and personal right will emerge in you—things on which Jesus placed no value. He was against these things as being the root of everything foreign to Himself—". . . for one's life does not consist in the abundance of the things he possesses" (Luke 12:15). If we don't see and understand this, it is because we are ignoring the underlying principles of our Lord's teaching.

Our tendency is to lie back and bask in the memory of the wonderful experience we had when God revealed His will to us. But if a New Testament standard is revealed to us by the light of God, and we don't try to measure up, or even feel inclined to do so, then we begin to backslide. It means your conscience does not respond to the truth. You can never be the same after the unveiling of a truth. That moment marks you as one who either continues on with even more devotion as a disciple of Jesus Christ, or as one who turns to go back as a deserter.

"AND EVERY VIRTUE
WE POSSESS"

". . . All my springs are in you" (Psalm 87:7).

Our Lord never "patches up" our natural virtues, that is, our natural traits, qualities, or characteristics. He completely remakes a person on the inside—". . . put on the new man . . ." (Ephesians 4:24). In other words, see that your natural human life is putting on all that is in keeping with the new life. The life God places within us develops its own new virtues, not the virtues of the seed of Adam, but of Jesus Christ. Once God has begun the process of sanctification in your life, watch and see how God causes your confidence in your own natural virtues and power to wither away. He will continue until you learn to draw your life from the reservoir of the resurrection life of Jesus. Thank God if you are going through this drying-up experience!

The sign that God is at work in us is that He is destroying our confidence in the natural virtues, because they are not promises of what we are going to be, but only a wasted reminder of what God created man to be. We want to cling to our natural virtues, while all the time God is trying to get us in contact with the life of Jesus Christ—a life that can never be described in terms of natural virtues. It is the saddest thing to see people who are trying to serve God depending on that which the grace of God never gave them. They are depending solely on what they have by virtue of heredity. God does not take our natural virtues and transform them, because our natural virtues could never even come close to what Jesus Christ wants. No natural love, no natural patience, no natural purity can ever come up to His demands. But as we bring every part of our natural bodily life into harmony with the new life God has placed within us, He will exhibit in us the virtues that were characteristic of the Lord Jesus.

> And every virtue we possess
> Is His alone.

YESTERDAY

"You shall not go out with haste, . . . for the LORD will go before you, and the God of Israel will be your rear guard" (Isaiah 52:12).

Security from Yesterday. ". . . God requires an account of what is past" (Ecclesiastes 3:15). At the end of the year we turn with eagerness to all that God has for the future, and yet anxiety is apt to arise when we remember our yesterdays. Our present enjoyment of God's grace tends to be lessened by the memory of yesterday's sins and blunders. But God is the God of our yesterdays, and He allows the memory of them to turn the past into a ministry of spiritual growth for our future. God reminds us of the past to protect us from a very shallow security in the present.

Security for Tomorrow. ". . . the LORD will go before you . . . ." This is a gracious revelation—that God will send His forces out where we have failed to do so. He will keep watch so that we will not be tripped up again by the same failures, as would undoubtedly happen if He were not our "rear guard." And God's hand reaches back to the past, settling all the claims against our conscience.

Security for Today. "You shall not go out with haste . . . ." As we go forth into the coming year, let it not be in the haste of impetuous, forgetful delight, nor with the quickness of impulsive thoughtlessness. But let us go out with the patient power of knowing that the God of Israel will go before us. Our yesterdays hold broken and irreversible things for us. It is true that we have lost opportunities that will never return, but God can transform this destructive anxiety into a constructive thoughtfulness for the future. Let the past rest, but let it rest in the sweet embrace of Christ.

Leave the broken, irreversible past in His hands, and step out into the invincible future with Him.

Subject Index

SUBJECT INDEX

Subject Index

SUBJECT INDEX

SUBJECT INDEX

SUBJECT INDEX

SUBJECT INDEX

SUBJECT INDEX

SUBJECT INDEX

Subject Index

SUBJECT INDEX

SUBJECT INDEX

SUBJECT INDEX

Subject Index

SCRIPTURE INDEX

Scripture Index

SCRIPTURE INDEX

SCRIPTURE INDEX

Scripture Index

SCRIPTURE INDEX

Scripture Index

SCRIPTURE INDEX

SCRIPTURE INDEX

SCRIPTURE INDEX

NOTE TO THE READER

The publisher invites you to share your response
to the message of this book by writing
Discovery House, P.O. Box 3566,
Grand Rapids, MI 49501, U.S.A.

For information about other Discovery House books,
music, or DVDs, contact us at the same address
or call 1-800-653-8333. Find us online at dhp.org
or send e-mail to books@dhp.org.

NOTES

PRAYERS

NOTES

PRAYERS

NOTES

PRAYERS

NOTES

PRAYERS

NOTES